"Finally! – a great book discussing and explaining the what, when, why, how and importance of techniques organizations should utilize in determining their staffing needs, and then going about sourcing, finding and hiring the best people for the various jobs found today at all levels in organizations. This is a don't miss for HR Practitioners!"

— *Kathryn McKee, SPHR, SHRM-SCP, Past Chair of Society for Human Resource Management, Lecturer, UCSB*

"Greene provides a solid, pragmatic, and comprehensive review of human resource practices that yield results. Fully energized to cover current topics, the book belongs on every HR practitioner's desk. As our world changes, HR must adapt to new challenges; this book will help to meet those challenges 'head-on.'"

— *Robert J. Butler, SPHR, CCP, USA*

"Dr. Greene has managed to bring an updated and realistic approach to the issues and challenges facing today's HR professionals. He has focused on the linkage between strategy, program management and execution in a way that is essential for proper success of HR initiatives. The field has had a need for a text that reflects the reality of today rather than a recycled version of past practices."

— *Peter Ronza, CCP, SPHR, President, Pontifex Consulting Group*

Strategic Talent Management

Clearly written and providing actionable strategies, this book explores new paradigms for workforce management to enable human resource managers and the organizations where they work to thrive in today's turbulent business environment.

Robert Greene goes beyond the many human resource management books currently available, to deal head-on with the new realities of talent management, including such factors as the "gig economy" and globalization. The book focuses on attracting, developing and effectively utilizing human capital. It begins with human capital planning, and then explores strategies and programs that can attract and retain the workforce an organization needs. A range of sizes and types of organizations and different working relationships are considered, as Greene demonstrates how to evaluate the effectiveness of strategies that fit specific contexts and will sustain the viability of an organization's workforce into the future.

Postgraduate students of human resource management, as well as current HR professionals and managers, will find this practical book an indispensable resource.

PowerPoint slides and test banks are available to support instructors.

Robert J. Greene, PhD, SPHR, GPHR, SHRM-SCP, CCP, CBP, GRP is the CEO of the consultancy Reward Systems, Inc., a Principal with Pontifex and a faculty member for DePaul University in their MSHR and MBA programs. He has over 40 years in the human resources field and is the author of three other books and over 100 articles. He was a principal designer of the SPHR/PHR, CCP and GRP certifications and has developed and taught professional development programs for several professional associations. He was the first recipient of the Keystone Award, bestowed by the American Compensation Association (now World at Work) for attaining the highest level of excellence in the field.

Strategic Talent Management

Creating the Right Workforce

Robert J. Greene

Routledge
Taylor & Francis Group

NEW YORK AND LONDON

First published 2020
by Routledge
52 Vanderbilt Avenue, New York, NY 10017

and by Routledge
2 Park Square, Milton Park, Abingdon, Oxon, OX14 4RN

Routledge is an imprint of the Taylor & Francis Group, an informa business

Library of Congress Cataloging-in-Publication Data
A catalog record for this title has been requested

ISBN: 978-0-367-42736-8 (hbk)
ISBN: 978-0-367-42691-0 (pbk)
ISBN: 978-0-367-85468-3 (ebk)

Typeset in Bembo
by Deanta Global Publishing Services, Chennai, India

Visit the eResources: www.routledge.com/9780367426910

Contents

Acknowledgments

The encouragement received from many friends and colleagues convinced me this book would be a complement to my previous work, and also be a contribution to the field.

My parents and brother Richard encouraged me in every way during my formative years. My wife Dorothy has acted as my editor, as well as encouraging me to continue my education. My son John encouraged me with his enthusiasm for my writing and teaching. An additional motivation is my desire to have my two granddaughters, Grace and Alice, be proud of me, at least when they reach the age when they can understand what I write.

All of these sources of inspiration and support have earned my deepest gratitude.

Introduction

Consider ...
If what allows an organization to be successful is:
Not only what it owns, but what it knows ...
Not only what it knows, but how fast it learns ...
Not only what technology it has, but how it uses it ...
Not only how good its products are, but how good customers think they are ...

Then how important is it to have the *right* workforce?

In order to succeed in today's competitive environment, an organization must develop and execute a human capital strategy that ensures that it has the talent it requires, that it utilizes the talent effectively and that it invests in developing people so that they remain productive into the future.

The human capital strategy must be derived from the context within which the organization exists and must be a good fit to that context. Figure 0.1 illustrates how human capital (human resource) strategy should be derived from the organizational strategy, which needs to be derived from the context within which it must be executed.

The vision and mission of an organization establish the desired end state and the optimal path to realizing its objectives. The internal and external realities influence how things can and should be done. The culture of the organization defines the values and beliefs that guide its people and influences both what they do and how they do what is required. The business strategy influences the type of workforce the organization needs and how it will be managed to produce a competitive advantage. And the structure of the organization defines individual roles and their relationship to each other. Each organization must understand its context and then develop a strategy that fits that context, since there is no one human capital strategy that will work well in every organization. What works is what fits each unique organizational context at a specific point in time.

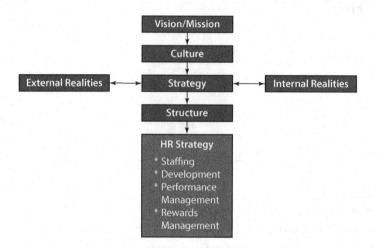

Figure 0.1 Deriving HR Strategy From Origanizational Context.

Given the dynamic nature of today's environment strategies must be dynamic. If external factors change it may require a different human capital strategy in order to function within the altered arena. And changing the strategy may require alteration of all systems.

An organization's human capital (talent) is always a critical resource. Adequate financial, operational and customer capital are also required for success, although their relative criticality varies across organizations and changes over time. Despite the increased power of technology being heralded today all that is done in an organization must be created by and directed by people … those that are doing the work, directing the work or developing the technology that will do the work. And the right workforce is the only sustainable competitive advantage, since competitors often have access to the other forms of capital under the same terms. The workforce that provides a competitive advantage must be built … it cannot be bought. And it must be nurtured with the appropriate investment in sustaining its viability.

Talent management strategies have historically been influenced by an underlying assumption that a stable workforce is desirable. In the 1950–1980 period, organizations such as IBM attracted and retained talent for extended periods. Public sector organizations tend to have employees who stay for extended periods, and even for their whole career. But as the lifetime of products shortened and the economy became more turbulent an increasing number of organizations found that their talent needs were changing more rapidly and the rate of churn in the workforce was increasing. The shorter amount of time that people spent in one organization was attributable to both organizational and individual needs. Individuals often find they can progress in their careers more quickly if they move more often. Rapid movement also may result in a more rapid escalation in their compensation. The increase in the turnover rate has prompted organizations to realize they have to compete more aggressively for the talent they require.

In order to attract, retain and motivate the talent an organization requires for success in today's competitive market it must be viewed as an employer of choice. Much as organizations brand their products, they must brand themselves as employers in order to be a preferred place for talent to apply their skills and knowledge. The first step in the development of a talent strategy is to define the knowledge, skills, abilities and behaviors the organization needs. Once its needs are defined an organization must be able to attract the right people. This requires a value proposition that is attractive to the people the organization needs and wants. Some organizations attempt to establish their credibility as a desirable employer by communicating impressive-sounding mission statements and cultural profiles. Websites receive massive investments in an attempt to attract the right people because of the increased use of web-based search activities by those seeking opportunities. Claims like "our people are our most important asset" and "we have an employee-friendly culture" are common. But since these are claims made by the organization they may be viewed as self-serving, reducing their believability for potential candidates for employment. And those considering the organization can visit websites that report the perceptions of actual employees, which can contradict the organization's claims, so organizations must be concerned about their social media image.

People will respond positively to organizations that aspire to do the right things and that appear to be successful. They also will prefer organizations that provide them with an opportunity to realize their goals. Research in psychology has determined that the three elements needed for individuals to feel deeply committed to what they do are: (1) autonomy, (2) competence and (3) relatedness. If candidates seek personal development, they will view organizations that invest heavily in human capital development positively. If they want short-term rewards they will opt for organizations that seem to offer premium rewards packages. If they are most concerned about doing meaningful or socially responsible work, they will prefer organizations known for exhibiting corporate social responsibility and be less impressed by those focusing solely on financial rewards. If they want to work on projects on a flexible basis, they will look for indications that the organization may accommodate their desired employment relationship. And if they are security-oriented they may be more impressed by generous benefits packages than would people more focused on short-term direct compensation. Finally, they will prefer organizations that place a high value on their occupation. Few IT specialists believe their occupation is the most highly valued one in a hospital. The doctors and other health care professionals are central to the hospital's mission and critical to its performance, making them the key to success. The IT specialist is more likely to prefer an organization that values their capabilities highly, unless they believe in the mission of health care organizations and wish to contribute to it alongside others similarly committed.

A major issue for people considering a relationship with an organization is what type of organization fits their priorities. Some wish to enter employment in a large, diverse organization that can offer a wide range of opportunities. Others would prefer to join a small and/or emerging organization ... perhaps one that was started by someone in their dorm room or garage. Yet others don't want to work for any organization, although they do want to do work for organizations.

This book, like the vast majority of others related to managing human capital, will address the issues most often faced by mid-range and large organizations, since they are the types of organizations that will have a Human Resources function and will have the resources to develop formal strategies and programs to attract, retain and motivate the required talent. But this book will also explore the question: "Do different types/sizes of organization have the same challenges and what impact does that have on talent management?" The fundamental challenges related to managing talent are the same no matter what the size, but the strategies that are required in order to be successful will differ.

The single-person organization is unique in that the founder must first decide what will be done and then how it will be accomplished. That person's time and financial resources must be invested in the right things in pursuit of the right strategy. But as soon as there are two or more "employees," similarities with all other organizations begin to materialize. There must be decisions about who invests and how the proceeds of the organization's business will be allocated. And the work that must be done must be assigned to the right party. This of course does not necessarily require the same type of formality in managing talent that is necessary in larger organizations. Reading this book and others on human capital management may seem a poor investment of time for those in very small organizations. But most small organizations want to grow and emerge into mid-range and larger organization. Understanding the issues related to people management that larger organizations face should be considered an investment in the future.

Too many startups grow dramatically, only to spin out of control and expire. People's Express was an example of a start-up that experienced explosive growth due to its low cost strategy, but growth became so seductive that management forgot an organization needs to have the people capable of dealing with the growth and maintain the discipline to stay within its capacity to perform. Southwest Airlines demonstrated discipline and grew to be a major airline. Its focus on the culture and on the workforce contributed to its success. Some of the high-tech startups in the 1990s experienced astronomical growth in their value after going public, even though they never produced a profit. Many failed because their business plan was flawed. Others failed because they could not execute their strategy. Many lessons were learned about managing human capital. One lesson is that you may be able to attract top talent with the promise of short-term wealth but may not be able to keep that talent when reality bites and the stock price crashes. People are subject to cognitive bias and they over-estimate the likelihood of success (Las Vegas is tangible evidence of this). When they decide to join an organization providing stock, rather than an old, stodgy bureaucracy offering only salaries and benefits, they may suspend rational thinking and assume their wealth is guaranteed. Stock price escalation made many temporary "paper millionaires," but subsequent events often made it necessary for their employers to tell them that their wealth was short-lived. The victims of this scenario of course blamed the organization, rather than their own judgment, and many humbly marched across the street to the stodgy bureaucracy seeking employment that would more reliably enable them to support themselves. Past history has taught us a lot about the differences between organizations and about how a human capital strategy should be designed to fit the nature of the organization. The fundamental lesson is that what works is what fits and this principle should guide the development of talent management strategies.

The business strategy of an organization will impact the type of talent it requires. The organization must first identify its comparative advantage (what it should focus on, given the alternatives) and then find a way to gain a competitive advantage. 3M identified leadership in adhesive technology as its "edge" and then focused its R&D on developing products that would produce a competitive advantage. Walmart chose to compete based on price, which required it to focus on world-class logistics and an emphasis on cost control. The two organizations consequently pursued the creation of a workforce that enabled them to execute their strategy. And each needed to decide who they could compete with based on their strategy and the workforce created to execute it. Walmart knew that Nordstrom's offered different products to different market segments and chose not to compete with them directly. As a result of the contrast between their chosen strategies each created a workforce suited to their strategy. However, some occupations were critical to both, such as logistics and IT professionals, so it was necessary to compete for specific types of talent. This can necessitate having different value propositions for different types of talent.

Once candidates have been attracted by the organization's value proposition and have decided to pursue a potential relationship with the organization it is necessary to recognize the right talent and then to manage the selection process effectively. One of the most important things to do is to honestly portray what employment will be like in the organization. Decades of research have established that the most effective device for avoiding unwanted turnover in the first 12–24 months is a "realistic job preview."[1] This entails telling the truth … the whole truth. It inoculates the candidate against the shock they experience when they discover aspects of working for that organization that are not ideal. And it begins the employment relationship on an honest, transparent basis.

Recently, the author orchestrated a session with members of a client's executive team that resulted in lists of the "good stuff" and the "not so good stuff" associated with working in the organization. That summary was used in a recruiting brochure and put on the organization's website. It was also communicated during selection interviews. Although some seemingly qualified candidates might have been lost as a result of the honest portrayal it is likely they would have left anyway, after the organization invested considerable resources in hiring and training them. False promises are dangerous … a recent public sector client continued to claim they rewarded performance, despite giving across the board step increases every year. That hypocrisy created cynicism, rather than motivation.

The final step in the employment process is the "onboarding" of new employees. Proper orientation and attention to ensuring new employees know what they need to know and have what they need to have in order to be successful are mandatory. By creating a formal process that is used for all new employees the organization can ensure that there is consistency and that the early socialization of new hires is aligned with the culture of the organization. Assigning highly competent people to act as counselors should be viewed as an investment and a commitment to effectively integrating new people into the organization.

Once an organization is clear about what type of people they need and how they want them to contribute to the organization's success it is much easier to decide what kind of staffing, development, performance management and rewards management strategies are appropriate. How effectively and appropriately the organization structures itself and designs individual roles will have a major impact on workforce effectiveness. How heavily the organization invests in developing its people will significantly impact how well the viability of the workforce will be sustained. And how effectively and appropriately an organization defines, measures, manages and rewards performance will have a major impact on employee engagement and motivation.

All facets of talent management must be assessed in light of the context within which work will be performed. The roles on offer must be well-designed, which means effective in producing the desired results and promoting engagement by appealing to those with the talent needed. These strategies can be communicated to employees and potential employees as the employer value proposition. And it is important that the proposition is communicated in the way that the desired audience will accept most readily. Clear, honest and complete descriptions of the employer brand and the components of the value proposition should be developed and then delivered via the media most used by the intended audience. And if needs change the value proposition should be evaluated to determine whether it will enable the organization to compete for the talent it needs. A "we have always done it this way" philosophy can condemn an organization to live in a past that does not fit current reality and impedes its ability to remain viable into the future.

A major development over the last decade has been the increased use of people who are not employees to do the work of organizations. This has produced what some have called the "gig economy." As contractors, consultants and free-lancers become a significant part of an organization's talent pool the strategies used to define, measure, manage and reward performance face new challenges. When knowledge and skills are in short supply organizations must compete for the talent that possesses what the organization needs to succeed. This real-ity has challenged organizations to also brand themselves as talent utilizers of choice, as opposed to only being employers of choice. The value proposition they offer to the market must result in attracting and retaining the needed tal-ent and motivating that talent to focus on contributing to the organization's success. Many strive to be recognized as a "best employer/talent utilizer" for different types of people. Since neutral entities compile these awards, they will be likely to be more believable than claims made on the organization's website or by its recruiters.

Since 2007 the economy has been turbulent. Currently there seems to be positive growth globally, although economists are divided as to how stable the upward trend will be. The decade that has passed has convinced many that their journey into the future will be more like a rafter facing permanent whitewater, rather than someone riding a roller coaster that has fairly predictable cycles. One must adapt quickly to change when facing whitewater. Accomplished rafters create a navigation strategy based on river maps, supplemented by obser-vations from the shore. But by the time the map is interpreted and the shore observations made the path forward through whitewater has changed. So the important skills for a rafter are agility and possessing a wide range of capabilities that can be utilized to deal with whatever happens. It is the same with organiza-tions. Strategies must be developed that would be robust in a number of pos-sible futures. Agility is insurance against assuming what has worked will work in the future.

The need to be an agile organization has made traditional planning (work-ing towards a single future) ineffective in many cases. Scenario-based plan-ning is increasingly used to prepare for whatever might materialize. And talent management strategies must be sufficiently pliable to change when the context changes. In American football, there is an opportunity to assess the situation before each play and select what seems to be the best strategy. After each play the results can be analyzed and the next play selected. In world football (soccer), there are no huddles and players must utilize a general objective and base their actions on what evolves. Organizations should consider which game is most appropriate to play in the dynamic environment they face today.

This book focuses on attracting, developing and effectively utilizing talent. It begins with human capital planning and then explores strategies and programs that can attract and retain the talent an organization needs. As mentioned ear-lier, different types of organizations and different working relationships will be considered when evaluating the effectiveness of different strategies.

Creating, developing and effectively utilizing the right workforce is funda-mental to success. But organizations must also define, measure, manage and reward performance effectively and appropriately. Balanced scorecards are still useful in providing information about organizational performance, but although the things that are measured (financial, operational, customer and workforce performance) may remain the same, the relative importance of each and what constitutes adequate performance must be defined dynamically. As what the organization needs changes so must its offerings to the talent markets. Designing roles that will appeal to people is critical, whether they are filled by employees or outsiders performing defined units of work. Defining, measuring and appraising individual performance must be done continuously, so that everyone clearly understands what is expected, how current performance compares to standards and what can be done to improve. And performance must be rewarded equitably, competitively and appropriately.

Performance and rewards management strategies are the focus of *Rewarding Performance: Guiding Principles; Custom Strategies*[2] and *Rewarding Performance Globally*.[3] This book focuses on attracting and retaining the required talent utilizing staffing and development strategies that fit the context and that will sustain the viability of the workforce into the future. The appendix provides a primer on analytics, as well as cognitive bias. A review of that material is recommended, especially for those who feel they need an improved understanding of analytical tools and processes. The rapid infusion of technology in talent management processes makes it necessary to understand how analytics can be used to increase efficiency and effectiveness. The material provides a basic grounding in statistical measures and how they are best applied to practical issues. There is also a discussion of how human bias can influence the interpretation of analytical results and how to best integrate human intuition and judgment in the decision-making process.

Notes

1 Cascio, W. *Managing Human Resources* (New York: McGraw-Hill, 2006).
2 Greene, R. *Rewarding Performance, 2nd ed.* (New York: Routledge, 2019).
3 Trompenaars, F. & Greene, R. *Rewarding Performance Globally* (New York: Routledge, 2017).

Chapter 1

Human Capital Planning

"We will face issues and deal with them as they present themselves" is a philosophy that might work in a stable and predictable environment. Such is not the world of the 21st century. Dramatic change in the economic, social and technological environment has made it difficult for organizations to formulate strategies until the future has fully materialized. But organizations must have competent and committed workforces in place at all times. A dramatic rate of environmental change can obsolete current knowledge and skills and create new demands. And as making significant changes to workforces quickly enough is devilishly difficult, the danger of a misalignment between what is needed and what the organization has is increased.

If it has taken ten or more years for someone to acquire the knowledge and skills required to be a skilled typesetter, then that person may be incapable of retraining to work with computerized front-end systems, a role requiring very different skills, in a very short period of time. Yet that was the experience of a large number of newspaper employees when their employers adopted new technology. And many skilled systems and programming technicians competent to work on mainframe-based systems found that they lacked the skills to replace legacy systems with network-based systems when the year 2000 (Y2K) rendered the old systems inoperable.

Although people are capable of learning new things, the process can require extensive training that takes a considerable amount of time and requires considerable investment. In the cases of the newspaper and Y2K transitions, most of the employing organizations had waited too long to train their current employees to become competent to utilize the new technology. When human capital requires a long time to adjust but organizations do not plan well enough to allow for that time the remaining option is to change out the workforce.

When employers attempted to acquire the talent required to effectively face the Y2K event, they quickly realized they were forced to compete in a labor market where the new skills were in short supply and the demand was enormous. As one learns in Economics 101, if demand exceeds supply the price is driven up. So even if an employer is able to acquire the required talent, a premium will be paid. The displacement of the typesetters resulted in newspapers facing industrial disputes and even violence because there were no ready solutions to the problem of having large numbers of employees who were no longer needed ... and who had few skills in demand in the labor market. The lesson that should be learned from these experiences is that waiting to worry about fire prevention or fire insurance until one's house is ablaze is not a feasible strategy.

Another source of shortages of human capital is the passage of time. Employees age and because this happens gradually organizations often suffer from the boiled frog scenario ... the consequences of not acting are not recognized until it is too late. Several recent studies have shown that there is a critical need to do workforce planning that is not being done. The Water Research Foundation did a study of the water utility industry and concluded that: (1) more than 50% of the current workers with critical skills will not be at their utility in ten years, (2) the supply of capable workers will be inadequate and (3) utilities are grossly underinvesting in training aimed at developing replacement workers. Several studies have found that the majority of workers who are 55 and older (about 30% of the workforce) say they will not postpone retirement. The two findings may work together to produce the perfect storm: a large percentage of workers eligible to retire and intending to do so. Optimists point to other studies that say the game is changing and that people will delay retirement or never fully retire at all. Combining the two predictions produces little but confusion. So the best an organization can do is to focus on continuous analysis of the demographics of its workforce and plan in a way that acknowledges that the future may bring surprises or shifts in the plans of employees.

There are different views of planning, particularly when the environment is turbulent. When change is dramatic and rapid some will believe that planning is fruitless, since what will emerge in the future is unpredictable. A few decades ago, many organizations developed ten-year strategic plans they expected to be viable in the future. These plans often were printed and widely distributed so everyone knew where the organization was headed. As the environment became more unpredictable, placing all bets on a specific future became untenable and scenario-based planning became more widely used. Scenario-based planning mandates defining alternative futures ... often an optimistic, a pessimistic and a most likely future. Organizations then test possible strategies against each alternative future and attempt to refine them so they will work reasonably well in all of the futures that might manifest. Royal Dutch Shell was an early adopter of scenario-based planning and was the most successful in dealing with political turbulence that produced supply swings and erratic prices in the oil industry.[1]

In order for scenario-based planning to work, it is necessary to develop environmental scanning capabilities and forecasting models that enable organizations to track what is happening. This assists in predicting what the future will bring, even though predictions are at best approximations. It is not unreasonable to be skeptical about the ability to forecast, but there is research that identifies characteristics that produce better, albeit not precise, forecasts.[2] A ten-year plan is often useful to guide decisions that have a long-range impact, but it is necessary to continuously update it based on current and emerging environmental realities. Organizations must operate in a manner that is consistent with the current context and ensure strategy co-evolves with the environment. What works is what fits … now.

Human capital planning has the same challenges as other types of business planning. For example, cities that are growing need to plan for infrastructure that will be adequate to meet the demands of the future … roads, power generation facilities, water supplies and police/fire protection. All of these services require people to create them and to manage them and it takes time for them to learn to do the required work. And organizations planning to expand their customer base need to be able to service that base. For example, Amazon is continuously acquiring warehouse space and transportation capabilities. It must then staff these facilities. In some cases, organizations decide to outsource work, which can alleviate the necessity of having the required amount of employees and facilities to do everything. But they still need people to make decisions about allocating work and managing it. Most organizations have planning functions, but few of them are concerned with human capital planning. And many Human Resource (HR) departments do not have the expertise or management support to do effective human capital planning. That lack of planning can result in keeping organizations from executing their business strategies.

Human Capital Planning Systems

Figure 1.1 is a model that illustrates a typical human capital planning process. The component steps in the planning process illustrated are:

1. Identify critical roles/occupations.
2. Determine the adequacy of the current workforce.
3. Identify gaps that exist today.
4. Project demand in one, two and five years.
5. Identify gaps that will exist in the future if no action is taken.
6. Define sources of additional people and ways in which people will be lost.
7. Develop a strategy to close gaps and ensure future workforce viability.

It is important to differentiate workforce planning from replacement planning and succession planning. Replacement planning is used to identify an individual who would replace a specific employee if they were to exit the organization or become incapacitated. It is very short-term in nature and serves the purpose of ensuring the organization can operate if unexpected personnel losses occur (e.g., pandemic outbreak, turnover, death/disability, winning the lottery, etc.). Succession planning is more long-range and looks at aggregate supply and demand in a specific occupation or role (e.g., Engineers). Human

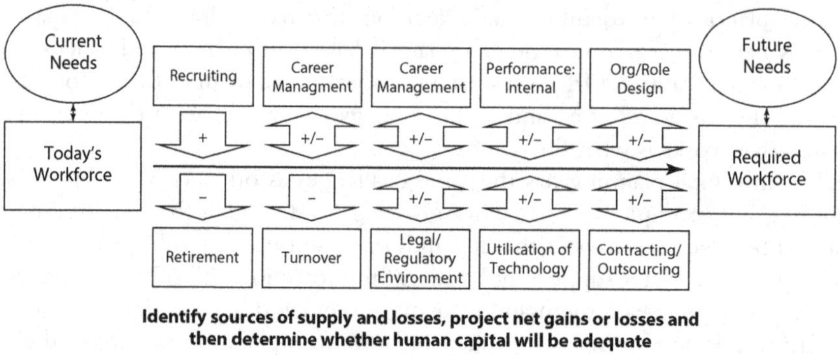

Figure 1.1 Human capital planning model.

capital planning as it is dealt with here is both short- and long-range and looks at external factors as well as internal factors that will impact the supply-demand balance in the workforce.

Human capital planning should be done systematically. If it is not, the organization will deal with surges in demand on an ad hoc basis, which can create gaps, overlaps and inefficiencies in how it staffs. Figure 1.2 is a skill/occupation-specific model that projects how well the organization will be staffed in critical areas. The first step in creating this model is to survey the management team to identify the skills/occupations that are critical to the organization. The criticality of an occupation can certainly vary by organization, depending on

Critical Skill	Supply Today	Demand Today	Demand in 1 yr; 2 yrs; 5 yrs	How long to develop?	Gaps: Supply/ Demand	Strategy For Closing Gaps
			1yr: 2yrs: 5yrs:	< 1yr: 1–2yrs: 2–5yrs:	1yr: 2yrs: 5yrs:	
			1yr: 2yrs: 5yrs:	< 1yr: 1–2yrs: 2–5yrs:	1yr: 2yrs: 5yrs:	
			1yr: 2yrs: 5yrs:	< 1yr: 1–2yrs: 2–5yrs:	1yr: 2yrs: 5yrs:	
			1yr: 2yrs: 5yrs:	< 1yr: 1–2yrs: 2–5yrs:	1yr: 2yrs: 5yrs:	

Figure 1.2 Assessment model.

what the core capabilities are. For example, a utility operating power plants or water treatment plants may identify control room operators as being critical to daily operations. Lacking adequate numbers of qualified people in specific roles could cause them to fail in their primary mission. On the other hand, administrative personnel with general skills may not be identified as critical. By focusing on critical skills, an organization can focus its resources on ensuring its viability. Skilled software designers are critical to a firm whose business is software, but they may be viewed as necessary yet not critical by an organization, if it can outsource projects or hire contractors.

Once a critical skill is identified, the previously described process can be applied to that skill. An additional element in this model is the determination of how long it takes to bring a worker who is qualified to enter the role up to the minimum standard of performance in that role. If the organization finds that there will be a substantial gap between supply and demand in one to two years and it takes three to four years to develop an entrant, it becomes apparent that a potential crisis already exists, as time is too short to train someone without the required skills. This is a critical concern when some jobs have to be filled with people holding licenses or certifications. Most formal credentials have an experience requirement as well as a test to determine competence. If a Lead Water Treatment Plant Operator needs a license that requires ten years of experience, then people cannot be fast-tracked in a shorter period of time.

Table 1.1 is an example of a detailed workforce flow analysis for control room personnel in a utility. It combines estimates with projections of likely

Table 1.1 Workforce Flow Analysis

	Treatment Plant Operators		
	Entry Level	Journey Level	Senior/Lead
Current staff	4	6	10
Current demand	2	12	6
Gaps (current)	(2)	6	(4)
Demand: 1 yr. out	3	12	6
Losses projected	1	(1)	4
Gaps: 1 yr. out	0	7	4
Demand: 2 yrs. out	3	13	7
Losses projected	2	2	7
Gaps: 2 yrs. out	2	10	12
Demand: 5 yrs. out	3	14	8
Losses projected	4	5	10
Gaps: 5 yrs. out	6	16	23
ADDED SUPPLY NEEDED			
Current	0	6	0
1 yr. out	0	7	4
2 yrs. out	2	10	12
5 yrs. out	6	16	23

events (e.g., the number retiring in a given year and/or the likely turnover) to provide an estimate of the magnitude of shortages. Once deficit positions are identified, it becomes necessary to consider alternative actions, such as attracting fully qualified people from other organizations or adopting accelerated training programs. Bringing in people from outside can result in inflated salaries and inequity relative to existing employees, as well as impacting the career opportunities of existing employees. However, if it is not possible to develop current employees in time, this may be unavoidable, and it solves the problem of having no one to perform critical operations. The age demographics of an industry may present yet another challenge. If the other organizations employing the talent required have the same issue (pending retirements), sourcing from the outside is not a feasible solution. If an organization cannot develop people to fill the gap or attract senior people from other organizations, it may be necessary to contract the work out. Some would argue that making projections five years out is sheer speculation and indeed things can change. However, the option (not planning) is not viable. And planning is at the very least like rain dancing … it may have no impact on the rainfall but it makes the dancers feel they are doing all they can.

The pace of globalization of trade has created new challenges for organizations who want to do business outside of one country. In order to create and service customers across borders, an organization must first convince potential customers that they should buy the goods and services that it has on offer. Then they must deliver the product to the customers. Crossing borders generally means crossing cultures and this often creates new demands for those responsible for marketing. Naming a car Nova and then attempting to sell it to Spanish-speaking people can prove to be fruitless. A car that does not go rarely is in great demand. Those supplying the products must therefore understand the customer and be able to communicate in a manner that creates a positive image. The University of Phoenix attempted to transfer their educational model from the United States to Europe, investing in infrastructure, only to find out that potential students in some countries in Europe were not interested in attending school at night while working full time. So the domestic organization that wishes to become a multinational may discover that their employees need new competencies in order to be effective. Needing to speak a foreign language is a hurdle that can be addressed by investing in language training or by utilizing translation technology, but being able to understand different cultural orientations is a much more challenging requirement to meet.

Multinationals have alternative sources for staffing their international operations. They can hire citizens of the host country who may already possess the required understanding of the cultural orientation of potential customers in that country. Or they can invest in training their employees in the headquarters country so that they can work effectively across cultures. Sending a headquarters employee to a foreign country on an expatriate assignment is one approach to managing foreign operations. But the assignee must possess the necessary understanding of the prevailing culture in order to be effective. Having employees cross-trained in cultural communication operate remotely from headquarters using technology is also an option. But the fundamental change that globalization makes necessary is the need to add cultural competence to the competency model used to select and evaluate employees.

Once the planning is complete, the organization is faced with developing a human resource management strategy and supporting programs that will produce the desired results. The remainder of this chapter will identify the requirements for success and discuss strategies/programs that will help the organization meet these requirements in general terms. More detail on each will be provided in subsequent chapters.

Attract the Right People

In order to ensure that the organization is capable of competing for the available talent, it is prudent to first define the "best fit" employee profile. The organization's culture, the competencies it determines are required to perform the roles and its rewards philosophy will all have an impact on the type of candidate the organization wishes to attract. This means that the organization must develop its "brand" as an employer and communicate what that means to potential candidates. It also requires that an honest value proposition be put forth so that those considering application know what to expect.

By honestly describing itself as an employer, an organization can become a preferred choice for candidates. And the honesty will attract the right candidates. Netflix describes its value proposition as consisting of premium pay, opportunity to use one's skills and the chance to do interesting and challenging work. It also admits to having high-performance expectations and limited job security. The picture that paints will be an attractor for those who accept the brand. Google offers meals, fitness facilities, transportation, concierge services and other attractive benefits but does not hide the fact that if someone is not actively contributing at a high level they will not be employed for long. There are organizations that actively contribute to charitable causes and others that take steps to take care of the environment. The socially responsible profile can also be the tipping point for some candidates when they select an employer from among multiple options. It is very difficult to project a false persona today, largely due to social media. Websites such as Glassdoor.com offer present and past employees with the opportunity to provide their assessment of what it is like to work for organizations. Employers are often criticized unfairly but still must convince potential candidates that the brand they present is accurately defined. Branding is marketing but, as with marketing products, the truth will be known.

Selection processes must be valid in order to be effective. This means they should result in hiring the right people. There are a number of tools available to assist in finding the right person. The most commonly used technique is the one-on-one unstructured interview, which involves a recruiter or manager having a discussion with a candidate and evaluating the interviewee on the basis of that conversation. Regrettably, this has been shown to be the least valid approach to selection. In fact, research shows it has very little power to predict the success of the candidate if this is the sole basis upon which a hiring decision is made. This will be discussed further in Chapter 4.

Once the selection is made, the organization must invest in a viable "onboarding" process that ensures new employees are smoothly transitioned into the workplace. If all of these requirements are not met, then the usual consequences are difficulty in recruiting and/or unacceptable losses through turnover. Effective processes will be explored in Chapter 6.

Develop People Appropriately

The MIT study of the global auto industry conducted several years ago found that U.S. organizations invested far less in hiring new employees and in training new people than Asian and European organizations with U.S. operations.[3] It was the first major study that identified this reality. That pattern appears to continue, according to further research. This may be due partly to the fact that U.S. accounting principles mandate treating training as a short-term expense (which reduces profits), with no certain future benefit (at least no definable financial benefit). Treating employees as a cost rather than an asset results in a "cost minimization" perspective. If employees are viewed as assets it changes the perspective, as it is often prudent to invest in assets, while it always is prudent to minimize costs. Most organizations do accept that training is necessary if people are to perform well. There is also a recognition that employees must share knowledge across the organization if what is known results in effective utilization. But the highly individualistic culture in many U.S. organizations breeds competitiveness for larger salary increases and individual bonuses and promotions, which can impede the willingness of employees to share their knowledge with peers and to codify it in procedures. Knowledge dissemination through on-the-job training can be a very effective tool, but employees have to be willing to share their know-how with their peers. Additionally, in organizations subject to downsizing employees often retreat into a protective mode, believing they compete for jobs. A culture that values and rewards knowledge sharing can help to increase dissemination; assuming how rewards are determined does not override the appeal to share.

There are significant obstacles to the dissemination of knowledge and to the application of best practices in many organizations. This makes employee development more difficult, or at least more expensive, because of the additional need for formal training. Some of the resistance to sharing knowledge can be overcome by celebrating and rewarding those who make others more effective. The author has found that adding "Contribution to the Effectiveness of Others/the Unit" as a factor to performance appraisals can help to show employees that this is valued. Productivity, quality of work and dependability/ adherence to policies are individual measures and adding the contribution factor makes measurement better suited to interdependent work.

Better career management can help reduce the need for formal training that requires people to be off the job while training. Much lost time can be avoided if career paths are well-thought-out and communicated, and developmental assignments are used to allow employees to accumulate knowledge and skills while being productive. Career planning can also be a positive in retaining people, particularly those who have been entering the workforce during the last decade. Since the lifelong employment contract has expired, the "big two" for attracting and retaining the recent cohorts entering the workforce have been "pay me well" and "keep me marketable."

Maximize the Available Supply

Organizations that have experienced low levels of turnover often relax their recruitment efforts and/or lapse into using the same strategy for transitioning in new employees. But skill shortages are likely to occur for some occupations as technology advances. So it is prudent for organizations to become more proactive and innovative in developing sources of supply. Employee referrals are extremely effective if they are valued and rewarded. Identifying and developing nontraditional sources can also produce a high yield on investment. Alliances with educational institutions, job fairs, open houses and marketing campaigns can help to inform the outside world about opportunities. And increased investment in training can expand the capabilities of current employees, increasing the supply. Sourcing talent is the topic for Chapter 2. Training and development are discussed in Chapter 7.

Skilled trades personnel are becoming more difficult to find in many areas in the United States, and it may be necessary for organizations to band together to create training programs in technical schools. This role has historically been filled by unions, but as unions became less prevalent a void was created. By demonstrating that there is an unfilled need, community colleges may be enticed into developing technical programs that provide additional qualified candidates, particularly if organizations support students with internships and the prospect of employment. In industries in which females or minorities are underrepresented, it may be possible to rethink recruiting strategies to reach this growing segment of the labor force. And as jobs requiring significant physical effort become less prevalent utilizing older workers may be a winning strategy for expanding supply. Talent platforms have become more common, acting as talent intermediaries. They can provide access to freelancers, reducing the difficulties faced by staffing functions in organizations associated with finding these widely dispersed individuals.

Maximize Productivity

If people are made more productive, it may take fewer of them to get the job done. Many organizations are shifting from seniority-based wages and salaries to instituting merit pay and incentive programs to provide a reason to increase performance. "What you measure and reward you will surely get more of" is a concept supported by behavioral research. There has been a shift from step-rate systems (pay incremented by longevity) to merit-based or skill-based pay programs over the past several decades. Although public and not-for-profit organizations still use programs that pay for performance sparingly, the competition for people with the private sector and the benefits of offering incentives are beginning to increase their adoption of merit pay and incentive programs.

Investing in capital equipment and technology is another source of increased productivity. If skills are more expensive or unavailable, investing in technology may prove to be a good strategy. Also, redesigning work processes can take out unnecessary work and reduce staffing and shorten timelines. In some cases, redesigning what people do and/or reallocating specific responsibilities can increase productivity and also lessen the number of incumbents required in occupations that are in short supply. If Engineers spend a substantial amount of their time doing administrative work, that work can be performed by people capable to do it (i.e., Project Administration Specialists), and reassigning that work can reduce the number of Engineers required.

There is an increasing utilization of artificial intelligence and machine learning technology and this has created a concern that robots and algorithms will replace people. To date, it seems more likely that technology will be used to do work that has specifically defined procedures and that it will alter the nature of the work performed by some people, rather than obsoleting people. But if the skills required change it is necessary to change the competencies of current employees. It is clearly in the best interests of organizations to continuously evaluate technology and to make decisions about the allocation of work. But given the reluctance to invest in training it may be difficult to ensure productivity is maximized by being certain competent people utilize the technology that is employed.

Transfer and Utilize Knowledge Effectively

Many organizations are investing in "knowledge management" programs that are designed to share best practices and critical information more widely and more efficiently. By promoting a sharing culture and recognizing contributions to the organization's knowledge all employees can be made more effective and more likely to create and share new knowledge. Creating an internal "yellow pages" directory that refers people to documents or people knowledgeable in specific areas makes it easier for employees to deal with situations they have not faced before. It also makes it possible to recognize the experts as being valuable resources, which can be an effective way to recognize their capabilities. It is advisable to invest in turning tacit knowledge (the know-how people carry around in their heads, often unaware of it) into explicit knowledge that is available to others. Databases that are coded by subject can supplement work procedures and manuals.

It is also necessary to create a culture that encourages informed emulation (called legal theft in one organization), which makes it clear that reusing practices is not the sign of someone who lacks imagination, but rather ingenuity in another form. Technology can be useful in dissemination but just because people can share information does not guarantee they will, particularly if they believe it is not in their best interests. The culture of the organization is a major factor in encouraging or impeding dissemination and if individuals compete with each other for their share of fixed budgets it makes sharing seem a poor strategy. But if incentives tied to organizational or unit performance are also used the desired cooperative sharing can be encouraged.

Redesign the Organization and Employee Roles

Work design can have a profound impact on productivity and employee satisfaction. There is a rich literature in organizational design and in designing workplaces/work roles. Job enlargement (often called cross-training) is widening the variety of things that are done. It can be a strategy for increasing productivity, as it produces a more flexible workforce that can be shifted to meet changing workloads. Job enrichment, which gives people more responsibility for their work, can also contribute to satisfaction and to fewer "handoffs" between people (e.g., having people handle quality control for the work they do).

There has been much discussion about the concept of a job becoming obsolete, but this varies across roles and workplaces. The model for effective role design that is most supported by research is one that promotes: (1) appropriate skill variety, (2) understanding why the work is important, (3) appropriate autonomy and (4) continuous measurement and feedback.[4] In cases in which a given process and defined rules must be adhered to (e.g., accounting), it is reasonable to assume organizations will consider automating some processes. When people must jump from one activity or project to another, there may be less focus on a specific list of tasks they are to perform and more on what they need to contribute to achieve the desired results.

The use of work teams in place of individual jobs has become more prevalent where it makes sense. But the use of teams should be limited to situations where the work process lends itself to this strategy and when there are people available who are capable of operating effectively as a team member. Certainly, more work is done in a project mode and project management tools should be applied where appropriate.

Manage Losses Due to Retirement

For many organizations, the biggest challenge will be replacing the retiring Boomers, particularly if they have spent all or most of their career with one employer. If the employer has a defined benefit pension plan that enables employees to retire with full benefits when their age and years of service total a specified number, it is reasonable to assume that many will exercise that right and do so as soon as they are fully vested. And because U.S. laws limit the ability of some employees to continue to work for an employer while they are receiving pension benefits from that organization there are limitations with regard to the way in which they are retained after retirement.

It is possible to extend career management strategies beyond the time when an employee ceases to be a full-time, permanent employee. If an organization needs to train new personnel, it could create a training contract with retiring employees to accomplish the training. Having a retiree spend one week a month or one day a week running a focused training program may allow the organization to utilize the retiree as a contractor and to accomplish what otherwise would have been a difficult challenge. Although mentoring and other on-the-job approaches can theoretically accomplish the same thing, it is often found that daily work demands cause underinvestment in training time, with dire consequences when the experienced person leaves.

Many organizations have created the ideal incentives for pushing out everyone eligible for retirement, no matter how badly they are needed or want to stay. Overly generous retirement plans, fully paid retiree health programs and other rewards for past service may provide more value to those who leave than those who stay. Employees who are eligible for full retirement at a fairly young age can begin to receive the income stream from the pension plan and move on to collect a second income from another organization. Conversely, defined contribution plans lend themselves to encouraging continued service more than defined benefit plans, since additional benefits can accrue beyond the normal retirement. Also, those who are relatively secure financially are in a position to contribute more to these plans in their later years.

Manage Losses Due to Turnover

The most potent approach to ensuring a viable workforce into the future is to avoid losing any valued employees when it is inconvenient. Organizations with very low turnover of incumbents with critical skills and who are top performers will certainly have less of a challenge than those suffering large losses of these people. But as so many competitors will be likely to be facing the same challenges, they will probably be doing their best to spoil the party by focusing on the organization's best people as a desirable source of talent.

All of the approaches already mentioned will help to minimize dysfunctional turnover. Well-designed jobs in organizations with attractive cultures and generous rewards will certainly promote retention, as will career planning programs that invest in employees. The best strategy is to do all the things with a positive impact on turnover and avoid those with a negative impact. One approach to countering the effects of turnover is not giving up when someone leaves but to maintain "alumni relations." By making it clear in exit interviews that someone is welcome to knock on the door in the future and by periodically reminding them that this is still an option, organizations may find that losses can become future sources of supply.

One of the most effective retention strategies is to aggressively communicate the value of the compensation and benefits package to employees. One of the tragedies for many organizations with generous employee benefits is that employees take them for granted and grossly underestimate the financial value of that which is provided. For example, most organizations would find that employees estimate the expenditure on benefits by the employer at something less than half of what it is. Furthermore, if asked what the benefits would cost if they were acquired directly by the employee, the estimates will almost certainly be far less than half of the true cost in most cases. The U.S. health care system relies heavily on employers to provide health insurance, which is not the case in many countries with national health care systems. So, when Toyota does not have to build benefits costs into its pricing and GM has more health care costs than steel costs in each car costs, who wins the competitive face-off?

Failure to provide comprehensive individual employee benefits statements on a regular basis misses an opportunity to better inform employees about the value of their benefits. Current technology has made providing these statements relatively easy and inexpensive. Another way to increase the perceived value of the benefits package is to compare what the organization provides with what is typically provided by other employers. This type of competitive analysis needs to be done periodically, to ensure that current trends toward limiting benefits and increasing the portion of total costs contributed by employees are recognized and that realistic values are placed on what is provided by the employees. Organizations that have historically not asked employees to contribute toward the cost of their health care will experience resistance when beginning to charge employees even a nominal amount. But the noise level can be reduced if the economic necessity for these actions is clearly communicated and if the communication is accompanied by tangible comparisons to what is happening in other organizations.

There is another approach to benefits that can further increase the perceived value to employees. Providing a "flexible" package that enables individuals to pick from equal value options gives them the freedom to choose those things with the most value and appeal to them. The traditional benefits package in the United States was designed for a male employee with a wife and 2.1 children. Given the diversity of workforces today, that is clearly a flawed approach. Pooling all types of time off, offering a range of health care packages and ensuring that employees understand how to create tax-free accounts to pay premiums and deductibles are all strategies that cost nothing except the time and attention of HR specialists knowledgeable about the options. Employees are intelligent enough to understand when programs make them better off by providing what they want at the best possible out-of-pocket cost.

Outsourcing Work

Not all work performed by an organization needs to be performed by employees. Many organizations are accustomed to contracting out large projects, such as building new infrastructure, but most perform work that is ongoing with employees, either full-time, part-time or seasonal. Organizations are increasingly finding that work not critical to their core capabilities can often be done better by other organizations specializing in that work. For example, it is unlikely that a hospital is going to be "world class" in IT, Accounting, Payroll and other administrative processes that are recurring and transactional in nature. This is true because the best-qualified people in these fields will not aspire to work in a hospital, as they understand that the organization's primary mission is not closely related to what they do. As a result, they are far down the list of which skills are critical. It may also be that the hospital does not see the need to fund the development of the most advanced systems and therefore the employees will be unlikely to stay up with the "state of the art" in their field.

By working together, organizations could represent a viable business for an outsourcing provider and enjoy state of the art systems and processes without each having to make a large investment in creating them on their own. Alliances and joint ventures between multiple organizations have become more common in many industries: newspapers share distribution services and printing operations; organizations of all types use the same providers to process their payrolls. It is unlikely that organizations will outsource activities that are critical to their success, but the current popularity of outsourcing demonstrates that it is not necessary to do some of the things organizations are doing if they will struggle to do them well and effectively. A final consideration is the culture, which is often (and many would argue appropriately) focused on core capabilities that produce competitive advantage. Having the most innovative and leading-edge administrative systems may be a low priority for an R&D organization, frustrating administrative professionals who are trained to make their work as good as it can be. This may create conflicts and lead to dissatisfaction and turnover.

Manage the Challenges Created by Globalization

Globalization has impacted how many organizations do business. Supply/logistics chains have become globalized in order to procure the best available commodity at the best price as quickly as possible. Talent management has also been globalized. Even if an organization employs people in a single country it is still likely to have a diverse workforce. Due to the mobility of talent, if the organization does not go "there" talent will come "here." And technology has also made it possible for people to do work "there" without coming "here." The result has been workforces that are more culturally diverse, which presents another set of challenges in managing people. Even though a shortage of engineering graduates in the United States could be dealt with by employing the plentiful supply of graduates in India or China a number of preconditions must be met. Experts have evaluated the competence of graduates in other countries and found a large percentage are not capable of performing adequately in a multinational organization. In many countries the standards for granting degrees are lower than they are in the developed world.

Another obstacle to utilizing foreign personnel is the reality that some may not be able to enter the country they are being hired to work in. For example, the United States tightly controls H1-B visas so tightly that allocations are typically used up the first day of the year. It may be possible for a multinational to have the talent work remotely in their home country, rather than move to the headquarters country. Satellite offices are being set up across the United States to avoid people having to face high cost of living and unattractive commutes, so it may be possible to create these offices outside the United States. Much research and development is being done in "centers of excellence" in places like Singapore and it is possible that a Silicon Valley–based organization can create similar talent colonies elsewhere.

The other major challenge associated with having a culturally diverse workforce is getting people to work effectively across cultures and getting them to accept organizational human resource policies and programs as equitable, competitive and appropriate. Beliefs and values are often deeply imbedded through socialization, and if how an organization does things is at odds with how an employee thinks they should be done it can create conflict. Whether an organization accommodates cultural differences and how it does so can be a major determinant of the ability to utilize people with different cultural orientations. Those interested in cross-cultural challenges can refer to the book *Rewarding Performance Globally*.[5]

Conclusion

Despite the uncertainties about whether there will be a shortage of workers in the near future and how large it will be, it is not wise to assume the organization will be able to deal with whatever happens when it happens. There have been shortages in some occupations, often lasting as long as three to five years per crisis (the time it takes to replenish the supply and redirect people in formal education programs to "hot" occupations). There will always be shortages for some organizations and for some critical skills, at least for short periods. The biggest mistake is not trying to plan for the future and waiting until the crisis is unarguably afoot.

Scenario-based planning techniques should be applied to workforce planning. By looking into the future and formulating a "worst case," a "best case" and a "most likely" scenario, an organization can develop strategies that are reasonably robust when one of the possible futures becomes the present. This type of planning equips the organization to respond more quickly and appropriately because it has thought in advance about its responses to a range of realities and has implemented processes and programs to help it deal with what occurs.

How an organization views talent will have an impact on how it manages talent. If people are thought to be capable of significant development, based on the belief that everyone has some kind of talent and potential, the strategy for building the right workforce may be one of investing heavily in making all the people all they can be. But if the belief is that the top performers are the ones that create success investment in development may be focused on the chosen few. Organizations rarely have adequate resources for development and the temptation is to focus on the few showing the greatest promise. Chapter 4 will address strategies for selecting talent and Chapter 7 will address development strategies.

Notes

1 Schwartz, P. *The Art of the Long View* (New York: Currency Doubleday, 1991).
2 Tetlock, P. & Cardner, D. *Superforecasting* (New York: Crown, 2015).
3 Womock, J., Jones, D., & Roos, D. *The Machine That Changed the World* (New York: Rawson Assoc., 1990).
4 Hackman, J. & Oldham, G. *Job Redesign* (Reading, MA: Addison-Wesley, 1980).
5 Trompenaars, F. & Greene, R. *Rewarding Performance Globally* (New York: Routledge, 2017).

Chapter 2

Determining Talent Requirements

In order to be successful in creating and developing the right workforce for an organization, the characteristics of that workforce must be defined. A staffing strategy defines how an organization plans to get the talent it needs. It first has to know what it needs.

Figure 2.1 is a model that defines the steps that are required for attracting, developing and retaining the talent the organization requires. The first step is to develop the "success profile," which involves defining the competencies, knowledge, skills and motivational fit a workforce must possess. The next step is to develop a strategy for sourcing the talent required, which will be discussed in Chapter 3. Once a pool of qualified candidates is identified those offering the best fit to the organization's need must be selected and brought into the organization. This process will be discussed in Chapter 4. And in order to sustain the viability of the talent pool people must be developed, their contributions evaluated, and those contributions rewarded.

The only sustainable competitive advantage for an organization is a competent workforce that is committed to the organization's success. All other forms of capital can be obtained by competitors under similar conditions. But a competent and committed workforce cannot be purchased ... it must be built. It is also important for an organization to realize that yesterday's successful workforce may not be ideal for the evolving environment. As IBM shifted from focusing on equipment in the form of mainframe hardware and personal computers to providing technical services, the required mix of knowledge, skills and abilities it required in its workforce underwent dramatic change. Had it stayed its course it would have become less relevant in a world that changed what it valued. The strong culture IBM had created was an obstacle to adapting, since it was so imbedded, but the organization invested in changing its talent pool to fit the new service-oriented strategy and modified its culture to fit its business offerings.

Knowing that the existing workforce does not fit the context that has evolved is a critical realization. But changing out a workforce is much like reprogramming the software that guides an airplane while it is in flight ... it has to stay on course during the transition. And navigating in a dramatic environment

Figure 2.1 Strategic staffing.

is more like playing world football (soccer) than playing American football. There are no huddles to evaluate the last play and to decide on the next one, defining each player's role in advance. Time outs are also limited. So the talent strategy has to be managed using environmental scanning and scenario-based planning, as described in Chapter One. Executing the talent strategy must be accomplished by reacting to unanticipated conditions and adjusting play to fit the new reality, much like soccer players do. And there are challenges created by the inability to freely substitute. In organizations, talent substitution may face legal and economic barriers, as well as social pressures.

In much of Asia, it has been common for large organizations to hire employees with the expectation that they will be there for their entire careers. In contrast, the "employment at will" doctrine prevalent in the United States (I can fire you any time for any reason, or for no reason at all) seems on the surface to enable immediate replacement of large numbers of employees whose usefulness has declined as a result of environmental change or resets of the strategy. But the ease of replacement is not as great as it seems on the surface. Terminating employees viewed as obsolete and hiring another group of employees with the skills now needed can create large legal obligations, excessive costs and strong social reactions.[1] If an organization's brand sends the message that people are the most disposable asset, rather than the most important asset, its ability to attract top talent may suffer.

Workforce planning can help organizations anticipate changing needs and give them adequate time to change the nature of its talent pool in a manner that exacts fewer costs. It is easier to modify a plane's software while it is on the ground and it is easier to retrain people when they are offline. If there is adequate time to retrain current employees to meet the new requirements then terminations and new hires can be kept at acceptable levels. There is of course an issue if the type of employee currently employed is not capable of being retrained. This means that controlling churn must be a significant factor in deciding who is hired in the first place. If employees who have done routine coding work on IT systems must now use advanced techniques to develop new cyber security software in order to be useful they may lack the required native intelligence and/or quantitative analysis knowledge. Knowledge gaps can only be closed through training if the person has the requisite intelligence to be developed, if there is adequate time and if the organization is willing to make the investment.

Microsoft, Google and other tech firms have stated that they hire the smartest people and then figure out how to utilize them, rather than hiring for a specific type of work. The underlying assumption is that when the nature of the work changes employees will have the capability to adapt. Managing talent as a diversified asset portfolio, much like experts suggest financial portfolios should be managed, is a sound principle. If a dynamic environment exists there will be high levels of uncertainty about the appropriate mix of investments. In order to be effective in that kind of environment the organization must ensure the talent portfolio is diversified in a manner that results in acceptable performance, no matter what materializes. On the other hand, if the environment is stable it might be optimal to create a specialized portfolio that is ideal for the current realities.

For an organization to benefit from having intelligent and knowledgeable employees the employees must be willing to share their knowledge when it will benefit the organization. Knowledge management is a critical activity, particularly in today's environment. The CEO of HP once stated that if HP knew what it knows and was able to use it across the organization it would have an immediate and significant positive impact on performance. Hiring smart people could result in everyone competing to be the smartest person in the room, a common characteristic among highly intelligent people. This is not a mindset that facilitates sharing the best ideas. An organization must shape the culture to be supportive of knowledge management, which will let employees know this is important and that sharers are valued much more highly than hoarders. Palo Alto Research Center (PARC), a subsidiary of Xerox, invented many of the components necessary for modern computing. But Xerox failed to gain financial benefits from commercializing the innovations due to a failure to effectively share knowledge across the organization. The scientists doing the inventing viewed the innovations as an end. The lack of communication and understanding across the organizational silos caused Xerox to ignore the commercial potential and the result was that the inventions were given away. Much of what was learned as a result of the Saturn experiment never was transmitted to General Motors, due to an apparent inability to consider other ways of selling cars. If an organization fails to understand and communicate the criticality of knowledge management there will be little incentive for employees to share what they know and to collaborate with other parts of the organization to maximize performance.

The fundamentals of sound knowledge management are well known. It is critical to first identify the different types of knowledge. Tacit and explicit knowledge differ in that the former must be transferred from person to person while explicit knowledge can be codified into manuals, operating procedures and other forms of communication that can be accessed by individuals.[2] Tacit knowledge is something someone knows but cannot fully explain to someone else in a manner that enables them to apply that knowledge immediately. It is much like muscle memory, that athletes achieve through repetitive simulation of physical activity. Executing something again and again can hard wire the ability to do it instinctively into the nervous system. The same is often true when someone faces a situation and somehow knows exactly how to act, even though the situation is not a carbon copy of something experienced in the past. The human brain is capable of filling in spaces, as long as a gestalt exists to provide a framework.

Tacit knowledge exists in the minds of employees, but does not appear in the procedure manuals, principally because it is difficult to write step by step instructions that enable someone to acquire and use it. Actions often appear to be instinctive even though they are in fact guided by knowledge possessed by the person. Tacit knowledge can become inaccessible to the organization when the possessor retires, terminates or just refuses to make it accessible to others. In Chapter 1, the importance of workforce planning was discussed and one of the benefits of anticipatory planning is that there is time to codify tacit knowledge before it exits with an employee. Much of tacit knowledge transmission must occur using an approach similar to the apprentice and craftsman interaction that over time turns the apprentice into a craftsman. Side–by–side actions can create mental memory that enables the apprentice to build an inventory of experience and knowledge.

Many organizations use mentoring and shadowing programs that simulate this process and enable tacit knowledge to be captured, even if remains as tacit knowledge, but now it is also possessed by the recipient. Knowledge is a unique asset … it can be given away again and again while the giver still possesses it. So in organizations where a significant part of intellectual capital is in tacit form there must be a knowledge-sharing culture created. This has an impact on the type of workforce required. Some years after the first moon landing NASA admitted that it would have to relearn how to go to the moon again, because it had "forgotten" how to do that. The best strategy to overcome that would probably be to bring back the people with that tacit knowledge and have them repeat past behavior. That however may not be possible.

The alternative to hiring employees is to retain qualified personnel under contract to do work. The emergence of the "gig" option makes it possible to avoid the extensive investment in employing personnel. This may become attractive when there is not enough work of a particular kind to be done on a sustained basis, which is what justifies an increase in the current staffing level. Although this option seems on the surface to be ideal an organization must worry about workforce continuity as well as ensuring those doing the work are engaged and committed to achieving the organization's objectives. If the work has a known duration it may be possible to manage short term spikes in workload with temporary staff. And if the work is a one-time project, the required knowledge and skills that will not be needed in the future using outsiders may be preferable to employing additional staff.

What Is the "Right" Workforce?

The "right" workforce is the one that best fits the current context and that is capable of remaining viable into the future. But the characteristics of the current environment and of what will manifest in the future must be known in order to ensure the workforce is a good fit. Figure 1.1 in Chapter 1 provides a model for continuous realignment of the workforce as things change. It requires that the organization first evaluate the adequacy of the current workforce against current requirements. Then it calls for the assessment of the sources of talent and the probable losses over time. Projections of what the workforce requirements will be at various times (one year, two years and five years) are then made, to determine whether the talent needs will be met. This aggregate view of the workforce needs to be supplemented by definitions of the requirements at different levels.

Organizations must make strategic business decisions before talent management strategies can be formulated. The first step towards defining the required workforce is to decide what the organization will do. Nike, Apple and other organizations choose to perform selected tasks and to outsource others, such as manufacturing. This decision has an impact on workforce requirements. There still might be a management structure for the manufacturing function, which will be charged with overseeing the activities of contractors, but those doing the work will be managed by other organizations. Within organizational functions, such as human resources, some activities might be outsourced, rather than being performed by employees. Many organizations outsource activities that are highly routinized, such as payroll. Since a contractor typically has extensive experience and performs the activities for other customers it is likely that they will be more proficient and efficient in doing the work. And if the work is cyclical, requiring significant effort at specific times, with gaps in between, outsourcing or using part-time/seasonal employees becomes more attractive, since using a staff consisting of full-time employees is too inflexible to fit the requirements imposed by uneven work demands.

Technological advances have also created new alternative ways of getting work done. Work that can be defined specifically can be controlled by algorithms that specify how decisions are made. Manual work can sometimes be done by robots. It is also possible to do more work remotely and asynchronously, using communication technology. This means in some cases those perform-ing the work may not have to be co-located, globalizing the talent market. Contractors, consultants and freelancers become viable options when work can be completely defined and outcomes clearly specified.

Another approach is crowdsourcing, where individuals voluntarily do defined blocks of work for an agreed-to reward or just the chance to win a contest. This approach enables freelancers to connect directly with the organi-zation. But intermediary organizations can also be used. These intermediar-ies identify qualified candidates and facilitate the process that creates a link between the people doing the work and the organization needing the work done. Referred to as "talent platforms," UpWork, oDesk, TopCoder, Tongal, Amazon Mechanical Turk, Business Talent Group and others have been cre-ated to source talent and to provide a structure for matching talent to task. These organizations are task/project focused and can arrange for short segments of projects that have been deconstructed to be done by many different people. The book *Lead the Work* discusses these alternative strategies in more detail.[3]

The use of outsiders creates different management challenges than those faced when managing employees. When a manager deals with a subordinate employee there is an established authority structure. When contractors or free-lancers are directed without that kind of authority it changes what managers must do and how they do it. This is often overlooked when the allure of having the ability to retain people when they are needed and let them go when they are not makes outsourcing work attractive. It must also be recognized that the work of outsiders and employees must be integrated once it is completed and this can be difficult if the outsiders use different techniques than employees.

When Boeing designed and manufactured the Dreamliner the work was parceled out to different countries, presenting enormous integration challenges. Compatibility was critical when the parts had to be assembled like a jigsaw puzzle. The space industry has experienced conflicts across country borders, such as when one subcontractor uses the metric system, but another does not. With parts of the Dreamliner being designed and built by different parties the concern is whether they will all fit when they must be assembled into a plane. On the surface, this approach may seem overly risky but Boeing had little choice. The airlines in the rest of the world are typically state-owned and those airlines could threaten to purchase from Airbus if they did not get a "piece of the action" from Boeing (including technology transfer, intellectual capital development and jobs for locals).

Organizations are subject to having their brand damaged by contractors doing things that are a violation of agreed-to principles. Using child labor or exposing people to dangerous or damaging work environments can occur half-way across the world when direct control is not possible. But Nike or Apple will be held accountable for atrocities that become public knowledge. Foxconn practices caused Apple to be accused of abusing workers, even though Apple did not employ or manage them. The swoosh and the apple are brand symbols worth enormous sums, as long as they are not associated with actions that violate customer values and expectations. There can also be damage to employee morale when work that is viewed as leading edge and valued in the marketplace is handed over to outsiders. Outsourcing work can be viewed as a threat to employment security and/or an indication that the organization does not value or respect employee capabilities. If employees are not allowed to learn new technology they are prone to believing career opportunities are scarce and they may consider departing to organizations willing to commit to continuous investment in maintaining skill currency.

Shaping the Workforce

Once an organization has identified the work that will be done there must be an assessment of what specific functions and occupations must be capable of doing. Within a function, such as human resources, some activities may be suited to outsourcing. As mentioned before payroll is a process that requires detailed knowledge of laws and tax codes. These must be adhered to, and changes must be monitored and incorporated into the process. When doing payroll for a globalized workforce those responsible will require interpretation of and compliance with numerous different legal and regulatory requirements across countries. The payroll process can be specifically defined and all requirements can be built into algorithms that can efficiently and effectively produce the desired outcomes. But whoever does the work must be sufficiently knowledgeable about a wide variety of requirements as to how things are done.

DuPont attempted to use stock options to celebrate an anniversary, no doubt thinking that holding stock would make employees think like and behave like owners. When the program was rolled out globally it was found that a majority of the 50-some countries posed challenges. In some the possession of stock in a foreign company was illegal. The taxation of the awards varied from taxing the value upon issuance to taxing it upon exercise to taxing it upon sale. When the administrative challenges had been addressed they could have cost more than the value of the awards. And not knowing about different laws and tax codes is no defense. In situations like this, it may be advisable to have the internal compensation staff use expert outside resources available to deal with this type of complexity.

If there are requirements that certain occupations must be staffed by people with specific credentials competency models can be developed that incorporate the qualifications. These models specify the knowledge, skills, abilities and behaviors that are required for employees in occupations. Table 2.1 is a competency model for human resources practitioners. It defines what employees must be competent to do and what the qualifications are for each competence level. Competency definitions are compliments to job descriptions. They are extremely valuable tools that can guide employee selection and career progression.

Table 2.1 Competency Model: Human Resource Management

HUMAN RESOURCE PROFESSIONAL COMPETENCY MODEL

BUSINESS COMPETENCIES	EMERGING PRACTITIONER	ACCOMPLISHED PRACTITIONER	SENIOR/LEAD PRACTITIONER
STRATEGIC PERSPECTIVE: analyzes trends and synthesizes information from all relevant sources; develops vision and works with others to realize; has long-term perspective	Knows mission and strategy of organization; looks for ways to meet objectives; understands the need to frame decisions and actions in broad context	Understands how HR strategy and programs fit into organization strategy; designs HR programs to support strategy; evaluates effectiveness of programs in facilitating success	Assists in formulating HR strategy and plans; projects future objectives for programs and plans to replace or revise them so they will fit the objectives as they change
ORGANIZATIONAL KNOWLEDGE: knows the organization; (context, products, customers and financials); has understanding of functional roles; selects strategies/plans based on clear objectives and their expected impact on organizational results	Knows about organizational context, its culture and how it is organized; works to understand roles of functions and business units and their needs; learns about internal and external customers and suppliers and how HR strategies and programs impact them	Understands how the structure functions; knows the culture and its implications; applies knowledge to design and administer HR programs in a manner that fits the specific context of the organization	Assists in assessing the culture and the organization structure and in reshaping them to fit organizational needs and realities; evaluates the extent to which HR programs support the HR strategy and assists in modifying the strategy to be effective given external and internal realities

BUSINESS KNOWLEDGE: knows about industry and related industries; understands economic/competitive forces; knows what is required for success; knows what knowledge/skills are critical and labor market realities for them	Knows about the economics of the organization and its businesses; works to understand the human capital needs of the organization and the realities of the external environment/labor markets	Understands how economic realities impact performance of the businesses and the overall organization; designs and administers HR programs in a manner that contributes to business success	Assists in evaluating HR strategies and programs to determine their business impact; ensures programs are cost-effective and based on sound business principles; evaluates strategy and programs continually to anticipate the need for change
CUSTOMER/ SUPPLIER KNOWLEDGE: knows key customers (internal & external) and suppliers and understands their needs/priorities; adopts strategies to meet their needs and uses programs and processes to meet them	Knows about the needs of internal and external customers and how HR programs impact them; develops relationships with customers and works to understand how HR can make them more effective	Understands what HR strategies/programs can do to satisfy customers and make them effective; designs and administers HR programs that satisfy customer needs while ensure they are cost-effective	Assists in developing an HR service model that identifies needs of customers, suppliers and venture partners and that utilizes cost-effective processes; monitors HR's performance; adjusts programs as required; recommends modifications to improve service

(Continued)

Table 2.1 Continued

	EMERGING PRACTITIONER	ACCOMPLISHED PRACTITIONER	SENIOR/LEAD PRACTITIONER
TECHNOLOGICAL KNOWLEDGE/ SKILL: knows about what is available and adopts appropriate tools; searches for new applications of technology based on their probable fit to context and their cost-benefit balance	Understands the commonly used tools and is proficient in using them; works to develop knowledge of emerging technologies and how they can be applied in HR	Understands how technology impacts HR service levels and cost-effectiveness; assists in recommending technology to improve service and/or lower costs	Assists in planning the acquisition/ application of technology to increase HR effectiveness; directs implementation and evaluates the impact on service levels and costs

HR PROFESSIONAL COMPETENCY MODEL

TECHNICAL COMPETENCIES	EMERGING PRACTITIONER	ACCOMPLISHED PRACTITIONER	SENIOR/LEAD PRACTITIONER
STAFFING Recruiting; selection; placement; workplace/ role design; workforce planning	Understands staffing concepts, techniques and processes and develops competence in applying them in program design/administration	Administers staffing programs; makes recommendations on program revisions to improve effectiveness	Evaluates effectiveness of staffing strategies/ programs; refines existing programs and develops new ones; directs implementation, communication and training

DEVELOPMENT Human capital assessment; career planning/management; training; education	Understands HRD concepts, techniques and processes and develops competence in applying them in program design/administration	Administers HRD programs; makes recommendations on program revisions to improve effectiveness	Evaluates effectiveness of HRD strategies/programs; refines existing programs and develops new ones; directs implementation, communication and training
PERFORMANCE MANAGEMENT Performance models at all levels; performance planning, measurement, feedback, development and contribution review (appraisal)	Understands concepts, techniques and processes and develops competence in applying them in performance management program design/administration	Administers performance management programs; makes recommendations on program revisions to improve effectiveness	Evaluates effectiveness of performance management strategies/programs; refines existing programs and develops new ones; directs implementation, communication and training
REWARDS MANAGEMENT Direct compensation; employee benefits; recognition/non-financial rewards; employee ownership	Understands rewards concepts, techniques and processes and develops competence in applying them in program design/administration	Administers rewards programs; makes recommendations on program revisions to improve effectiveness	Evaluates effectiveness of rewards strategies/programs; refines existing programs and develops new ones; directs implementation, communication and training

(Continued)

Table 2.1 Continued

EMPLOYEE/LABOR RELATIONS Employment policies; health, safety & security; ethics; communication; leadership; legal/regulatory compliance	Understands E/LR concepts, techniques and processes and develops competency in applying them in HR program design/administration	Administers E/LR programs; makes recommendations on program revisions to improve effectiveness	Evaluates effectiveness of E/LR strategies/programs; refines existing programs and develops new ones; directs implementation, communication and training
PERSONAL COMPETENCIES	EMERGING PRACTITIONER	ACCOMPLISHED PRACTITIONER	SENIOR/LEAD PRACTITIONER
Learning Agility/Creativity: Open to new concepts; observes, listens and absorbs new ideas; creates new approaches; adapts to new conditions	Develops knowledge of ideas and concepts to create varied repertoire; is flexible in realizing, accepting and adapting to change	Actively seeks new ideas and techniques; tries new approaches; accepts contextual change and attempts to adapt to new requirements	Scans external sources for new ideas; leads others in search for better ways to design and administer programs.
Cultural Understanding: Understands the similarities/differences between values and beliefs; open to different approaches; leverages benefits of diversity	Develops knowledge of the perspectives of others; actively works to accommodate and respect differences when performing job	Evaluates policies and programs to ensure they respect cultural differences; makes recommendations for changes	Takes initiative to find approaches to work that will fit the beliefs and styles of others; evaluates policies to ensure they appropriately consider the impact on different cultures

Competency			
Flexibility/ Adaptability: Willing to consider new/conflicting ideas; adjusts to different contexts and requirements; does not resist needed change	Open to new ideas; adapts behavior to fit changes	Open to new models; searches for behaviors and approaches that will better fit changes in context	Open to new paradigms; anticipates need for change and proactively initiates actions to make necessary changes
Integrity/Honesty: Represents beliefs, values and ideas candidly; shapes actions based on laws and principles rather than on expediency	Adheres to legal and regulatory requirements and to values/policies; reports violations of laws/regulations and of organizational values and policies	Ensures programs are administered in a manner that is compatible with organizational values; identifies violations and takes appropriate action	Acts as role model; helps others develop behaviors that enable them to maintain integrity; takes appropriate action when violations of laws, values and ethics occur
Communication Effectiveness/ Ability to Influence Others: Able to convey information in manner fitting audience; able to influence others to consider alternatives and to accept recommendations	Effectively expresses self in manner understandable to target audience; receptive to views of others and exerts appropriate influence	Evaluates how well programs have been communicated and recommends how employee acceptance and understanding can be improved	Effectively dialogues with all internal and external parties; exerts influence on policies and strategies; develops communication strategies for new programs

(Continued)

Table 2.1 Continued

HR PROFESIONAL COMPETENCY MODEL

PERSONAL COMPETENCIES	EMERGING PRACTITIONER	ACCOMPLISHED PRACTITIONER	SENIOR/LEAD PRACTITIONER
Interpersonal Skills: Able to work with others to make them effective and achieve desired results; builds needed relationships	Interacts with others as required to share knowledge and exchange information; builds network of contacts	Interacts with others to coordinate activities with parties at interest; creates effective relationships with others	Motivate others to create effective working relations; facilitates sharing of ideas and knowledge across organizational units
Planning/Organizing Skills: Scans environment for emerging trends and plans for needed responses; organizes people and manages resources to produce needed results	Plans and organizes work to meet priorities/ deadlines; allocates time and resources to meet established objectives	Structures project management plans for assigned areas; evaluates results vs. plan and redirects resources as appropriate	Identifies long-term trends and requirements; develops robust alternative scenarios to deal with requirements imposed by the context
Analytical/Synthesis Skills: Able to analyze situations using quantitative and qualitative methods; able to integrate information to understand what responses are required	Develops analytical skills through study of concepts and methods; translates data into usable information	Analyzes effectiveness of processes and programs; determines what changes are required and recommends when implement in order to increase effectiveness and efficiency	Diagnoses context and identifies factors that impact results; integrates information in order to develop strategies for dealing with issues

	HR FUNCTIONAL MANAGER	HR DIRECTOR: Small Organization	HR EXECUTIVE: Large Organization
Change Management Skills: Recognizes/accepts need for change; defines requirements and develops plans, involving appropriate parties; directs process to produce needed results	Develops skills required to implement modifications to programs	Leads change initiatives and takes responsibility for assisting line managers in creating opportunities for motivating others in the execution of the change processes	Identifies need for changes to culture, strategy or policy; develops change plans and directs their execution; acts as role model for desired behaviors
Leadership Skills: Able to create vision others can understand; motivates and aligns efforts towards objectives; adapts approach to those being led	Directs aspects of assigned projects as appropriate; provides guidance to involved parties	Leads and provides direction for projects; defines roles for tam members, allocates responsibilities and motivates team to achieve objectives	Develops vision of successful organization and communicates it to others in a manner that guides effective action and that produces the desired results

BUSINESS COMPETENCIES	HR FUNCTIONAL MANAGER	HR DIRECTOR: Small Organization	HR EXECUTIVE: Large Organization
STRATEGIC PERSPECTIVE: *analyzes trends and synthesizes information from all relevant sources; develops vision and works with others to realize; has long-term perspective*	Assists in formulating HR strategies and plans; projects future objectives for programs and develops plans to replace or revise them as appropriate	Formulates HR strategies and plans; projects future objectives for programs and develops plans to replace or revise them as appropriate	Formulates HR strategies and plans; projects future objectives for programs and directs planning to replace or revise them as necessary

(Continued)

Table 2.1 Continued

| ORGANIZATIONAL KNOWLEDGE: knows the organization; (context, products, customers and financials); has understanding of functional roles; selects strategies/plans based on clear objectives and their expected impact on organizational results | Assists in assessing the culture and organization structure and in reshaping them to fit organizational needs and realities; evaluates the extent to which HR programs support the HR strategy and assists in modifying the strategy to be effective given external and internal realities | Assesses the culture and organization structure and develops plans to reshape them to fit organizational needs and realities; evaluates the extent to which HR programs support the HR strategy and assists in modifying the strategy to be effective given external and internal realities | Assesses the culture and organization structure and develops plans to reshape them to fit organizational needs and realities; evaluates the extent to which HR programs support the strategy and assists in modifying the strategy to be effective given external and internal realities |
| BUSINESS KNOWLEDGE: knows about industry and related industries; understands economic/competitive forces; knows what is required for success; knows what knowledge/skills are critical and labor market realities for them | Assists in evaluating HR strategies and programs to determine their business impact; ensures programs are cost-effective and based on sound business principles; evaluates strategy and programs continually to anticipate the need for change | Ensures HR strategies and programs have a positive business impact; ensures programs are cost-effective and based on sound business principles; evaluates strategy and programs continually to anticipate the need for change | Ensures HR strategies and programs have a positive business impact; ensures programs are cost-effective and based on sound business principles; ensures the evaluation of strategy and programs continually to anticipate the need for change |

| **CUSTOMER/SUPPLIER KNOWLEDGE**: knows key customers (internal & external) and suppliers and understands their needs/priorities; adopts strategies to meet their needs and uses programs and processes to meet them | Assists in developing an HR service model that identifies and meets needs of customers, suppliers and venture partners and that utilizes cost-effective processes; monitors HR's performance; adjusts programs as required; recommends modifications to improve service | Develops an HR service model that identifies and meets needs of customers, suppliers and venture partners and that utilizes cost-effective processes; monitors HR's performance; adjusts programs as required; formulates and implements modifications to improve service | Directs and leads the Development of a HR service model that identifies and meets needs of customers, suppliers and venture partners and that utilizes cost-effective processes; monitors HR's performance; oversees the adjustments to programs as required; formulates and implements modifications to improve service |
| **TECHNOLOGICAL KNOWLEDGE/SKILL**: knows about what is available and adopts appropriate tools; searches for new applications of technology based on their probable fit to context and their cost-benefit balance | Assists in planning the acquisition/application of technology to increase HR effectiveness; assists with implementation and evaluates the impact on service levels and costs | Evaluates the need for the acquisition/application of technology to increase HR effectiveness; directs implementation and evaluates the impact on service levels and costs | Determines and recommends the need for the acquisition/application of technology to increase HR effectiveness; directs implementation and evaluates the impact on service levels and costs |

(Continued)

Table 2.1 Continued

MANAGEMENT KNOWLEDGE/SKILL Knows sound management principles and is capable of applying them; effectively utilizes financial, operating and human resources	Directs activities and staff within own area of responsibility; selects subordinates, develops them and defines, measures and rewards their performance; assists in the management of the HR function	Formulates HR staffing plan; directs HR activities; selects subordinates, develops them and defines, measures and rewards their performance; ensures effective management of functions by subordinates	Formulates HR staffing plan; oversees HR activities; selects subordinates, develops them and defines, measures and rewards their performance; responsible for HR functions being effectively managed

HR PROFESSIONAL COMPETENCY MODEL

TECHNICAL COMPETENCIES	HR FUNCTIONAL MANAGER	HR DIRECTOR: Small Organization	HR EXECUTIVE: Large Organization
HR STRATEGY Aligning HR strategy with organizational context and objectives	Develops strategies in own functional area that fit the organizational context and contribute to executing the HR strategy	Formulates and develops an HR strategy that fits the organizational context and contributes to meeting objectives and oversees the development of HR functional strategies that support the HR strategy	Responsible for achieving a HR strategy that fits the organizational context and contributes to meeting organizational objectives and ensuring its viability into the future

HR FUNCTIONS
Fully knowledgeable about strategies, programs and methods that enable Staffing, Performance Development, Performance Management, Rewards Management and Employee Relations to be effectively performed

Defines objectives for the HR function(s) managed; designs a structure, staffs the function and manages personnel to achieve the function's objectives.

Directs the design and operation of all HR functions; ensures each function is staffed appropriately and defines the objectives assigned to each. Manages all HR functions directly or through subordinates and evaluates the performance of each, based on meeting HR objectives and contributing to organizational results.

Responsible for the design and operation of all HR functions; ensures each function is staffed appropriately and defines the objectives assigned to each. Manages all HR functions through subordinate managers and evaluates the performance of each, based on meeting HR objectives and contributing to organizational results.

INTEGRATING HR FUNCTIONS
Ensuring functional strategies fit together and produce desired results

Evaluates how effectively own functional strategy integrates with other HR functional strategies and with the overall HR strategy

Ensures that HR functional strategies are appropriate, that they integrate effectively and that they produce the desired results

Responsible for HR functional strategies being appropriate, that they integrate effectively and that they produce the desired results

(Continued)

Table 2.1 Continued

HR PROFESIONAL COMPETENCY MODEL

PERSONAL COMPETENCIES	HR FUNCTIONAL MANAGER	HR DIRECTOR: Small Organization	HR EXECUTIVE: Large Organization
Learning Agility/ Creativity: Open to new concepts; observes, listens and absorbs new ideas; creates new approaches; adapts to new conditions	Scans external sources for new ideas and trends; leads others in search for better ways to design strategies and administer programs	Scans organizational environment, using external sources for new ideas and trends; leads others in search for better ways to design strategies and administer programs	Scans the organizational environment, using external sources for new ideas and trends; leads others in search for better ways to design strategies and administer programs
Cultural Understanding: Understands the similarities/differences between values and beliefs; open to different approaches; leverages benefits of diversity	Takes initiative to find approaches to work that will fit the beliefs/styles of others; evaluates policies to ensure they consider the impact on different cultures	Responsible for identifying approaches to work that harmonies the organizational needs with the beliefs/styles of all parties; evaluates policies to ensure they consider the impact on different cultures	Responsible for identifying approaches to work that harmonies the organizational needs with the beliefs/styles of all parties; evaluates policies to ensure they consider the impact on different cultures
Flexibility/Adaptability: Willing to consider new/conflicting ideas; adjusts to different contexts and requirements; does not resist needed change	Open to new paradigms; anticipates need for change and proactively recommends actions to make changes as necessary	Open to new paradigms; anticipates need for change and proactively initiates actions to make changes as necessary	Open to new paradigms; anticipates need for change and proactively initiates actions to make changes as necessary

Integrity/Honesty:
Represents beliefs, values and ideas candidly; shapes actions based on laws and principles rather than on expediency

Acts as role model; helps others develop behaviors that enable them to maintain integrity; recommends appropriate action be taken when violations of laws, values and ethics occur

Acts as role model; helps others develop behaviors that enable them to maintain integrity; ensures appropriate action is taken when violations of laws, values and ethics occur

Acts as role model; helps others develop behaviors that enable them to maintain integrity; ensures appropriate action is taken when violations of laws, values and ethics occur

Communication Effectiveness/ Ability to Influence Others:
Able to convey information in manner fitting audience; able to influence others to consider alternatives and to accept recommendations

Effectively dialogues with internal and external parties; exerts influence on policies and strategies; develops communication strategies for new programs

Effectively dialogues with internal and external parties; exerts influence on policies and strategies; responsible for the development of communication strategies for new and existing programs

Effectively dialogues with internal and external parties; exerts influence on policies and strategies; responsible for the development of communication strategies for new and existing programs

(Continued)

Table 2.1 Continued

HR PROFESIONAL COMPETENCY MODEL

PERSONAL COMPETENCIES	HR FUNCTIONAL MANAGER	HR DIRECTOR: Small Organization	HR EXECUTIVE: Large Organization
Interpersonal Skills: Able to work with others to make them effective and achieve aggregate results; builds needed relationships	Motivate others to create effective working relationships; facilitates sharing of ideas and knowledge across organization	Motivate others to create effective working relationships; facilitates sharing of ideas and knowledge across organization	Motivate others to create effective working relationships; facilitates sharing of ideas and knowledge across organization
Planning/Organizing Skills: Scans environment for emerging trends and plans for needed responses; organizes people and manages resources to produce needed results	Identifies long-term trends and requirements; develops robust scenarios to deal with requirements imposed by the context	Identifies long-term trends and requirements; develops robust scenarios to deal with requirements imposed by the context	Identifies long-term trends and requirements; develops robust scenarios to deal with requirements imposed by the context
Analytical/Synthesis Skills: Able to analyze situations using quantitative and qualitative methods; able to integrate information to understand what responses are required	Diagnoses context and identifies factors that impact results; integrates information in order to develop strategies for dealing with issues	Diagnoses context and identifies factors that impact results; integrates information in order to develop strategies for dealing with issues	Diagnoses context and identifies factors that impact results; integrates information in order to develop strategies for dealing with issues

Change Management Skills:			
Recognize/accept need for change; defines requirements and develops plans, involving appropriate parties; directs process to produce needed results	Identifies need for changes to culture, strategy or policy; develops change plans and directs their execution; models desired behaviors	Identifies need for changes to culture, strategy or policy; responsible for developing change plans and directing their execution; models desired behaviors	Identifies need for changes to culture, strategy or policy; responsible for developing change plans and directing their execution; models desired behaviors

Leadership Skills:			
Able to create vision others can understand; motivates and aligns efforts towards objectives; adapts approach to those being led	Develops vision of successful organization and communicates it to others in a manner that guides effective action and produces the desired results	Responsible for the development of a vision for the organization that enables it to be successful and communicates it to others in a manner that guides effective action and produces the desired results	Responsible for the development of a vision for the organization that enables it to be successful and communicates it to others in a manner that guides effective action and produces the desired results

Another issue that must be addressed is what the staffing levels must be. Once the work that will be performed by employees is determined the "how many" question must be answered. And if all work in the human resources function will be done by employees it is not only necessary to decide on the number of incumbents needed in specific roles but also on the distribution of incumbents across the competency levels. It is necessary to evaluate the work and to decide what level of competence is needed for each activity. Using Table 2.1 the organization may decide that 10% of the work requires a senior/lead person, 60% an accomplished level person and 30% an emerging practitioner. The staffing level for each of the competency levels can then be determined and this staffing model can guide staffing and development strategies. If the organization already has too many senior-level incumbents, future hires should be brought in at the emerging or accomplished level. Having a senior perform routine work means the person is too expensive for that work and it is likely the person will not be too happy doing it. And having an emerging practitioner doing work that requires a senior level of competence is a risky action, especially if the activity is critical and inadequate performance is costly.

Aligning the workforce mix with the work mix over time can be accomplished by using the type of model provided in Table 1.1 in Chapter 1. By continuously monitoring the age demographics of the employee population organizations can anticipate when losses due to retirement are apt to occur. This can lead to focusing developmental investments on what will meet the challenges associated with losses of talent. Historical turnover rates can also enable projections to be made and the implications of likely turnover can be factored into staffing plans. The planning model in Chapter 1 provides a roadmap for dealing with these issues.

One of the tendencies of managers that must be dealt with is the desire to play it safe and over-hire. When a senior engineer is expected to leave there is temptation to replace the person with someone who can immediately operate at that level of competence. But if the function already has an overly rich skill mix this will exacerbate the excessive cost of the staff. Managers may resist hiring people lacking full competence, since they will require more training and supervision, but it must be made clear to them that one of their responsibilities is to staff all work at an appropriate level and that they are expected to develop people appropriately.

Once the work to be performed by employees is defined and the required competency level for each role is determined an organization may consider the type of employee it wishes to employ. Selecting employees based on personality is thought by some to be risky, since it lends itself to bias in favor of others who are similar to those making the selection decisions. If personality tests are not validated to ensure they are not impacted by gender, age, religion, ethnicity or race, there is a potential risk that this will result in illegal and inappropriate discrimination. But despite the challenges there may be a justification for measuring and considering personality rather than just technical competence.

Competency models include required behaviors when how someone does their work is important, such as in customer-facing roles. But organizations often hire based on job descriptions, that define physical and/or mental capabilities, but do not address personality. Ryan Leaf was picked ahead of Peyton Manning in the NFL draft, based on superior athletic ability as determined by using quantitative measures of performance. But Leaf failed and Manning became a Hall of Fame candidate. Because of personality the team would not perform for Leaf, while Manning exhibited a style of leadership that rallied the team around him. This is an example of using a selection model that is deficient in capturing relevant measures.

There is yet another consideration when an organization decides what its talent requirements will be. That is the specificity level at which roles are defined. Some types of work require the design of fully defined jobs. If incumbents of a job have fully specified duties and working procedures that must be done in a specific manner they must be selected and/or trained to ensure they can execute the work processes required. Electricians are required to adhere to codes when performing tasks. That requirement makes it necessary to ensure they know the codes and are able to perform in a manner consistent with their specifications. But an organization might choose to develop their building and maintenance staff to do fill broader roles (i.e., doing machine maintenance and instrument repair).

When a broader range of skills is required it impacts hiring specifications, training requirements and how people are paid. Skill-based pay systems may be used to reward employees who become multi-skilled, increasing the motivation for them to learn more things.[4] And a candidate's ability and willingness to become competent across a broad range of skills should be a consideration when staffing the role. Career paths require incumbents to acquire the qualifications to move through the levels, but if they lack the ability to acquire them movement will be impeded. Motorola implemented technology in their manufacturing processes, only to find that employees lacked the necessary numeric skills to function effectively using the new methods. This required the creation of training programs that filled the gaps left by an inadequate educational system at the high school level. A utility the author consulted with faced the same problem and established a program with the local community college that all new hires for specified jobs attended to address this same issue.

Professional roles can also be defined specifically or more generally. A human resources practitioner may be specialized in compensation management or may be more of a generalist who has a working knowledge of all the disciplines within the HR function. How the HR function is staffed will be impacted by the organization's philosophy. The advantage of having specialists with deep knowledge in a function is that it enables them to deal with the more complex issues related to their specialization. But specialists may be inclined to diagnose and deal with issues from their narrow perspective. The compensation specialist is inclined to presume the loss of a valued employee was due to compensation issues, while an employee relations specialist might assume that the causes were something else. When specialists do not have sufficient knowledge outside their discipline, they are less likely to be able to determine the real cause. On the other hand, if the entire HR staff is made up of generalists, they might be able to consider a broad range of causes but may not be capable of resolving the issue once the cause is determined, since they lack the in-depth knowledge to do so. Some organizations have resolved this issue by cross-training generalists in diagnosing the causes of issues and even though they lack the depth to resolve the issue they know where to refer it so it can be resolved. And employees need to know when to ask for additional resources. When an issue that is unique or more complex than normal it may necessitate augmentation using outside resources.

When organizations utilize work teams another issue presents itself … are team members classified as team members, or into specific jobs? If everyone on the team is expected to learn all facets of the work performed by the team and if they are expected to do whatever it is that needs to be done at the time how their performance measured and how are they rewarded becomes an issue.[5] In some cases project team members are expected to deal with issues related to their area of expertise and may remain classified into jobs based on their specific knowledge and skills. If they are expected to do whatever is required they would need a broader range of capabilities and might be rewarded differently than employees classified into specific job.

The Impact of Leadership

Leadership is a topic that probably has generated more books, articles, seminars and training programs than any other aspect of management. Prescriptions for successful leaders abound … follow Attila the Hun, Jesus or Jack Welch. Yet each suggests there is a best style for all organizations at all times. This contradicts the research that supports contingent adoption of different styles, to fit different contexts. An organization in crisis may need one type of leader, while one with decades of consistent success may require another.[6]

In today's globalized environment each organization that operates outside a single country must fashion a philosophy about how it manages its operations in different parts of the world. One perspective is to adopt a global philosophy relative to talent management and a single style of leadership. Many organizations attempt to utilize the same strategies and programs world-wide, subject to customization based on legal, economic, cultural and logistical realities. Since talent has become more globally mobile this may result in an increased supply. Yet there are factors that influence how effective people will be based on where they are located.[7] Other organizations source and utilize talents within regions and attempt to employ the same strategies and programs within each region. Others treat operations within each country as independent operations and use the same talent management strategies and programs within each country. And in countries such as Italy and Spain, it may be prudent to be sensitive to differences between regions and attempt to fit strategies to regional contexts.

Nike and Apple place their manufacturing operations in Asian countries, where labor is relatively inexpensive. But even though an organization may be open to having work done anywhere there are factors other than labor costs that must be considered. Historical events may make the use of talent from one country in another difficult, even within a region. Despite being at peace the relations between Japan and Korea still suffer from the memories of past wars. The Middle East has numerous cross-border issues, a function of historical events. Some countries demand that locals be employed and that the number of foreign workers be limited. The impact of cultural differences may challenge the organization to manage talent differently depending on the cultural orientation of employees.

The relationship between the headquarters country and the foreign operations will have an impact on the type of talent needed in each location and how that talent should be led. For example, if a multinational has an ethnocentric management philosophy all policy decisions will be made at headquarters and other locations will operate in the manner prescribed for them. Little is expected from the foreign locations except for compliance with headquarters direction. At the other extreme are multinationals that locate centers of excellence globally, based on the availability of the right kind of talent. A U.S. organization may locate sophisticated manufacturing operations in Singapore, R&D functions in Israel and basic manufacturing operations in Vietnam. Each of these centers are expected to innovate and develop the organization's global capabilities in their area of specialization. The role of foreign operations will have a major impact on what type and level of talent is required in each of them and will influence who manages these operations.

Ethnocentric organizations will typically use expatriates to set up and manage foreign operations, based on the belief that local personnel might not be capable of conforming to the way the organization wants things done. Japanese multinationals tend to use expatriates in key management roles in foreign locations, to ensure control and conformance with the organization's way of conducting business. Japan has always been a culturally homogenous country, and this has much to do with how it socializes employees and who makes decisions. This has an impact on talent selection and management in foreign operations. Other multinationals, such as many U.S. firms, use formal role definition and management by objectives systems for managing performance to control expatriates. The Japanese approach relies on those on international assignments being adequately socialized into the Japanese and organizational culture. The U.S. approach provides a job description and set of objectives, which means guidance is provided using formal specifications, rather than alignment with culture, to exercise control.

The global perspective will impact the type of talent used in all operations. If there is "by the numbers" guidance a broader range of candidates can be utilized in both local national and international assignee roles. If local operations are expected to provide innovation and exert leadership in specific aspects of the organization's operations the quality of talent will need to be aligned with what the organization requires.

The most extensive research project dealing with the effectiveness of leadership styles across the world is the GLOBE study.[8] The study examined the six most common styles of leadership across ten cultural clusters and then evaluated how effective these styles were and what alternative styles might produce better results. Within each of the leadership styles, dimensions were defined and their effectiveness evaluated as well. One of the findings was that in the United States the most common style was one that relied on high power distance ... in effect, a hierarchical, top–down approach. But when a large sample of people were asked whether that style was appropriate its effectiveness scores were one of the lowest. A leadership style focused on emphasizing a performance orientation was believed to be the most appropriate one by those surveyed. Charismatic leadership was found to be more effective in Anglo cultures than in the Middle East. Conversely, self-protective leaders (self-centered; status conscious; face saving) were most effective in the Middle East and least effective in Anglo, Germanic European and Northern European cultures.

An analysis of 21 global leaders who effectively functioned in unique contexts showed the importance of context, in addition to the nature of the organization, in determining how effective a particular style of leadership can be when faced with a specific set of circumstances.[9] The evidence refutes the notion that there is one best style across contexts.

Conclusion

Sourcing and selecting talent will be discussed in Chapters 3 and 4. But before the right talent can be acquired each organization must define the type of talent it needs in each role. And the roles may differ ... in the scope and depth of capabilities required ... in the way work is segmented and assigned ... in the native intelligence, technical knowledge and personality required to be successful in the role. But one more requirement for ensuring the right people are able to be successful is to design roles that enable them to perform. There is a bountiful literature on job/role design and the characteristics of sound role design.[10] First, there must be an appropriate amount of skill variety built into the requirement so that incumbents feel their capabilities are being utilized and that the work is not mind–numbingly repetitive. There are roles that require strict adherence to fully specified processes (i.e., arming explosive devices) but the duties can be expanded to ensure employees do not lapse into an auto-pilot state of mind. Second, there must be an understanding of the tasks that are required and how they fit into the overall result. Third, incumbents must believe what they do is significant ... that doing it well makes a difference. Fourth, an appropriate amount of autonomy must be allowed ... being able to decide how to best do what needs to be done. And, fifth, there must be continuous measurement of performance and feedback provided to the employee so there is an understanding of how well things are going and perhaps how to do them better. Effectively utilizing talent will be discussed in more detail in Chapters 5 and 6.

The right talent cannot produce the desired results unless the context within which people work is appropriate. Well-designed roles ... a knowledge-sharing culture ... effective measurement of performance ... supportive management. All of these conditions must exist if even the best qualified people are on board.

Notes

1 Cascio, W. *Responsible Restructuring* (San Francisco: Berrett-Koehler, 2002).
2 Nonaka, I. & Takeuchi, H. *The Knowledge Creating Organization* (New York: Oxford Press, 1995).
3 Boudreau, J., Jesuthasan, R., & Creelman, D. *Lead the Work* (Hoboken, NJ: John Wiley & Sons, 2015).
4 Greene, R. *Rewarding Performance, 2nd ed.* (New York: Routledge, 2019).
5 Greene, R. *Rewarding Performance, 2nd ed.* (New York: Routledge, 2019).
6 Bardwick, J. *Danger in the Comfort Zone* (New York: AMACOM, 1995).
7 Trompenaars, F. & Greene, R. *Rewarding Performance Globally* (New York: Routledge, 2018).
8 House, R. *Culture, Leadership & Organizations* (Thousand Oaks, CA: Sage, 2004).
9 Trompenaars, F. *Twenty-One Leaders for the 21st Century* (Oxford: Capstone, 2001).
10 Hackman, J. & Oldham, G. *Work Design* (Reading, MA: Addison-Wesley, 1980).

Chapter 3

Sourcing Talent

To know where to look for talent an organization needs to clearly know what it needs. Staffing the workforce should be guided by a strategic perspective. Figure 2.1 in Chapter 2 presented a model that can be used to make decisions about what kind of talent and how much talent is required. The cyclical nature of the model illustrates the necessity of continuously evaluating the business strategy and what the critical success factors are. As has already been discussed the dynamic environment that exists today, and probably will persist into the future, can mandate modifications to the business strategy, which in turn can impact what the right workforce is, where the right talent can be sourced, how the right people can be selected, how talent must be developed and how the organization evaluates and rewards performance. The strategies for executing these processes follow the sequence in this chapter and in the chapters to follow.

When sourcing talent organizations usually seek someone to fit a job opening. But there are also programs that source candidates based on their long-range potential, rather than a fit to a specific role. My first job out of undergraduate school was in Johnson & Johnson's executive development program. Candidates were screened for their suitability to become future executives in this esteemed organization. There was no clear career path communicated to candidates and accepting a position was really accepting a potential future rather than a specific job. I did not know what my job would be once hired and did not think to ask. J&J promised extensive training in all facets of business as a part of its program, in lieu of any certainty about what one's "day job" would be. Because I was a beneficiary of this program, I viewed it as a sound concept. But had I been a senior HR executive I would have asked what the organization was getting for its investment. Hiring someone to fill a job opening makes sense ... does hiring on potential rather than current competence make sense as well?

Since most people are hired for a specific role in an organization and their suitability is measured based on the qualifications for that role the criteria that are utilized in making selection decisions are different than they were for the executive development program I entered. So, should organizations decide to hire based not only on current qualifications for the job opening, but also on the candidate's potential for the future? And should employee development and career management strategies evaluate both? Considering both seems advisable. Employees are generally desirous of career progression and personal growth so anticipating the path they are likely to follow over time can preclude hiring someone who is qualified to do a job but not capable of progressing. The selection criteria used should therefore be broad enough to evaluate both the immediate and the longer-term fit of a candidate to the organization. If workforce planning is adequate, there should be guidance as to what talent will be needed in the future as well as what is needed today.

The suitability of candidates may be established based on numerous criteria and using multiple processes. Southwest Airlines uses panels of flight attendants to evaluate candidates for flight attendant openings, to determine if they will fit into the team environment. Even things like having a sense of humor may weigh on the selection. Cabin crews need to work together and integrate their efforts so compatibility can be a legitimate factor in selection. Fit to the culture is a consideration for many organizations when hiring employees. Selecting someone for a customer facing role should be based on somewhat different criteria then those used for selecting a coder who will perform a contract assignment working halfway across the world with no personal contacts. Investing in a comprehensive evaluation of what the organization needs is a necessity, to ensure that the search is for the right talent.

Technology has provided tools that can simulate different combinations and predict the outcomes that would result from making decisions about the ideal combination. NBA teams have begun to use AI tools to determine the best mix of players for a particular situation (behind or ahead at the moment; last second need for a three-point goal; based on opponent's current mix). By having data on each player's capabilities and on the results of past strategies a prediction can be made about the best approach. Organizations can do the same thing with their staffing strategies. Determining objectives by using key performance indicators (KPIs) and evaluating past results that occurred with specific strategies can enable a projection to be made about the best talent mix for producing the desired results. The book *Moneyball* described the characteristics that Oakland A's used to evaluate and select players based on a rationale. In order to make the playoffs (a lofty objective for the team with the smallest player payroll) the team would have to win a lot of games. It was also assumed that in order to win a lot of games the team had to score a lot of runs. That objective led to selection of players based on individual on base percentages, which had been determined to be the best predictor of run totals through the use of analytics.

Once an organization knows what it needs and determines the talent it needs to achieve its objectives it must find sources for acquiring it. There are numerous approaches. Globalization opens the sources up geographically. It has also become increasingly possible to utilize outsiders instead of employees. Effective talent development can increase the capabilities of current employees so they can do more. Technology makes it possible to have some work done by software or robots. Alliances and joint ventures can provide access to the talent of other organizations. A sign in front proclaiming "Help Wanted" can still identify the opportunities that exist in an organization. Web sites can provide information on the organization and the talent it needs, as well as branding it as a preferred employer/utilizer of talent. And social media has become a major source of information about opportunities. The approaches for developing potential sources are numerous, but finding the right ones and mining them to produce the needed talent is the key to building a viable workforce.

Traditional approaches to sourcing are still viable in many cases, but many have become less powerful attractors due to the development of other tools. Twenty years ago, if someone was looking for employment the principal source of information about opportunities was the local newspaper. For educated professionals, there were some media sources that identified opportunities nationally. Placement agencies acted as intermediaries as well, making it possible for recruiters to meet face-to-face with candidates. Job fairs provided venues for contacts between multiple firms and job seekers. Many unions managed hiring shops and provided occupational training. Placement departments of universities acted as intermediaries between organizations and their graduates. Finally, personal referrals have always been a viable way to connect job seekers and organizations.

The sources for connecting with potential employees or contractors and freelancers have multiplied, attributable in large part to the development of the internet. Recruiting agencies have in many cases morphed into talent platforms, capable of providing people qualified to perform work on a contract basis. Since there has been an increased acceptance of having some work done using arrangements that do not involve hiring an employee, the prevalence of using contractors, consultants and freelancers has increased. There will always be work an organization will carefully control access to, especially unique processes that are critical to its performance. Intellectual capital that cannot be protected by patents or licenses, turning it into intellectual property, is typically cordoned off, done by trusted employees and often protected by agreements not to share the specifics of how things are done. And although intellectual property is theoretically protected in some countries it may be fair game, since patents, licenses and non-compete contracts are not enforced. Whether employees are actually a safer bet when intellectual capital cannot be legally protected is questionable. Non-compete contracts are often used in an attempt to avoid defection, but they are often challenged. Assuming that proprietary knowledge is protected if it is only shared with employees may turn out to overly optimistic. But there can be steps taken to reduce the loss of unique knowledge shared with contractors.

Although the increased mobility of talent globally seems to create a bountiful supply of knowledge and skills that might not have been available a decade or two ago there are potential obstacles to accessing talent across country borders. In the United States, there has been a shortage of graduates in STEM (science, technology, engineering and mathematics) fields for some time.

This presents a supply-demand imbalance, since the explosion of new technology has dramatically increased the need for people trained in these fields. To further exacerbate the shortage an increasing number of graduates want to start their own businesses or act as individual consultants, rather than becoming employees of established organizations.

Going abroad has its limitations for certain types of talent. For example, India and China are graduating a large volume of graduates in technical fields, but there are obstacles to effectively utilizing them. Laws and regulations vary across the globe and can sometimes create barriers to talent mobility. The H1-B visa cap shuts the door to people who otherwise would have come to the United States for employment. And experts have evaluated the competence of many of the graduates of some foreign schools and found them unqualified to meet the expectations of multinational firms. In order to fill the gap created by the shortage of U.S. graduates and the loss of some graduates to either the gig world or the entrepreneurial world organizations have been forced to find alternative strategies. In some cases, the jobs that would have been filled in the United States are exported overseas where the talent is. The issue of the lack of competence on the part of some graduates can be dealt with, since investments in training may be sufficient to bring the competence level of potential candidates up to the required level. Since employing people in low wage countries offers a cost advantage the investment in training may be offset by the savings in payroll costs.

Rather than attempting to recruit scarce skill sets domestically, many U.S. organizations have elected to locate staff outside the home/headquarters country. If an operation is to be established in a foreign country a decision must be made about the adequacy of local talent. This of course should have been a major consideration when deciding where to locate operations. The decision to locate in a developing country is often based on the cost of labor. If the organization is trying to decide whether to establish operations in Germany and India utilizing relatively unskilled labor India may be the preferred choice since it has a larger supply of unskilled labor and the cost may be as little as 1/20th of what it would be in Germany. But there are other considerations as well. If skilled craftsmen are being sought there might be a larger existing pool available in Germany, since the two-track educational system there generates a larger supply of this type of worker. Also, Germany is a member of the European Union and the free mobility of talent mandated by EU regulations can further expand the supply. Finally, the level of corruption and the ease of doing business may be considerations that, although not directly tied to the labor force, may have an impact on operations. Germany ranks 24th on Transparency International's Ease of Doing Business index while India ranks 77th. Germany ranks 15th on the World Bank's Corruption Index while India ranks 85th. Attempting to staff a workforce in India may take much longer than in Germany, due to the "license raj" that imposes bureaucratic processes, and the level of corruption in India may make it difficult for a U.S. company to adhere to the provisions of the Corrupt Practices Act, which has extraterritorial jurisdiction. A final concern is the quality of the educational system in a country being considered, particularly if the work requires people with high literacy and numeracy capabilities. So offshoring operations that will require sourcing local talent can be challenging.

Organizations can utilize expatriate personnel to set up operations in foreign countries as well as manage them on an ongoing basis. But in order to use expatriates the organization has to have people who are qualified and willing to work offshore. It can source talent from the headquarters country and/or from third countries. When people are relocated across borders it can present challenges for them. Family and career considerations may cause some qualified candidates to be unwilling to take international assignments. There is a significant percentage of families in the United States in which both partners have careers, which could result in the trailing partner being unable to work due to limitations on work visas. Concerns about educational disruption for children result in a significant number of candidates to decline. And there may be inadequate security and health care conditions, which can make an assignment unattractive. As a result, assuming the organization has an adequate number of qualified candidates may be overly optimistic.

Selecting women for international assignments can help to expand the supply of qualified candidates. In the United States, organizations have often excluded women because they believe they would be unable to accept and/or that they would not want to be assigned outside the country. This assumption is frequently mistaken and results in overlooking employees that would not only be able to go but increasingly see international experience as a way to increase their marketability. There can be concerns about whether a woman would be accepted in some cultures. Madelyn Albright, who served as Secretary of State, told attendees at an HR conference that her acceptance was enhanced by her disembarking from Air Force One. And experience has shown that in some countries where local women would not be considered in a role the fact that the organization selected a woman for an expatriate assignment was evidence that the person was truly exceptional. The scarcity of talent today makes overlooking otherwise qualified people a poor decision. Age and ethnicity are other personal characteristics that sometimes preclude selecting someone who might not "fit in" at the assignment location.

When sourcing talent outside the home country there may also be language and cultural issues that impede the effectiveness of foreign recruits. Language deficiencies can be addressed with training investments. But cultural differences may be so great that the organization may have to accept different ways of doing business in order for the conditions of employment to be acceptable to candidates. In the book *Rewarding Performance Globally*[1] co-author Trompenaars and I provide examples of how potential conflicts can occur when deciding that how performance is defined and rewarded will be done in the same way globally. Lincoln Electric, a Cleveland based organization, successful for decades using a pay for performance system, attempted to expand their business overseas. They found that in some cultures their approach was not accepted, which meant that they would either have to alter one of the cornerstones of their business philosophy or exit the country where the conflict presented itself. In several cases, they did the latter. And if an organization's brand and its value proposition conflict with cultural orientations in some parts of the globe what seems like a plentiful supply of talent may prove to be out of their reach. If locally based organizations are viewed at premium employers and foreign organizations are viewed with suspicion recruiting may be challenging.

Cultural differences within a workforce present a rather unique challenge. The organization has to decide who to accommodate and what form accommodation might take. If a U.S. firm with a local workforce begins to import employees from other cultures the diversity may impact the effectiveness of policies and programs. Cultural orientation may cause employees to view the workforce management strategies of the organization to be inappropriate. An employee may observe the Sabbath on Friday, Saturday or Sunday, raising scheduling issues. There are a number of management practices that can create conflict, especially performance and rewards management.

Performance Management: in most Western and Northern cultures managers are expected to appraise performance in a manner that involves direct communication with the employee about both the positive and negative aspects of the employee's performance. Being clear and direct is intended to apprise the employee of what is expected and how well those expectations have been met. People from cultures that place a high value on "saving face" may react to this type of appraisal very negatively and it may destroy the relationship with the manager. Those from high power distance cultures may also resist mutual goal setting, feeling it is inappropriate for the subordinate to challenge the superior. Those from cultures that take a long-term view of an employee's contribution, including factors such as longevity and loyalty, may find the short-term assessment of their performance to be unfair. Those who believe that external factors will have a major impact on results and who do not feel they possess internal control will find the "can do" mindset that underlies the management by objectives approach to be delusional. When speaking at a Middle Eastern conference in Dubai I was asked how people who believe outcomes are controlled by a higher power can be motivated to do their best, since they are not in control of what happens. The best I could come up with is to convince them that all of their capabilities are a gift and it is their responsibility to use them.

Rewards Management: hiring people from collectivist cultures (common in Asia, South America and the Middle East) may result in an expectation that rewards will be distributed on an egalitarian basis, since the employees will tend to believe that it takes everyone to produce results. When this exists, differentiation can disrupt group harmony. If the organization is a strong believer in paying for individual performance, it may be unwilling to adopt a more "socialistic" approach to determining rewards just to appease employees.

Reconciling these dilemmas is challenging and an organization should consider the implications of cultural diversity when sourcing talent across borders. One of the major challenges associated with operating globally is finding leaders and leadership styles that can be effective across borders and cultures. The GLOBE study produced insights into the type of leadership style that would likely be effective in different countries, as discussed in Chapter 2. When local operations are staffed with employees that are relatively homogenous in their cultural orientation the study findings can be used to select leaders for specific international assignments. If the leading candidate for a leadership position in a specific country utilized a style that was unlikely to be accepted in the local culture a dilemma presents itself. Does the organization attempt to change the style used by that person? Or is it assumed that somehow the person will be able to impose his or her preferred style in a way that will enable the person to be successful? Other research studies have provided cases where specific styles were effective or ineffective, and one of the findings is that a style might be effective at one stage of an organization's evolution but become ineffective as the context changes. The principle of contingent leadership effectiveness has been embraced for decades and in effect says what works is what fits … for a specific context at a particular point in time. An organization operating across cultures will almost certainly find that selecting leaders will best be done on a case by case basis, considering the context.

Management is thought to differ from leadership. It has been contended that management is managing the boxes on an organization chart and leadership is managing the white spaces in between the boxes. The nature of a management role should influence selection and development of candidates for specific assignments. Leadership effectiveness is impacted by alignment of style with culture, as demonstrated by the GLOBE study. Management effectiveness is impacted by the nature of the role and the characteristics of the manager. The bottom line is that leaders and managers must fit what they are expected to do and by the acceptance of those led/managed of the manner in which they do it.

Pooling Talent with Other Organizations

Organizations can enter into a number of different relationships with other organizations. Mergers, acquisitions, joint ventures and alliances can all result in a larger pool of talent. Each type of relationship has its own set of opportunities and challenges. For example, although mergers and acquisitions theoretically make the workforces of both organizations available to the new entity there may be issues related to compatibility. While consulting with an insurance company that was acquiring another insurance company a dramatic difference in culture was discovered. Regrettably, the due diligence process had not included an analysis of the two staffing strategies, performance expectations and rewards management systems. Employees in the acquired organization were used to having ample, if not excessive, staff levels. They were also used to relatively low performance expectations. And even though their pay was lower than employees at the acquiring company their low productivity more than obliterated the lower cost advantage.

Well-thought-out M&As can produce a talent pool that can elevate the performance of the new entity. The larger tech firms have been acquiring start-ups that have products they can use to increase their capabilities, as well as talent that can increase their intellectual capital. They may also be acquiring these organizations to eliminate a potential competitor, but even though that is the primary motive they can also enjoy the benefits of new knowledge and skill being available to them.

Joint ventures create a third entity, to which both organizations contribute capital and talent. Joint ventures are typically considered when neither of the organizations have adequate resources to take advantage of an opportunity. The Department of Energy has contractors managing the national research laboratories and has in many instances mandated that a private sector bidder must partner with a research university to create the contracting organization. It is often the case that the cultures of the two parties are very different and that the workforces have different expectations as to how they do their work and what they expect in return. The Palo Alto Research Center (PARC) was a part of Xerox and the incompatibility of their cultures led to inventions that advanced personal computing being given away because the parent could not see their commercial potential. Researchers are often focused on creating new knowledge while for-profit organizations are focused on creating new products. Mindsets can influence the way people work and can determine the value of their talent to an organization, making it difficult to fashion a management strategy that works for all employees. Another issue is raised when both parties contribute talent to the joint venture. If one sends their best people while the other does not it can create disputes and threaten the success of the relationship.

Alliances are cooperative ventures that do not create a new entity. One example is a pharmaceutical company that has a product that competitors do not have but lacks a salesforce in a region that can effectively sell it. A competitor might have that workforce and be willing to expand the product lines they sell in the region. Even though cooperating with an organization that is for other products a competitor may seem like a questionable strategy this approach could benefit both organizations. There typically are fewer talent management challenges presented by alliances compared to joint ventures.

Current Employees as a Talent Resource

One of the most overlooked sources of talent is the organization's current workforce. Employees who have already proven themselves to be solid citizens have many advantages. Since they are familiar commodities the uncertainty associated with new hires is minimized. Current employees are known to be imperfect, but since hiring from the outside is often based on a one-sided resume (imperfections not included) familiarity may be beneficial. But current employees may lack the specific competencies required when the organization begins doing new things. One of the obvious solutions is to train them to do the new type of work. But if they lack the ability to learn the work this may eliminate them from consideration. And if inadequate workforce planning results in too little time to develop employees this option is not viable.

It is commonly accepted that organizations typically utilize only a portion of the capabilities of current employees. It is likely their people have strengths that have never been recognized ... because they have never been utilized. Many people conclude they are not good at quantitative analysis because their experience with technical courses during their formal education was unpleasant. That does not mean they cannot expand their capabilities if given the appropriate training and the opportunity to do new things. Several of the growing occupations, many of which have insufficient supply, require coding skills. Code.org has developed skill development programs for children as young as five, supplemented by more advanced programs, which suggests this is a skill that can be learned by most people. A number of for-profit organizations and educational institutions offer coding "boot camps" that develop skills through intensive immersion for a relatively short time. If an organization is attempting to staff projects requiring coding skills, they might not even have to develop their own training programs. And they may discover current employees could do the work if given the tools. If employees want to be given the opportunity, even if that requires them to take courses on their own time, development becomes an attractive option. Time invested now for some employees may increase the likelihood of remaining employed in the future. Conversely, when an organization knows some skill sets are in the process of being obsoleted it is to its advantage to make this clear to employees and to offer them alternative opportunities if they possess the native ability.

Very few organizations can honestly say they thoroughly test newly hired employees to determine the full range of their capabilities and their potential for developing new ones. IBM developed an exam to test for computer programming aptitude decades ago, supplemented by programmed instruction modules that enabled those desiring the skills to develop them. This enabled people to find out whether they were likely to be successful in the field and provided a hands-on preview of what the work entailed. There was a selfish motive behind these offerings ... programmers were in short supply and the demand in IBM was expanding at an exponential rate. This of course does not guarantee that people who could be successful would opt to pursue the field, or to go to work for IBM, but increasing supply seems to be desirable. The rigid requirements involved with programming are viewed by many as lacking in opportunity to innovate and to use interpersonal skills. A lot of people do not want to sit in a cubicle and code. But it is surprising that so many organizations limit their assessment of a person's capabilities to determining their likelihood of success in the job they are hired for. By administering a battery of tests during the onboarding process they could identify current competencies and provide an inventory of strengths that could be used in career management systems.

In the 1950s, human resource accounting became a tool for talent management and led to the creation of what are often called "skills inventories." And in recent decades a number of additional techniques came on the scene, including assessment centers, vocational interest tests and personality tests. In-depth information on alternative approaches is available in comprehensive texts.[2] Utilizing inventories of the things people can already do and the things their knowledge, skills and abilities would enable them to do in the future can increase the effectiveness of workforce planning and career management systems. Yet there are many organizations focused singly on what will be required in the current role when doing the selection. This misses the opportunity to seek people who have capabilities that would be valuable over the long run.

An increasing amount of work is being done as "gigs." An often unrealized source of potential "gig-ers" may be the existing employees. Mining this source can preclude the necessity to go outside the organization and potentially around the world to find qualified candidates. There are benefits to be gained by considering employees. Many people feel stalled in their existing roles, even though they are working in the field they are suited to and have selected. Giving them an opportunity to expand their knowledge or just providing some opportunities to explore other options may be the antidote for them to begin browsing the websites of competing organizations to see what they might be offering. By informing employees of opportunities to work on projects using intranets and other forms of communication the organization can convince employees their capabilities and their preferences are both valued.

There are obstacles to internal mobility, particularly in highly structured organizations. Managers may resist their people being recruited to perform tasks outside their current job, since it disrupts the staffing of their unit. And even if an assignment is only temporary an employee may find the grass is truly greener in other fields, increasing the potential of turnover, even though it is internal. But it is incumbent on executive management to make it clear that employees are in fact an organizational resource, not just their resource, and that managers are expected to contribute to the talent pool of the organization.

In order to maximize the organization's knowledge of its employee's capabilities other employees may be encouraged to recommend peers for assignments. By working side by side with someone it often enables a colleague to gain a realistic assessment of what their peer is capable of. One of the characteristics most highly correlated with performance is conscientiousness ... in fact it is second only to basic intelligence as a predictor of performance. Fellow employees are perhaps the best source for determining whether someone is conscientious ... their knowledge is based on actual experience. Given the difficulty with using formal testing to measure how conscientious an employee is apt to be this approach can yield benefits. Many organizations use employee referral programs to identify outsiders who might be recruited, but these programs often do not scout talent internally. One source of information about employee potential is to use "360-degree assessment." Often implemented as a part of the performance management program assessments by supervisors, peers and subordinates could be a source of valuable insight into whether employees do what they are expected to do, persisting despite obstacles. And they may also provide information on knowledge, skills and abilities an employee has that are not a part of their current roles. But the questions that will uncover capabilities need to be asked as a part of the peer or subordinate assessments.

Using employees as recruiters also has promise. Programs that seek to develop referrals of outsiders from employees often provide financial incentives. Employees usually receive a specified sum when a referral is hired and often receive another sum when the referral has been employed for a period of time. It may not be feasible to offer financial rewards for those providing valuable information about their co-workers but 360-degree assessment programs can gather the information. Employees tend to be more forthcoming in providing peer and subordinate information if the program is used for development rather than for rewards and informing employees of the value of this information can provide an incentive to provide it.

Internship and Co-Op Programs

A traditional approach to identifying talent that may be useful in the future has been the use of internships and co-op programs. There are numerous alternatives, ranging from a summer internship to a multi-year co-op program. For example, students can be selected for a co-op program in their freshman year and work for the organization during the three summers prior to their graduation. In a field like engineering, people accumulate knowledge and skills as a result of their course work, with the level of complexity increasing as they progress through their programs. And by having them doing work that is consistent with their level of competence they can reinforce academic learning with practical experience. In some cases, the organization may have them work during the school terms, although their work schedules must be integrated with their studies. By the time someone has participated in the program for several years the organization will have a significant amount of knowledge about their capabilities and the participant will have a greater understanding of the organization. One of the opportunities this approach presents for multinationals is the ability to involve foreign students, who might otherwise be unreachable. Having a student from India or China complete the program would enable the organization to have a candidate for full-time employment in their home country or in the headquarters country. Returning them to their home country can minimize the uncertainty associated with international assignments, typically caused by the need to adjust culturally to a foreign country.

Another benefit of co-op and internship programs is that the organization and the participant have the option of having graduates continue their relationship with the organization as freelancers or consultants. If the work is project-based it may lend itself to sporadic utilization of individuals. And increasingly people are opting to work as independents rather than entering employment. Even when talent platforms pre-screen candidates for gig assignments there is considerable uncertainty about whether individuals will fit into the organization well. But if they have worked as interns or co-op participants that uncertainty can be minimized.

Retention Reduces Recruitment Demands

Managing turnover can reduce the need to source talent from the outside. Turnover can be necessary, or at least beneficial, if the type of workforce that will be needed does not match the current workforce. But losing talent that is critical to success can be damaging, since it creates a need to find a source of replacement talent. When an organization has a 10% turnover rate that may be viewed as too high, optimal or lower than expected. Comparing to other organizations can enable a judgment to be made. If competitors have 20% turnover rates, then the organization may believe it is doing something right. But what in what parts of the organization is turnover occurring? In which occupations is it happening? Is the turnover desirable (functional) or damaging (dysfunctional)? Aggregate rates are of limited usefulness and further analysis can improve assessments as to whether there is a turnover problem.

Figure 3.1 is an analysis of aggregate turnover, broken down by internal versus external, unavoidable versus avoidable and functional versus dysfunctional. Even after categorizing turnover rates by type it is necessary to evaluate the

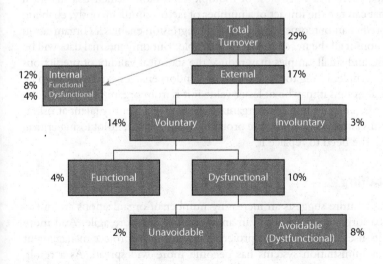

Figure 3.1 Turnover analysis.

impact of each type. Internal turnover can be indicative of career development, but it also can suggest people running away from certain roles or certain managers. External turnover that is involuntary is generally not a concern unless the wrong people are being shown the exit. Unavoidable turnover is also common and by definition there is little the organization can do to prevent it. The bottom line is that 29% aggregate turnover is an inadequate figure for deciding if there is a problem. The 12% of the total that is viewed as dysfunctional should be of greatest concern and is a more realistic way to decide if turnover is a problem.

As discussed elsewhere in this book, technological advances are providing new tools that may be useful for talent management. Predictive analytics can help organizations do a better job of sourcing and selecting the right kind of talent. And there are now tools that can help identify critical talent that might be prone to leave. By identifying potential leavers, the organization can initiate efforts to address concerns that might be prompting people to consider leaving. IBM has developed AI/machine learning capabilities for predicting who might be prone to leave the organization. These tools were developed for internal use but have been made available for purchase by other organizations. The software uses large amounts of internal and external data to identify the factors that predict voluntary turnover. Factors such as job tenure, internal pay comparisons, external pay comparisons, promotional history, length of commute and age are all tested to see if they correlate with past turnover. Although an experienced human resource professional may understand that all of these factors will impact the intention to leave attempting to evaluate the likelihood of departure for a large number of employees manually can be impractical. By identifying the criticality of specific individuals, the number of analyses can be reduced but the process remains difficult. In the Appendix, there is a discussion of multiple regression, which is a statistical technique that can test the impact of a number of factors simultaneously, enabling the user to predict an outcome. Using multiple regression enables an organization to do predictions if all the necessary data is available. But only internal data will be likely to exist, and small samples may reduce the statistical validity of predictions based on that sample. Using tools provided by vendors enables external data to be used as well, although it may be of lesser value if it is from organizations with dissimilar contexts (i.e., culture). If an organization is able to identify talent at risk, it can take actions aimed at lessening the probability of departure. Not losing critical talent reduces the need to replace it.

Project Staffing

The current literature suggests an increasing number of organizations are utilizing teams as a form of organization, in an attempt to be more agile. And more work presents itself in the form of projects, so the use of project management and project administration systems has become more widespread. As a result, project management/administration is evolving into an occupational discipline.

Since project management and team leadership require many of the same skills those successful at leading projects are probably going to be successful leading teams. There are formal programs leading to certification or other formal credentials, offered by the Project Management Institute (pmi.org) and by some educational institutions. Project work must be staffed differently than units with a stable purpose. Because of the importance of project work it is critical for organizations to be able to source talent that will enable successful project execution.

Staffing projects begin with a process known as "deconstructing work."[3] This entails the development of a project planning framework that defines blocks of work and establishes their relationships with each other. Figure 3.2 is an example of a project management plan. This example follows the PERT-CPM (project evaluation and review technique – critical path method) methodology. Each block of work (segment) defines what must be done, specifies the resources (talent, budget and technology) required and establishes a timeframe. All of the segments on the middle (critical) path must be completed on time, since any slippage will delay the entire project. Segments off the critical path have slack, which means there is more time available to do the work than would be required if a concentrated effort is made. The relationships between the segments establish the sequence that must be followed. In this example the feasibility study segment must precede and be completed before any other segments can begin, since the study will determine if the project will get off the ground. Once the work involved in each segment and the outcomes that must be produced are defined the estimated time required and the performance milestones can be established. The last step is to identify who will perform the work in each segment. Figure 3.3 illustrates the assignment of segments to the party that will do the work.

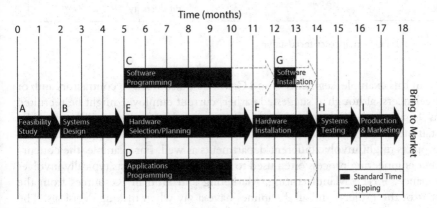

Figure 3.2 Project planning.

Segment	Milestones	Standard Time/Slack	Performance Criteria	Staff Eligible
A	Present feasibility study to management	2 mos. / 0	Quality of study	Project staff
B	Complete systems design	3 mos. / 0	On-time completion / quality / cost	Systems staff
C	Complete software programming	5 mos. / 2 mos.	On-time completion / quality / cost	Software staff
D	Complete applications programming	5 mos. / 4 mos.	On-time completion / quality / cost	Applications staff
E	Complete hardware selection/planning	6 mos. /0	On-time completion / quality / cost	Operations staff
F	Complete hardware installation	3 mos. /0	On-time completion/ quality/cost	Operations staff
G	Complete software installation	1 mo. /1 mo.	On-time completion/ quality/cost	Software staff
H	Run successful systems test	2 mos. /0	On-time completion/ quality/cost	Project staff
I	Produce/market system and deliver to market	2 mos. /0	On-time completion/ quality/ productivity	Project staff

Figure 3.3 Performance criteria/staffing.

In this example, segments C and G will be outsourced to contractors and/or freelancers, although as suggested earlier, current employee might be recruited as "gig-ers" to perform the work. The rest of the segments will be done by staff members of the internal department, in this case the IT department. Some projects might involve different departments as well. For example, the concurrent engineering process often used to develop new products typically involves Finance, R&D, Manufacturing, Marketing and Human Resources from the start of the project, and all disciplines have a say when making decisions. The often-used "have R&D design it and throw it over the wall to Manufacturing to see if they can make it … if not, send it back for rework" methodology has proven to be too costly and time-consuming, not to mention the frustration level it generates among those involved.

When work is done in teams, additional competencies may be required in order for someone to be successful. Some people have a deeply ingrained "I will do my work … you do yours" mindset, often attributable to their cultural orientation (the United States is one of the most individualistic cultures in the world). This type of mindset can keep teams from being successful, since knowledge sharing is required. Employees with a strong individualistic cultural orientation often have difficulty replacing "me" with "us" in their thinking about who contributed to the outcomes produced. And if they have only experienced merit pay programs, they might find team incentives, and even team-based performance appraisal to be misguided. Competitive behavior may be imbedded in their psyche and it may be difficult for them to share their best ideas and techniques with peers, which can impede knowledge dissemination. The "what you measure and reward you will get more of" principle argues for measuring and rewarding cooperative behavior rather than competitive behavior if overall team performance is the goal.

Once the sources of talent are identified a selection process must be put in place to decide which of the potential candidates is chosen. Talent selection is the topic of the next chapter.

Notes

1 Trompenaars, F. & Greene, R. *Rewarding Performance Globally* (New York: Routledge, 2017).
2 Cascio, W. *Managing Human Resources* (New York: McGraw-Hill, 2015).
3 Boudreau, J., Jesuthasan, R., & Creelman, D. *Lead the Work* (Hoboken, NJ: Wiley, 2015).

Chapter 4

Selecting Talent

Having a large supply of fully qualified candidates is a luxury every organization would prefer to have. During periods of low unemployment, such as the one that exists in 2020 in the United States, an adequate supply of people trained in many occupations is more difficult to find than when unemployment was higher during the economic crisis that began in 2007–2008 and persisted for several years. When the economy worsened the downsizing activity it precipitated created a temporary surplus of people. But many organizations were economically incapable of taking advantage of it. They needed to control costs because their revenues had declined. So hiring was out of the question, even though high-quality candidates were available with qualifications that are typically difficult to attract and retain.

Some organizations were in a position to take advantage of the situation and offered rewards packages that would have been laughable in better times. Desperation on the part of those needing employment resulted in organizations finding real bargains, at least temporarily. There are difficulties associated with taking advantage of a situation like this – when things get better economically it is not wise to stand in front of the exits, lest one be trampled by the departing talent. Many people know when they are being taken advantage of and it does not generally result in content workers.

As discussed in Chapter 1, workforce planning should be based on a long-range view of the talent the organization will need. This prevents short-sided actions such as taking advantage of people's immediate need for employment. In the United States, there have been instances that suggested some organizations believe that serial downsizing and upsizing is a viable strategy. The "employment at will" doctrine that prevails in the U.S. theoretically allows such a strategy, but there are significant problems created when taking this path.[1] Serial downsizing may do less damage to an organization's brand in the United States than it would in countries where longevity is encouraged and when there are laws/regulations that make terminations costly and even illegal. But even though an organization may feel it can survive the image tainting there are economic reasons for controlling large scale terminations.

First, terminating an employee will often result in significant additional cash outlays at the time of termination, which is the last thing an organization struggling to reduce costs wants. The value of vested rights to accrued vacation, sick leave time and pension benefits must be paid out. There may be severance pay policies that mandate significant settlements. Benefits may be extended beyond termination. Stock held by employees may have to be bought back. Unemployment insurance rate premiums may be increased based on the organization's experience rating. Outplacement programs might mandate costly assistance to those terminated. There will also be administrative requirements creating by the terminations that current staff may not be able to handle, necessitating the use of contractors.

In addition to the immediate economic costs an organization should consider the impact on the morale of survivors and on its employer brand. Survivors who are left with the same amount of work, to now be done by fewer people, will wonder if survival was the good news or the bad news. And becoming known as an organization that views employees as its most disposable, rather than most important, asset does not bode well for future recruitment.

There will always be limited supplies of highly qualified candidates in specific occupations. In the late 1990s, the desperate shortage of IT personnel skilled in designing network-based systems made dealing with the massive number of system conversions in order to deal with Y2K a nightmare for many organizations. As has been discussed earlier, workforce planning would have been a partial answer to the turmoil organizations went through. But there was a legacy to be dealt with as well, caused by the tendency of organizations to focus solely on candidate qualifications that are needed in the role they are being hired to play. Even though an organization might have a high potential program that considers future potential most recruiters are charged with assessing current competence for the roles to be filled today.

In Chapter 3, the discussion about sourcing talent internally highlighted the lost opportunity associated with not doing an assessment of incoming employees that identified the full range of their capabilities and their potential. When a new role is created within an organization there is often a tendency to assume that it will be necessary to go outside, since no current employees have played that specific role and/or demonstrated a capacity and willingness to fill it. This is partially attributable to the lack of knowledge about what employees know and are capable of and not taking steps to have them realize their full potential. The career interests of employees may also be a significant factor, since some may contribute their time if given the opportunity to learn something new and that they have an interest in. Even though it may be difficult to get candidates to declare their future aspirations there is a payback in anticipating how the person might fit in over the longer run.

Making staffing decisions without considering whether candidates are likely to fit the career paths most frequently followed in the organization makes the selection criteria deficient. Where possible it is valuable to determine if a candidate is someone who has demonstrated a willingness to learn. Organizations usually recognize the need to invest in current employee development, which can increase the probability that functional internal mobility will be possible. But it is important to attract people who will welcome continuous development and embrace changes in the roles they play. Some candidates will want to continue doing what they have been doing, with no aspirations to explore other occupations or to go into managerial roles. Having a stable core of employees in certain roles may be beneficial. But if no one is concerned about meeting future staffing needs the organization will be prone to stagnation. Another obstacle to mobility can be the practice of having an employee's manager absorb the costs of training people in his or her operating budget. By creating a corporate talent development account an organization can avoid this source of resistance to expanding employee capabilities. And although usage of the development account may need to be monitored managers should not be penalized for doing something that will benefit the organization, especially when it may actually make their job harder. Development will be discussed in more detail in subsequent chapters.

Selection Strategies

If an organization has done adequate workforce planning, as described in Chapter 1, and has identified both current and future needs it can define what its talent requirements are, as described in Chapter 2. When its' needs are clearly defined it can begin to source talent, as described in Chapter 3. Once the talent pool has been identified the process of selecting the right talent is the next challenge. As discussed in the Introduction and in Chapter 3, there are more options available for getting work done than simply hiring employees to do it. This reality can have an impact on the selection process, and the ability to assess the relative benefits of performing work with employees or outsourcing it becomes critical.

There are four options when selecting who is going to do the work that needs to be done. The organization can hire fully qualified people and put them right to work. Or it can hire people with the potential to learn how to do the work and develop them. Or if it cannot find anyone that fits either of those options it can change the definition of the work. And finally, it can have another outside party do the work. All have disadvantages and advantages.

Selecting fully qualified people. This is the most common approach. Most organizations wait until work needs to be done before management figures out who should do it, frequently resulting in a frantic search for qualified people. This unfortunate scenario is generally the result of inadequate workforce planning. But even if planning has been done and there is a need to hire someone it is still necessary to decide who will fill the role. If multiple candidates are eager to join the organization and they are at least minimally qualified a strategy for selecting the best talent is needed.

Staffing functions vary in their selection strategies. Unstructured one-on-one interviews are one option, even though this is the least valid of the several available tools according to research findings.[2,3] Despite the lack of predictive power this type of interview is still the most commonly used approach. Managers overestimate their ability to identify the best candidate based solely on an interview ... this is one of the common cognitive biases everyone is subject to. In addition to the lack of validity in selecting the best candidate this type of interview provides little protection against the tendency to favor people who are like the interviewer, or who the interviewer likes. Interviewers tend to prefer those who seem to be the easiest to relate to and are prone to concluding that those who agree with the interviewer's beliefs and values are the best choice. Racial, gender and age bias can become an issue, since there are no controls over the questions asked and how the decisions are made. And since diversity can have positive benefits allowing the "like me/I like you" bias to work against diversity.

As discussed earlier the work by Kahneman and Tversky identified a number of biases that degrade the quality of decisions.[4] They also identified the two types of cognitive activity ... System 1 (fast) and System 2 (slow). Many decisions do not require deliberation or calculation because prior experience or relative knowledge may make it possible to do things automatically. Qualified drivers are on a form of autopilot most of the time and execute maneuvers without conscious calculations. Unfortunately, System 1 is gullible, biased to believe information without question. Another problem with System 1 is that it is prone to stereotyping, since this is efficient and effortless. It leaps to a conclusion in cases where incomplete evidence has been processed, which is why candidates for leadership roles that "look like leaders" (or at least like the successful ones the recruiter is aware of) can have an unwarranted impact on the overall evaluation. And the recruiter's blood sugar level or the types of candidates interviewed before the current candidate can also influence evaluation. The time of day and the time since the last meal can cause variations in the thought processes of interviewers. Regrettably, this is also true with judges, resulting in uneven application of the law.

One of the most disturbing human tendencies is falling prey to the halo effect, which means the rating on the first selection factor can unjustifiably impact ratings on subsequent factors. So even the sequence followed when evaluating someone on a series of factors may have a substantial impact on the overall rating.

A significant problem with hiring fully qualified people is that they will tend to be expensive. Rarely does an organization have a surplus of highly qualified people knocking on the door. It is understandable that these high-quality candidates will expect higher pay rates than would candidates who are not competent in all aspects of the job. And these people may also be harder to find, since they often have to be enticed to leave other organizations. It is very common for fully qualified entrants to be paid at or even above the salary range midpoint. And bringing them in at a high rate may cause them to be paid the same as, or even more than current employees who have been with the organization for some time and who are just as qualified. This is called compression and compensation specialists know it can cause difficulties with longer service employees who view this as inequitable.[5]

A last consideration when seeking fully qualified people is how the organization establishes that the candidate is indeed fully qualified. Having done similar work may be one reason a person is viewed as qualified, but there are still questions about whether their experience translates across organizations. The quality of the person's work at prior employers is hard to determine. And having the same job title at the other organization does not establish that the work is the same. The technology employed, the autonomy the person had, and the resources provided may all have an impact on whether what was done equips the person to meet the organization's expectations.

Selecting Candidates with the Potential to Learn the Job. This approach can usually enable the organization to pay lower starting rates than would be required for fully qualified people. But it should be recognized that the person will require an investment in their training and may not be able to meet performance standards for some time. If the organization has an adequate supply of employees able to perform the work that must be done currently this approach can be viable. But if there is a shortage of current staff to perform the work required the delay caused by doing the necessary training may make this a poor strategy. If the total cost (starting pay plus training investment) is equal to what is incurred when hiring fully qualified people, it may also be prudent to consider future workforce needs. If the age demographics of incumbents indicate that a significant portion of experienced employees are likely to retire soon management must be certain training and development can be completed prior to the loss of the competent employees. The learning curve from entry to fully qualified may also be considered. If job holders require a license that can only be obtained with a set number of years of experience this can alter the experience requirements for new entrants.

Millennials represent about one-third of the current U.S. workforce. Those in their early 20s will be new graduates or people with limited experience, while those in their early to mid-30s possess more knowledge and skills, so one must be careful about assuming they are all the same. This cohort was found by Korn Ferry research to have different priorities than prior cohorts. They ranked the things they most value as follows: (1) recognition, (2) wellness programs, (3) work-life balance and (4) student loan assistance. Surveyed people felt they received far too little feedback about how they were doing and what they needed to do to improve and advance. And their desire for social and sporting events, grounded in a desire to be healthy and to have a rich social life, was not being fulfilled. Organizations counting heavily on Millennials must consider whether the culture and existing programs are going to be attractive to this group of potential candidates, or they are going to find attraction and retention more difficult in a competitive environment. The median tenure for this cohort is 2.8 years, down from 4.2 years for prior cohorts. The leading reason for the short tenure was largely due to the perception that professional development and advancement opportunities within a single organization were inadequate. These realities are going to have an impact on an organization's ability to compete effectively for this talent pool, unless steps are taken to change perceptions and employment decisions.

One of the decisions an organization must make is whether they hire recent graduates or people with work experience. Hiring specifications usually allow for a tradeoff between formal education and experience, but when selecting someone for a role it is necessary to evaluate the type of knowledge and skill required. If candidates are being hired to do electrical work the right qualifications should be determined based on what they will do. Designing electrical circuits may require someone with a BA in electrical engineering, while installing electrical equipment in a plant may favor hiring someone with experience in doing that type of work. Due to the advances in computing technology there has been a dramatic increase in the need for people to do coding of various types. Although employees in the IT function have most often been university graduates many organizations have recognized that many types of coding can be done by someone with technical training acquired in the coding "boot camps" that have proliferated. Experience and displayed competence may trump conceptual knowledge gained in higher education and the reality is that people without university degrees tend to be less costly.

Although university attendance has been placed on a pedestal in the United States, in many countries vocational training is considered to be a credible alternative. Germany has established dominance in some fields by creating a highly skilled pool of people using vocational schools and work-learn apprenticeships. The culture also reveres higher education and PhDs dominate the executive ranks in many organizations there. The "Herr Doctor" form of address signals the level of respect that higher education commands.

An ongoing debate about whether universities provide graduates with the knowledge, skills and abilities required in organizations has raged in the United States for many decades. Perhaps the most contentious debate is about the value of an MBA degree. This credential has been heralded as a ticket to enter the C-suite, or at least as a high-octane fuel for people with high career aspirations. Recent college graduates are generally thought to have the newest technical skills and ideas. But the World Economic Forum research has found that the gap between the skills people learn in school and the skills they need on the job is widening. Employers such as Google have found that the most important qualities of their highest performers are soft skills, such as critical thinking, communication, listening ability and empathy.

The National Association of Colleges and Employers (NACE) has developed a set of definitions for the competencies related to career readiness.[6] These are:

1. Professionalism/Work Ethic: Demonstrate personal accountability and effective work habits, integrity, ethical behavior, ability to learn from mistakes and responsibility for the interests of the larger community.
2. Critical Thinking/Problem Solving: Exercise sound reasoning to analyze issues, make decisions and overcome problems; able to obtain, interpret and use knowledge, facts and data; demonstrate originality and inventiveness.
3. Oral/Written Communications: Articulate thoughts and ideas clearly and effectively orally and in writing; has public speaking skills.
4. Teamwork/Collaboration: Build collaborative relationships with colleagues and customers representing diverse cultures; able to work within a team structure and can negotiate and manage conflict.
5. Digital Technology: Use digital technologies ethically and efficiently to solve problems, complete tasks and accomplish goals.
6. Leadership: Leverage the strengths of others to achieve common goals and use interpersonal skills to coach and develop others; able to manage own emotions and those of others and use empathetic skills to guide and motivate others.
7. Career Management: Identify and articulate one's skills, knowledge, strengths and experiences; pursue career goals and identify areas necessary for professional growth.
8. Global/Intercultural Fluency: Value, respect and learn from diverse cultures, ages, genders, sexual orientations and religions; demonstrate openness, inclusiveness, sensitivity and ability to interact respectfully.

These competencies are to some degree universal, although their relative importance will vary based on the type of career pursued and the occupation. If they are not being developed in university programs and they are critical for adequate performance in a role an organization may devalue the degrees held by candidates. One of the challenges facing those making selections is resisting the application of stereotypes. Because many of these competencies have been found to be lacking in university training that does not mean that any person lacks them. The school attended, the program completed, and the makeup of the individual can all help to determine whether the general findings apply to that person.

As organizations use team structures more frequently, they may find that selection models may require more focus on the ability of candidates to exhibit teamwork. In the United States, education often emphasizes individual competition when measuring performance. Few parents encourage their children to graduate in the middle of their class. Yet competing at the individual level can develop a perspective that does not easily lend itself to contributing to the effectiveness of others. A team consisting of members focused on outdoing each other is unlikely to be effective when work is interdependent. Adding a performance measure that rewards contributing to the effectiveness of others and the unit can help to encourage collaboration once people are employed. If that contribution impacts compensation and career progression it can at least encourage employees to develop the skills required to work collaboratively. But GPA and class-standing are usually factors that are heavily weighted by employers for new graduates so entrants may show up on their first day ready to compete … and be those least prepared to share.

Cognitive biases also have an impact on whether candidates are capable of being developed. It is more difficult to determine if someone has the ability to learn something than it is to determine if they have already learned it. As a result, hiring based on potential can be more difficult to execute well than it is when selecting fully qualified candidates. Since there is less tangible evidence the probability that System 1 will dominate the evaluator's thought process increases, and with it the probability that biases will have an impact.

Redesign the Role So Available Candidates Can Meet the Requirements. When employees remain in a role for a long time, they tend to pick up additional duties and responsibilities and become competent to perform them. They also fall into a pattern of how things are done. As the time when they must be replaced nears the organization may find they are trying to staff a hybrid job that few if any people would be able to do. If the retiring person has accumulated relatively unrelated duties rather than trying to find a direct replacement it might be wiser to redesign the role so that the qualifications required are likely to be found in candidates.

When consulting with an envelope manufacturer I found that over the years the company's maintenance people had drastically modified the equipment. Since envelopes are generally seen as a commodity and manufacturers must compete on price the organization continued to modify the equipment to increase productivity and reduce costs. The equipment was so modified that the original vendor's people were unable to work on it. The maintenance people who had been around for 20 or more years were paid at a level equivalent to engineers, since their contributions had given the organization a competitive edge. When I asked what the company would do when these people retired, they admitted they had not come up with an answer but certainly were working on it. What made it difficult is that they knew the supply of maintenance people available in the labor market could not do the job, at least not in the short term. Redesigning the roles was also a challenge since the equipment was the key to their competitiveness. I suggested they begin to focus on knowledge management incentives, that would encourage maintenance workers to pass their knowledge on to either current employees or new hires. In some instances, there was resistance on the part of incumbents, who were proud of being the "go to" people for issues related to productivity, and who wanted to retain that status. One strategy the organization adopted was the creation of a formal training regimen that allotted a percentage of the senior maintenance workers time to sharing what they knew. And they were paid incentives for doing it well.

When redesigning roles, it is also necessary to consider the pool of qualifications required in the unit. If some of the duties that had been in the job description can be covered by current employees someone who is qualified to do things others cannot currently do well can be selected. There is a tendency to attempt to combine roles into as few job titles as possible, but this strategy may be flawed. Like completing a jigsaw puzzle the shape of the pieces is dictated by the gaps that need to be filled. Carrying this "fewer jobs is better" philosophy to the absurd extreme would produce one job title ... employee. Given the increased use of outside talent the job title might more appropriately be worker. On the other hand, assuming everyone's role is unique can produce a classification system that is unwieldy.

Classifying technical professionals into career progression models has been discussed earlier. This represents a role-based, rather than a job-based perspective.[7] For example, employee roles can be defined as doing what needs to be done at the time, in a response mode (i.e., employees in IT, engineering and other technical occupations). A system crashes ... a production line performs poorly ... an employee's terminal won't talk to the network ... these are all examples of situations that require someone to respond and to remedy problems. Response mode jobs include fire fighters and police officers, who might have ongoing duties but whose primary function is to deal with events as they occur. Anyone who has tried to write a job description for employees whose work is done in a responsive mode realizes the best that can be done is to list the types of things the incumbent may do when needed. IT professionals are often working on several projects simultaneously, often in different capacities over time ... project manager on one project, individual contributor on others. This type of fluid work requires a different set of competencies than does a job that is stable. Managing people requires different skill sets than coding. Providing technical leadership requires the ability to persuade others when there is no formal authority to direct them. Organizations must be cognizant of such differences when selecting people who will be a good fit to the role. Supplementing qualification specifications with competency models can help provide a broad perspective, including interpersonal skills, needed behaviors and other personal characteristics that are relevant and required for successful performance.

Outsourcing the Work. As already discussed, an increasing amount of work is being done by parties not employed by the organization.[8] Now the selection issue becomes what kind of outsider to select to do the work. Turning over the complete unit of work to an outside party is one option. Payroll processing, printing, accounting work ... there are many types of work that could be outsourced. As long as the work can be clearly defined and needed outcomes can be fully specified turning over the full unit of work can result in lower costs, better quality or both.

Newspapers compete for circulation and advertising by providing the best journalism and the largest audience. Many of them enter into joint printing operations with other papers, since printing is not what gives them a competitive advantage. Every organization must decide what its comparative advantage is ... what it is or can be especially good at. It was pointed out in the Introduction that Nike and Apple believe their comparative advantage is gained by focusing on design and marketing. It is unlikely they could be world-class and cost-competitive in manufacturing so they turn it over to someone who can be. Correctly identifying comparative advantage enables an organization to focus on what it does best. If it then formulates an effective business strategy that enables it to gain a competitive advantage it will maximize the probability of success. Doing what one does best makes performing well a good deal easier.

Few organizations do well when they have to cope with erratic swings in work volume with a fixed workforce. Since it takes time to source and select talent and to get employees up to full competence the organization must plan ahead, so that staffing levels are adequate to meet demands. A stable workforce is generally not the best way to deal with widely fluctuating demands unless employees are able and willing to be flexible on hours worked. Organizations that face significant but predictable seasonal variations in demands commonly hire seasonal help. Chefs who work in resorts know that they might be in ski country for the winter months and water sport areas for the summer. Retailers hire large numbers of temporary help to meet seasonal demands ... few are looking for a Santa Claus in July. And the construction industry in some climate zones have employees who must deal with variable employment.

All these situations are predictable, while others are not. Economic downturns breed layoffs and surges in demand for skills result in scaled up hiring (i.e., Y2K for IT personnel). If work demand varies within a day, then part-time employees may be used to match staffing levels to work demands (i.e., peak-time tellers at a bank). But if the part-time employees cannot meet their income demands with part-time earnings, they may have to hold multiple jobs, which employers might view as a problem. Offering a 15- to 20-hour work week might attract full-time students but may not attract a sufficient number of qualified candidates. When the economy is booming, and unemployment is low the part-time employees who would rather work full-time may be able to find a new home where full-time work is available.

Appropriately selecting a mix of part-time and full-time employees is a major determinant of workforce effectiveness. This is an issue faced in industries such as retail. Costco employs a higher percentage of full-time employees than Sam's Club, a look-alike competitor. Often it is the cost of providing full-timers with benefits that cause organizations to only offer part-time work. But this approach can make it difficult to compete for the best talent. Costco justifies its higher pay and higher percentage of benefit eligible employees by factoring in their lower costs associated with turnover, which is lower than that of Sam's Club.[9] The Costco CEO also defends the expenditure by pointing out the income level of Costco customers is higher and that a better quality of employee is necessary to provide the level of service expected by those customers. But Costco must also consider whether offering more hours makes the staffing level less adaptable to swings in customer volume.

Part-time employees can be considered for full-time work when vacancies exist. The time spent as a part-timer can serve as an indicator of suitability of the person for full-time slots. Often organizations do not pay attention to the performance of part-timers and do not make an effort to identify the full range of their capabilities or to invest in training them. Given the uncertainty about the suitability of strangers when recruiting it would seem prudent to use what the organization knows about those who have been in a part-time role to evaluate them based on this more complete knowledge. Knowing that someone reliably shows up when they are supposed to and that they perform assigned work diligently is valuable information that can be used to predict their success in other roles. Résumés can be contrived to create a positive image and interviews have limited value in predicting success. Past behavior is the best predictor of future behavior and a history has already been established for part-timers. If someone can only be available for part-time work an organization might be well served by making an effort to identify obstacles to full-time work and considering a restructured schedule so the person can be utilized more fully. If a student can work three 12-hour days over the weekend, a new source of qualified talent becomes available, assuming that this fits operational needs.

Contractors can be retained in a manner that enables the organization to prescribe the type of skills required, the amount of time they are required, the volume of support required and the schedule. So outsourcing work that is subject to wide swings in volume may be the best option. Organizations that dramatically increased their IT staffing levels by hiring new employees in order to deal with the intense workload required to redo systems prior to 2000 often found they were overstaffed once the conversion was complete. On the other hand, those who used contractors to do the extra work were often able to adjust staffing to meet ongoing work volumes without terminating employees. Whether they had made the right decision from an economic perspective depended on what their contractor costs were compared to what costs would have been if another approach had been used. Since many organizations had no option because their current staff was too small or existing employees were incapable of doing the work this may be a meaningless analysis. And the failure to do workforce planning early enough to make other options available might have also limited their choices.

There can be concerns about whether outsiders will be as engaged in their work and as committed to sticking around until the work is done as are employees. Incentives can be created that demand high-quality results if the contractor's compensation is contingent on project completion and quality. Incentives can also be used to encourage contractors to train the organization's employees to effectively use the work product going forward. Contractors may view training client's employees as creating a new competitor for future work, but by making it clear that failure to adequately train employees will impact whether there is any future business can motivate the desired behavior. It can also be penalized by a financial adjustment if not done.

Non-profit organizations often use volunteers to augment their workforce. Hospital systems often have a designated Director of Volunteer Services who may have hundreds of people to manage. Deciding whether work can be done by volunteers may involve legal considerations, since some work requires specific licenses and certifications. There is also a concern about using people who employees might view as threats to their job security. And there are also concerns about whether people who do not have their income from employment at risk based on their performance will respond to direction provided by managers. Volunteers can provide expertise that an organization could not afford if it meant hiring an employee with the same qualifications. Over my career, I contributed several thousand hours to professional associations creating certification programs and designing and teaching professional development programs. There must of course be some attraction for people to provide their time without compensation. Wikipedia and some of the open source software have been created by volunteers and there may be no central body controlling their work. One could argue that an unpaid internship is a volunteer gig. Even though the motive behind the willingness to do free work is personal development and/or establishing a relationship that may lead to a paid job this source of labor can be taken advantage of. As a result, many universities will not involve themselves with helping students get internships that are not paid. Organizations dedicated to community development often have people who are employees of for-profit organizations provided to them on a part-time basis. These programs are typically supported by for-profit organizations because they send the message that contributing to society is important and that it helps to brand the organization as socially responsible.

Selection Methods and Processes

There are numerous methods available for making selection decisions.[10] The failings of the one-on-one unstructured interview has already been made clear and although this tool may be used as an element of a valid selection process it cannot do the job alone. Many selection processes are like hurdle races that require baton exchanges, since they involve a series of "tests," each of which candidates must pass before moving through the rest of the process. When in college, I was in Air Force ROTC and went through an exhaustive series of medical tests to see if I would qualify for fighter pilot, which was the only role I would accept if I were to join the Air Force. All of the candidates were queued up to take the eye test. My impatience caused me to ask why everyone was not spread out among the ten or so stations, to speed things up. I was informed that this was a hurdle system and that the largest percentage of failures were at the vision testing station. If your vision was not essentially perfect (and apparently the majority of those there eventually were told they did not qualify due to some vision issue) you would not be accepted. Those with adequate vision for other roles, such as Navigator, were channeled through future testing associated with that alternative role. When I reflected on the way the process was organized, I realized having everyone take all of the tests would have been a waste of resources.

A similar hurdle system was encountered when I was asked to rewrite the plumber exam for a large city during my PhD studies. The pay and benefits for plumbers were so good that the city would have hundreds of applicants for an opening and they wanted to use a process that enabled them to cope with that volume and do so in the most cost-effective manner. The written test was the Achilles' heel for plumber applicants, just like the eye test for fighter pilot candidates. Something like 70% of the plumber applicants failed the written test that covered codes and other specific knowledge needed by people doing the work. By doing the written exam first it reduced the number going on to the next stage. The next hurdle in the city's process was a performance test. This was very time and material consuming, so it represented a considerable cost to run people through this phase. By minimizing the number of performance tests using the written test as a screen the overall process passed an efficiency test. So hurdle systems are a good strategy when similar conditions exist.

There are some jobs that are physically demanding as well as requiring skills and knowledge and tests of physical capabilities should be used in these cases. Screening applicants for a fire department will involve strength and endurance tests, which will determine whether candidates have the native ability to do the job. I wondered why we were not tested for fear of heights when I entered jump school but I found the Airborne had another method of dealing with that condition … those who froze in the door at the 32-foot tower in week 2 were thrown out the door, based on the assumption the candidate was now over any fear of future exits from high places. We also had a few freeze events on the first live jump. And yes, the corrective action was the same as in the tower.

The National Football League teams utilize comprehensive processes when selecting their draft choices. Players are tested for intelligence, as well as physical ability. There are different "cut scores" (lowest passing score) for different positions. The highest cutoff is for the quarterback position and the second highest is for the left tackle position (the one most responsible for keeping the very expensive quarterback alive). The physical performance tests are extensive. Players are run through tests at the combines and individual teams often have their own performance tests. Medical tests are also extensive for obvious reasons. But sometimes personality can play a role in how effective a draft choice will turn out to be.

Ryan Leaf was picked ahead of Peyton Manning, based on athletic ability. Manning turned out to be a Hall of Fame candidate, while Leaf failed to last long in the league. Players would follow Manning and play for him, while

Leaf could not rally teammates around him, resulting in failure. The difference between the two was related to personality, which Webster's dictionary defines as "a set of distinctive traits and their characteristics." But in order to use personality as a selection criterion there must be a valid way to measure it. Whether personality tests can be good predictors of performance has been widely researched. Some studies have shown limited predictive power. A potential workaround in the Leaf-Manning case might have been to interview past teammates and coaches, to get a better insight into how one works. Organizations are largely precluded from using this approach, since it is generally not practical to gather this kind of information from previous employers. In fact, due to U.S. laws and the fear of lawsuits, an organization is lucky to get employment dates verified by past employers.

Other research indicates that personality tests can be helpful in predicting performance if the tests are focused on the appropriate personality characteristics.[11] The predictive power is small to moderate. The most widely supported characteristics used to define personality are the "Big 5," which are: Neuroticism, Extraversion, Openness, Agreeableness and Conscientiousness. All of these five are positively correlated with work performance, except neuroticism. Conscientiousness is the most consistent predictor of performance and when it is used along with Intelligence (General Mental Ability) its power is greatly enhanced, since GMA is the best single predictor. Predictive power varies by job type: professionals' performance is only predicted by conscientiousness (along with GMA), while manager performance is impacted by extraversion as well.

Making selection decisions should be based on measures that best predict success of candidates. Measures should be comprehensive and should include all things that contribute to the quality of prediction. So if personality will be an issue there should be an attempt to measure it, even if the measure is imperfect. Including all predictors makes the selection model *comprehensive*. It is also necessary for the model not to contain predictors that provide no value or even detract from the validity of the model. Including such factors *contaminates* it. There is an increasing focus on workforce analytics and organizations have much more data that can be used to improve the prediction power of things like selection models. The book and movie *Moneyball*, which was discussed briefly earlier in this book, illustrated an analysis of factors that contributed to the value of a baseball player. The Oakland A's had the smallest payroll in the league but aspired to make the playoffs. The manager hired an advisor to use quantitative measures to select players that would be more productive. A logic was developed: in order to make the playoffs the team had to win a lot of games. In order to win a lot of games it had to score a lot of runs. So measures that would select players who would contribute to scoring runs should be used. Admittedly "a lot" is an imperfect statistical measure, but it served the purpose. The advisor zeroed in on one measure ... on-base percentage. Not whether the player looked like an athlete or moved like an athlete. Not foot speed or strength. Just on base percentage. There also had to be an assessment of a player's fielding ability, since they had to play defense when not at bat, unless they would be a designated hitter. Failing to include that requirement would make the selection model *deficient*, meaning it did not include measures that were necessary. Using that model the team restructured itself through trades and made the playoffs. The opinions of the scouts had been superseded by analytics, even though they had many years of experience evaluating players. The movie *Trouble with the Curve* made the case for paying attention to the opinions of experienced scouts as well. And as is commonly found, adopting a "both-and" rather than an "either-or" approach to selecting factors seems the wise path to follow.

When a "best to work for" organization seeks candidates and is inundated by a large volume of potentially qualified candidates a hurdle system seems advisable. Cisco was one of the early adopters of software that screened submitted applications electronically using an algorithm. The company had enjoyed dramatic increases in their stock price and since they used stock options liberally many people sensed the prospect of early wealth. The use of algorithms to screen applicants based on the résumés submitted is common today. There are no doubt people who claim to be able to "beat the algorithm" by writing résumés in a certain way but that is difficult. It is understandable that organizations are not forthcoming with the details of what they look for in a resume, so it is hard to determine the validity and reliability of this element of a selection process. But caution must be exercised when creating selection algorithms, since they will do what they are told by the creator and nothing else.

Facebook suffered an embarrassment when it was discovered that it sent ads for STEM field jobs much more often to men than to women. On the surface this seemed to be gender-based discrimination, not something Facebook would like to be suggested in the media. The unintended pattern was the result of a cost-benefit analysis … women were more expensive to reach with ads. And the characteristics that measue suitability had been identified using male resumes. The algorithm did its job without considering consequences or such arbitrary things like the reaction of people to the results produced. "Guilty by algorithm" has not entered employment law in the United States as of yet, but …

Screening candidates for jobs that require technical competence and that produce tangible outcomes, such as programmer or graphic designer, may lend itself to performance testing. Organizations are increasingly asking applicants to display their level of competence by performing a task that is similar to the work they would be doing. One approach is to "crowdsource" by running an open contest and allowing people to submit their work. This can be as simple as writing code that will produce the desired result. It can also be as complex as producing a 30-second commercial for a product. The "winners" might be hired as employees. Or they may be paid a specified amount for producing something the organization can use. Many "gig-ers" are found this way and they may go on to do work for the organization on a contract basis. Another approach is to work with talent platforms, such as UpWork and TopCoder, who have candidates that they have tested and rated. When this is done the organization provides a full specification of what is needed, and the talent platform matches people to the requirements.

The more advanced tools technology has produced in recent years enable organizations to minimize the cognitive biases that people are prone to. When utilizing interviews, especially one-on-one unstructured interviews, bias is difficult to control. But using panel interviews with a standard set of questions can help to minimize individual biases. Some organizations are using automated selection tools such as video interviews that can be augmented by AI features. It is possible to develop psychographic profiles of candidates that were not possible in the past. Utilizing game-based tests can also refine the selection process. And realistic simulations are also possible to create that are much more sophisticated than previously used tools such as in-box exercises. Pilots are trained in simulators … crashes are less expensive in a simulation.

Selecting the "best" people one at a time may result in a pattern that raises other issues. There has been considerable legal and regulatory activity in the United States over the last 50 years focused on preventing illegal discrimination in hiring. The Equal Pay Act, Title VII of the Civil Rights Act, ADA, ADEA at the federal level and numerous laws and regulations at the state level are all intended to ensure equal access to employment. If the selection process used by an employer results in a statistically significant adverse impact on a protected class this constitutes prima facie evidence of illegal discrimination. When this is found to be the case the organization must defend the process based on business necessity or it will be found guilty of illegal discrimination. Discrimination based on age, gender, color, national origin, race, ethnicity, sexual preference or religion is illegal in the United States (also illegal in other countries, but many of them lack any significant enforcement).

Being found in violation of employment laws is not something an organization wants to experience. In addition to legal penalties there is also an impact on the employer brand of the organization. One of the most common sources of violation is the use of hiring requirements that are not necessary for someone to be able to perform the work required by the job being applied for. The landmark case of *Griggs v. Duke Power* established the concept of *bona fide occupational qualification*. Duke Power had required a high school diploma for jobs that did not require it. The result was that black applicants, who were far more likely to lack a diploma, were excluded in a larger percentage of cases than were white applicants. This case illustrated that wanting more than what is required to do the job may present an unwanted result, on top of the unnecessary extra cost of demanding excessive qualifications.

Managers have a tendency to ask for qualifications that are more than necessary. Playing it safe is a reasonable thing to do, since having new hires who struggle to do the job will require an investment in training and difficulty in getting the work done. If there is an inadequate supply of people with the necessary qualifications it may require hiring people who do not meet entry level requirements and then finding ways to deal with the knowledge/skill gaps. Hiring overqualified and underqualified people both have undesirable consequences, but if there is a supply–demand imbalance they may be the only choice. It is however prudent to discuss such situations with the candidate to be certain all parties recognize the realities and are comfortable with going ahead. Some candidates may react positively to entering an "above their head" situation, considering it an opportunity to grow, while others may be uncomfortable. Varied reactions will also occur when a candidate enters a role that they are overqualified for. Performing work that is viewed as unchallenging and tedious may not be ideal but if there is a prospect that the mismatch between capabilities and demands can be remedied in the future a candidate may elect to live with it. There is of course the option of redesigning roles and/or reallocating work. People react differently to these situations and by realigning staff assignments it may be possible to make the best of the situation.

A last consideration in selecting the best candidates is whether they will be content doing the type of work they will be expected to do. One could conclude that since candidates are applying for specific roles that they want to do the work required. But often economic necessity can cause people to force themselves to accept any job if the alternative is no job. And Help Wanted ads rarely paint a full picture ... like how it feels to do the job. Realistic job previews have been discussed previously but an organization should also consider building formal assessments of a candidate's preferences into the selection process. An organization that operated data centers used a 30-minute film showing potential applicants what it was like to be a Data Center Operator. Potential applicants were shown the film before completing an application. Every time the film was used there were fewer applications filed than the number of people viewing the film. One manager complained that applicants were being lost. The response from HR was that they would have been lost anyway, after being hired and trained, and that using the film to screen applicants was the low-cost approach. Going the extra mile to tell the truth can reduce unwanted turnover and lessen the percentage of incumbents who are miserable in their jobs. Considerable research has demonstrated that satisfied employees will treat customers better if they like their jobs so exposing customers to employees who would rather be almost anywhere else doing anything else is probably a bad practice.

So, what is the best process for selection? There are many sources of in-depth information on specific methods and processes for selecting talent.[12] There has been extensive research done on this topic and it is prudent for anyone responsible for making decisions related to talent selection to take advantage of this available knowledge. Mistakes in selection can be costly and relying on intuition or practitioner knowledge may not be adequate. High-quality decisions are worth an investment in careful design of selection processes.

Using Technology in Selection

Artificial intelligence and machine learning are providing potentials tool for improving selection. One of the ways to determine what will work in the way of staffing strategies is to find out what has worked and what has not. This enables those developing selection strategies to take advantage of having knowledge about past successes and failures and to apply the learned knowledge to future approaches. Creating a predictive model based on all available data can increase the success rate. Figure 4.1 describes the decision-making process for hiring.

The logic underlying this model is that people have to know about the organization, find its brand as an employer acceptable, determine that its current opening fits one's capabilities and objectives and decide to submit an application. Without that chain of events nothing happens, and no data is available for analysis. The number of hits on the organization's website can be taken as the number of people evaluating it and that is useful information. The percentage of people submitting an application can provide information about the apparent effectiveness of the website and the attractiveness of the job posting. It would be beneficial to know who did and who did not apply, so that the characteristics of each group could be analyzed. But unless there is a way to capture information about people visiting the website that is not possible, just as it is not possible to decide who pursued a newspaper or magazine ad and who did not. So data will be captured only on those who moved to the next step.

The most useful knowledge clarifies not only what has worked or not worked but *why*. Using machine learning past outcomes can be used to determine what will be likely to happen when specific selection criteria are used. Many organizations have concluded that using a particular set of selection criteria has resulted in a higher offer acceptance rate ... or that managers have found that those hired have "worked out." So it is critical to discover what lies behind the percentage of those applying, the percentage receiving an offer, the percentage accepting offers, the percentage actually joining the organization and

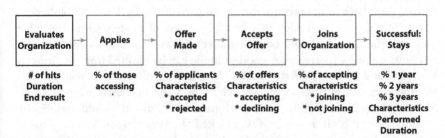

Data captured on all stages of selection. Results broken down by performance level and length of voluntary stays for all hires.

Figure 4.1 Analysis of selection process.

the percentage who are deemed to be successful and who stay long enough to make them a good investment. But if the characteristics of each person entering the process are not captured, they cannot be evaluated as predictors of behavior. For example, the qualifications of each applicant must be determined in sufficient detail to enable them to be considered as determinants of the eventual outcomes. These can be compared to the qualifications for the job opening and there can be conclusions reached as to whether a good match was required for someone to be made an offer, for them to accept the offer and for them to be successful. Organizations often ask for required credentials when openings are posted but later find out these criteria have little predictive power for determining who will apply, accept and succeed. This can enable the organization to refine its required qualifications. Requiring something that is not necessary will reduce the number of applicants, many of which may be qualified. U.S. employment law also precludes asking questions that might produce information that would be helpful in screening applicants. But compliance with the law overrides usefulness.

The reason machine learning and AI tools are so important is that it is very difficult for an organization to make an accurate assessment of the best predictors. With multiple factors impacting results the complexity soon exceeds the capacity of a human to analyze them. Theoretically, someone could use multiple regression to find out what enables the organization to predict success. Yet staffing professionals may lack the capabilities to do this. Because a factor cannot be evaluated for its relevance unless it has been included in the data gathering process an organization may have to err on the side of gathering too much information. But trying to get personal information or an excessive amount of information can reduce the willingness of those considering applying to provide information. Things that might be related to personality (i.e., asking someone if they play well with others in a way that is not offensive) may be good predictors but may also increase resistance to providing the information … and may result in inaccurate responses. Everyone thinks they are easy to work with. Asking what is tantamount to the person's opinion may not produce usable data. And the accumulation of some information may best be delayed until later in the process, when mutual interest has been established.

Building prediction models may be the purview of a data scientist but what goes into the models should be determined at least in part by someone with extensive staffing experience. A good example can be gleaned from the movies *Moneyball* and *Trouble with the Curve*. The data scientist in *Moneyball* focused on each person's on base percentage while the scout in *Trouble with the Curve* considered more intangible factors. Human intervention would enable the consideration of both. Ryan Leaf was picked ahead of Peyton Manning based on quantitative data related to athletic ability and no one considered personality factors, which turned out to be a primary determinant of success. Athletic ability was a necessary but not sufficient predictor … both players had adequate ability.

When Facebook was accused in 2018 of being gender-biased in the way they directed ads for STEM jobs, the CEO immediately denied intent to discriminate. But incorrect accusations have a regrettable habit of having an impact on perceptions. Although the analysis of the algorithm disclosed that the outcome was the result of a cost-benefit analysis, having nothing to do with male or female potential, it did not erase the impact. No malicious intent, but still an unfortunate outcome. Being accused of something publicly tends to have a lasting impact, even if subsequent retraction is forthcoming. Today "fake news" distorts perceptions even when it is clear upon examination that it was wrong.

Algorithms often do not incorporate factors that humans might have deemed necessary. Another example of a conflict between algorithmic software and human judgment became apparent in early 2019 when two crashes of Boeing 737-MAX aircraft were attributed to software that lowered the nose of the plane despite multiple attempts by the pilots to bring the nose up. Without alignment between human judgment and algorithmic directions catastrophes can occur … this time in the form of over 300 deaths.

Humans, even trained professionals, are prone to bias, such as favoring people who are similar. This can easily result in selection rates that indicate gender or racial preference. On the other hand, technology can apply analytical tools to spot adverse impact on protected classes and alert management that the pattern needs to be researched and the causes identified. But it is also necessary to recognize that algorithms are created by people. It is reasonable to presume that human biases will be factored into algorithms if there are not analytical tools for identifying bias and correcting the biased logic built into the technology. But if properly incorporated into the selection process machine learning technology can perform iterative analytics to identify bias.

The bottom line is that technology can enhance the ability of people to develop and use a predictive model. But it cannot fully replace the knowledge of experienced professionals that is required to evaluate the data analysis and augment it with human factors.

A final measure of success in selection is who stays, for how long and how well they perform. Attracting and hiring top candidates who are successful can power organizational performance, but if those people leave at inopportune times the cycle must be repeated, at great cost to the organization. There are consultancies offering services that include predicting who is prone to leave the organization and they are using AI and machine learning techniques alongside analysis of human factors by experienced staffers. Once an organization decides how many of a particular type of employee or contractor it needs it must also determine how long that person's services are needed. Key personnel leaving in the middle of a project can be devastating, as can someone in a critical role. Past experience captured in data can be useful in developing "who will go" models. But using data from the past to predict the future depends on the future being similar to the past, so caution must be taken to continuously evaluate the relevance of events taking place in a context that is different from the current context. An obvious example is when unemployment drops to very low levels. Experience data from a time when unemployment was high may not be a good source for developing projections.

There should be other factors considered when predicting turnover and many of these are difficult to render explicit. An employee who finishes a project and starts another answering to a different project manager may find the new work environment to be more or less acceptable. Very often performance appraisal ratings for a person change when the evaluator changes, despite efforts to use consistent standards when measuring performance. A student taking a class from someone who grades generously and then begins a class for someone with much more stringent standards will undoubtedly feel life has just become unfair … or at the very least, different. Personal chemistry with one's manager is also a major determinant of employee satisfaction. The reality is that someone showing no indication of considering an exit based on a quantitative model may abruptly leave because of something that was not built into the model. The HR function should be aware of the standards imposed by managers and attempt to create level playing fields so that employees believe there is consistency and equity across the organization. Monitoring performance rating distributions across managers can provide an early warning of inconsistency, making it possible to use tools like "frame of reference" training to reduce variation caused by personal differences.

An unfair action by a manager can easily trigger dissatisfaction, particularly among relatively new employees who have not been hardened by experience against the vagaries of being managed by people. And the technology that is available in an employee's pocket or on his or her wrist can instantly trigger a notification to the person's acquaintances that the organization is not the great place to work they thought it was. Social media has given each person a platform for broadcasting dissatisfaction to a wide audience. Although the technology also makes it possible to rave about the great place one works, human nature makes it likely that the effort will be more likely to be exerted when there is dissatisfaction. Hotels have found this out when providing comment cards … those who take the extra time to fill them out will not represent a random cross-section of guests and compiling the results will be likely to indicate an overly critical mindset.

A Global Perspective

Perhaps the most challenging selection challenge is finding people who can successfully manage foreign operations. In Chapter 3, the GLOBE study research was cited as a guide to identifying leadership styles that would work well in different countries. This is helpful but does not address the issue of whether an individual is the best choice for a foreign assignment. Psychological makeup is one of the most critical factors in determining a person's suitability for that role. This is a related but separate issue from leadership style. People can adopt a style of leading that is not consistent with their beliefs, values and personalities. But psychological makeup will assert itself when someone is attempting to function within a context that asks for behavior that is inconsistent with their makeup. Psychological tests are being used more in recent years for selecting international managers.[13] But their validity across cultures is still questionable. The psychometric properties of tests may not fit some cultures or cultural groups. If an organization is trying to select someone for a role it is important it should attempt to ensure that the tests are culturally neutral. As with other types of tests language facility may be a major determinant of someone's performance and this produces a form of bias in selection. A unique challenge when selecting candidates who must work with people who have a different cultural orientation is that the incumbent must not only have a makeup that fits the role but also that fits those (s)he must deal with.

Because of the potential limitations of psychological tests, it may be preferable to use assessment centers to select candidates that are a good cultural fit. By using role playing it is possible to observe not only what a person does in a situation but how they do it. If a manager is attempting to do a performance appraisal for several subordinates with differing cultural orientations observers can note whether the person is able to recognize the differing perspectives and to make adjustments to accommodate the orientation of each person being rated. For example, if the ratee is from a culture where saving face is important can the manager take steps to be less direct, particularly when discussing behaviors or results that did not meet standards. In some cases, an appropriate posture is to show emotion, while in others it is more effective to be highly controlled. If the ratee has a collectivist orientation emphasizing individual measurement may not be the best choice to gain acceptance of an evaluation. In Middle Eastern countries, religious beliefs may cause people to misinterpret performance appraisals as a means to evaluate the worth of the person, rather than one's contribution. Personal experience suggests using the term "contribution review" lessens the focus on the individual and shifts it to what has been done. And assessment centers may be an unfair way to evaluate the cultural IQ of a candidate if the person has not received any training to prepare them with the knowledge about what would be most appropriate in given situations. Research on the preparation for international assignments done by organizations suggest that there is inadequate training on cultural diversity and how to manage a diverse workforce.[14]

The philosophy an organization uses to provide direction to foreign operations will impact the type of manager that would best fit a specific situation. For example, if headquarters provides specific policies and controls operations centrally it would be important that candidates are fully socialized to the way the organization manages. On the other hand, if each foreign operation is viewed as a separate entity, often termed a multidomestic approach, a candidate capable of adapting to local realities might be the better choice. So native intelligence, emotional intelligence and cultural intelligence may all be factors considered but the relative weight given to each should be based on the context within which the person must function.

Notes

1 Cascio, W. *Responsible Restructuring* (San Francisco: Berrett-Koehler, 2002).
2 Lawler, E. *Reinventing Talent* (Oakland, CA: Berrett-Koehler, 2017).
3 Cascio, W. & Aguinis, H. *Applied Psychology in Talent Management* (Thousand Oaks, CA: Sage, 2019).
4 Kahneman, D. *Thinking Fast and Slow* (New York: Farrar, Straus & Giroux, 2011).
5 Greene, R. *Rewarding Performance, 2nd ed.* (New York: Routledge, 2019).
6 www.naceweb.org/career-readiness/compentencies/career-readiness-defined.
7 Jesuthasan, R. & Boudreau, J. *Reinventing Jobs* (Boston: Harvard Business Review Press, 2018).
8 Boudreau, J. & Jesuthasan, R. *Lead the Work* (Hoboken, NJ: Wiley, 2015).
9 Cascio, W., Boudreau, J., & Fink, A. *Investing in People* (Alexandria, VA: SHRM, 2019).
10 Cascio, W. *Managing Human Resources* (New York: McGraw-Hill, 2015).
11 Barends, E. & Rousseau, D. *Evidence-Based Management* (London: Kogan Page Limited, 2018).
12 Cascio, W. & Aguinis, H. *Applied Psychology in Talent Management* (Thousand Oaks, CA: Sage, 2019).
13 Scullion, H. & Collings, D. *Global Staffing* (London: Routledge, 2006).
14 Trompenaars, F. *Riding the Waves of Culture* (Burr Ridge, IL: Irwin, 2004).

Chapter 5

Utilizing the Talent of Employees

One of the most critical responsibilities that managers have is to effectively utilize talent. Once an organization has done its workforce planning, defined the "right" workforce, identified the sources for attracting the talent required and selected the right people it is necessary to effectively utilize that talent. In this chapter utilizing employees effectively will be discussed. In Chapter 6, utilizing talent from outside sources effectively will be addressed.

Utilizing talent focuses on the capabilities an employee has currently, while developing talent is a form of investment in enabling people to grow and to realize their full potential, as well as being capable of adapting to the organization's future needs. Development is the subject of Chapter 7.

First Steps to Effective Utilization

Since all components of the organization's human resource management systems must be integrated into a coherent process the next step after selecting the right talent is to "onboard" the people. This is a popular term for orientation or placement. It is the front end of the employment experience and is intended to begin the employee's relationship with the organization on a positive note. Cruise directors must start the adventure by ensuring all passengers know where their cabins are, but also what to do if the ship sinks. First things first, so lifeboat drills before going to the buffet.

Employment attorneys advising organizations in the United States try to ensure new employee orientations emphasize that the organization follows the "employment at will" doctrine, that establishes the right of the organization to terminate employees at any time, for any reason, or for no reason. This can be viewed as a poor way to begin a relationship, but compliance with laws is necessary and making promises relative to employment security that cannot be met are unwise.

Written policies and material presented in orientations make employees aware of what the laws are and how the organization functions within the law. They also provide insights into what drives decisions about their lives in the organization. Orientations have a major impact on the mindset and expectations of those entering an organization. They should be structured as a process that will make the new employees feel welcome, advise them of policies regulating their employment and provide them with an understanding of the culture. It is good professional advice from legal counsel not to make promises or commit to anything that the organization might not be able or willing to abide by in the future. Calling employees "permanent" sends a false message in the mind of many legal advisors. If the value proposition is that the employee has a job for as long as they want to stay and for as long as the organization wishes to keep them that philosophy should be made clear.

Aligning Employee and Organizational Culture

The organization's culture should be one that facilitates employee acceptance and provides a setting conducive to performance. Many organizations attempt to describe the company's culture to new employees. Yet culture is like the water the fish swim in ... it affects everything they do even though they are not aware of it. If one were to ask a fish why the water was so blue the answer would be "the what?" Defining organizational culture can be like measuring a moving cloud with a ruler. Having attended orientations that attempted to define culture and its meaning to employees I am convinced this is one of the most difficult things to accomplish. Underlying culture are deep-seated beliefs and values and they define appropriate behavior. These beliefs and values should be reflected in policies that are intended to elicit and guide the behavior of members. Everyone wants to know what is expected of them and how they should behave in specific situations. But creating a list of all rules and the preferred behavior in any situation that might arise is not possible. At best an effective description of the prevailing culture can nudge people in the desired direction when they encounter situations, even though they might have to work out what their specific actions should be on their own. Understanding the values helps to make decisions when specific guidance is not available.

An organization's policies should specify how the organization ensures compliance with laws and regulations, as well as how decisions should be made. Policies convey an aspect of the culture. Edgar Schein defined culture as how organizations resolve issues related to internal integration and external adaptation. Others have suggested it is a set of principles and guidelines that have been agreed on and that are intended to promote the desired behavior. Sometimes the way an organization deals with laws and regulations can provide insights into culture.

The Foreign Corrupt Practices Act is a U.S. law with extra-territorial reach, meaning it governs behavior of U.S. organizations no matter where their business is being conducted. It prohibits bribes being paid to foreign government officials to gain a business advantage or to promote a specific outcome. If the sales representative of a U.S. organization operating in another country is told by a government official that there must be a significant cash payment in order for the organization to be considered as a vendor, it places the sales agent in a difficult situation. Although the Act allows "facilitation payments" if they are for processing expenses incurred by the agency doing the procurement the difference between such a fee and a bribe is fuzzy. And if it is clearly a bribe but all competitors are paying it what the sales agent should do now becomes even more problematic. Not making the payment means no business.

If an organization approves the bribe verbally but does not document the approval this sends a message about the culture ... business ahead of ethics or legal compliance. If the organization does not approve the bribe but does not discipline a representative who pays it without approval, and even pays commission on the realized sales volume, that sends a similar message. If on the other hand a representative paying the bribe is terminated the guidance is different ... follow the law or suffer the consequences. So how management reacts to scenarios like this will provide guidance to employees as to what behaviors are expected of them. Prescribing behavior when a specific situation is confronted helps guide actions. But not every situation can be so defined. And each situation may occur in a different context so even past practice may not be clear guidance. Often story telling is a medium for giving employees insights into what constitutes acceptable behavior and what is not sanctioned.

Some organizations believe their mission statement suffices as a definition of their culture. It is true that a good mission statement sets the stage for establishing priorities and emphasizing what the organization views as important. Walmart's mission statement establishes its purpose as enabling lower income people to purchase things that they would like to have but have not been able to afford. That sends the message that Walmart competes by being a low-cost provider. This can be further interpreted to suggest that efficiency is valued, and that waste is abhorred. It is also a signal suggesting how employees should set priorities and make decisions ... to a degree. But mission statements alone cannot do what a clear understanding of the culture.

Figure 5.1 is a culture assessment questionnaire that has been used to define culture and evaluate its effectiveness. It is derived from cultural anthropology research and can be used to identify what employees believe the culture to be, what they think it should be and how they think "is–should be" gaps should be closed. These assessments are made for each of the dimensions, with employees providing their perceptions and opinions. This instrument can be used in a process that not only helps to define the culture, but also how it might be altered to serve the organization better. By having a cross-section of employees, or all employees, complete the questionnaire the organization can determine what they believe and how they would recommend better aligning the culture with what will serve the organization best. There are of course limits to the accommodations an organization would be willing to make in shaping the culture.

> *"Organizational culture is like a chameleon -a creature of such variegated hues that, while everyone acknowledges its splendor, few can agree on its description"*
> Charles Hampden-Turner

CULTURAL ASSESSMENT

NAME:_____

TITLE:_____

DATE:_____

Relative to each of the dimensions on the following pages, indicate what you believe the organization's prevailing culture currently IS and then what you believe the culture SHOULD BE to best support the organization in fulfilling its mission. Place an "I" in the appropriate position on the scale to represent IS and an "S" to represent SHOULD BE. A (3) indicates a balance between the two polar positions ('1' and '5') or signifies that both are present to a significant extent.

Once you have indicated IS and SHOULD BE if you find that there is a significant gap on a dimension, provide your assessment of: 1) why the gap, if any, exists (if you believe IS and SHOULD BE are relatively close indicate "N/A"); 2) how critical it is to close the gap; and, 3) what would be required to close the gap and how it should be done in your opinion. Enter your comments on separate pages, cross-referencing them to the appropriate dimension.

Reward Systems, Inc.
1. PERFORMANCE IS DEFINED AS:
(1)------------------------(2)------------------------(3)------------------------(4)------------------------(5)

(1)ORGANIZATION MEETING ITS GOALS   CUSTOMER SATISFACTION(5)
* business plans must be met   * customer must be satisfied
* superiors evaluate performance   * customer evaluates performance *
sound internal systems critical   * service levels/processes must be
   and must serve organization   acceptable to customer

2. PERFORMANCE IS DETERMINED BY:
(1)------------------------(2)------------------------(3)------------------------(4)------------------------(5)

(1) ACTIONS OF INDIVIDUALS/UNITS   EXTERNAL FACTORS (5)
* effort/resources applied determine results   * uncontrollable forces determine results
* outcomes under organizational control   * people should accept/adapt to conditions
* there is no "try" – only "do"   * efforts should focus on doing the best
   given the realities that exist

3. PERFORMANCE IS TYPICALLY ATTRIBUTED TO:
(1)------------------------(2)------------------------(3)------------------------(4)------------------------(5)

(1)A FEW KEY INDIVIDUALS   ALL EMPLOYEES/UNITS/FUNCTIONS(5)
* focus is on individual results   * focus is on group/unit/team results
* belief in self-determination   * belief in shared destiny and that it
* a few people determine performance   takes everyone to succeed
* performance is on competitive basis   *contribution to effectiveness of unit/others
   and relative rank is "score"   is considered part of performance

Figure 5.1 Culture assessment questionnaire.

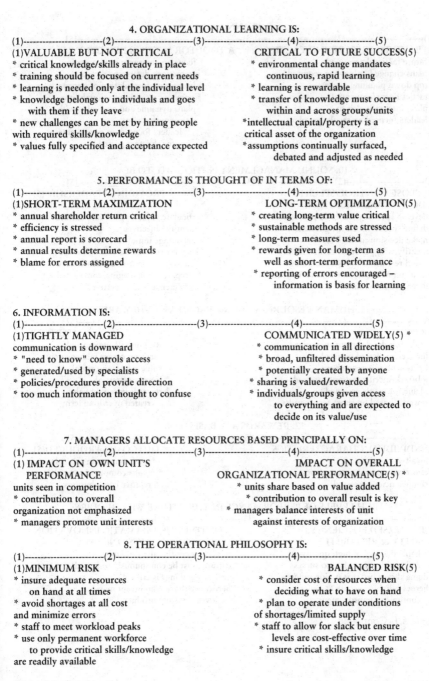

4. ORGANIZATIONAL LEARNING IS:

(1)------------------------(2)------------------------(3)------------------------(4)----------------------(5)

(1)VALUABLE BUT NOT CRITICAL

* critical knowledge/skills already in place
* training should be focused on current needs
* learning is needed only at the individual level
* knowledge belongs to individuals and goes
  with them if they leave
* new challenges can be met by hiring people
with required skills/knowledge
* values fully specified and acceptance expected

CRITICAL TO FUTURE SUCCESS(5)

* environmental change mandates
  continuous, rapid learning
* learning is rewardable
* transfer of knowledge must occur
  within and across groups/units
*intellectual capital/property is a
critical asset of the organization
*assumptions continually surfaced,
  debated and adjusted as needed

5. PERFORMANCE IS THOUGHT OF IN TERMS OF:

(1)------------------------(2)------------------------(3)------------------------(4)----------------------(5)

(1)SHORT-TERM MAXIMIZATION

* annual shareholder return critical
* efficiency is stressed
* annual report is scorecard
* annual results determine rewards
* blame for errors assigned

LONG-TERM OPTIMIZATION(5)

* creating long-term value critical
* sustainable methods are stressed
* long-term measures used
* rewards given for long-term as
  well as short-term performance
* reporting of errors encouraged –
  information is basis for learning

6. INFORMATION IS:

(1)------------------------(2)------------------------(3)------------------------(4)----------------------(5)

(1)TIGHTLY MANAGED

communication is downward
* "need to know" controls access
* generated/used by specialists
* policies/procedures provide direction
* too much information thought to confuse

COMMUNICATED WIDELY(5) *

* communication in all directions
* broad, unfiltered dissemination
* potentially created by anyone
* sharing is valued/rewarded
* individuals/groups given access
  to everything and are expected to
  decide on its value/use

7. MANAGERS ALLOCATE RESOURCES BASED PRINCIPALLY ON:

(1)------------------------(2)------------------------(3)------------------------(4)----------------------(5)

(1) IMPACT ON OWN UNIT'S
    PERFORMANCE

units seen in competition
* contribution to overall
organization not emphasized
* managers promote unit interests

IMPACT ON OVERALL
ORGANIZATIONAL PERFORMANCE(5) *

* units share based on value added
* contribution to overall result is key
* managers balance interests of unit
  against interests of organization

8. THE OPERATIONAL PHILOSOPHY IS:

(1)------------------------(2)------------------------(3)------------------------(4)----------------------(5)

(1)MINIMUM RISK

* insure adequate resources
  on hand at all times
* avoid shortages at all cost
and minimize errors
* staff to meet workload peaks
* use only permanent workforce
  to provide critical skills/knowledge
are readily available

BALANCED RISK(5)

* consider cost of resources when
  deciding what to have on hand
* plan to operate under conditions
of shortages/limited supply
* staff to allow for slack but ensure
  levels are cost-effective over time
* insure critical skills/knowledge

Figure 5.1 Continued

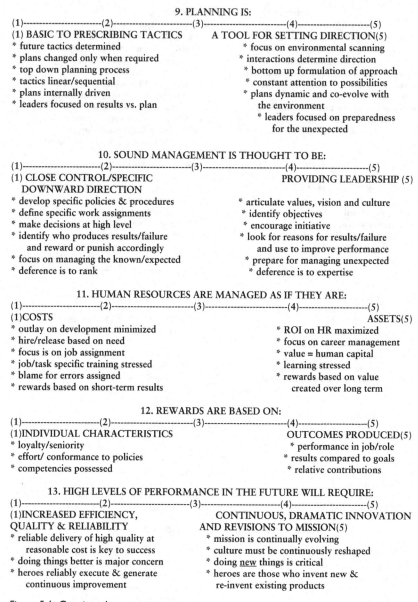

9. PLANNING IS:

(1)----------------------(2)------------------------(3)--------------------------(4)----------------------(5)

(1) BASIC TO PRESCRIBING TACTICS
* future tactics determined
* plans changed only when required
* top down planning process
* tactics linear/sequential
* plans internally driven
* leaders focused on results vs. plan

A TOOL FOR SETTING DIRECTION(5)
* focus on environmental scanning
* interactions determine direction
* bottom up formulation of approach
* constant attention to possibilities
* plans dynamic and co-evolve with
  the environment
* leaders focused on preparedness
  for the unexpected

10. SOUND MANAGEMENT IS THOUGHT TO BE:

(1)----------------------(2)------------------------(3)--------------------------(4)----------------------(5)

**(1) CLOSE CONTROL/SPECIFIC
DOWNWARD DIRECTION**
* develop specific policies & procedures
* define specific work assignments
* make decisions at high level
* identify who produces results/failure
  and reward or punish accordingly
* focus on managing the known/expected
* deference is to rank

PROVIDING LEADERSHIP (5)

* articulate values, vision and culture
* identify objectives
* encourage initiative
* look for reasons for results/failure
  and use to improve performance
* prepare for managing unexpected
* deference is to expertise

11. HUMAN RESOURCES ARE MANAGED AS IF THEY ARE:

(1)----------------------(2)------------------------(3)--------------------------(4)----------------------(5)

(1)COSTS
* outlay on development minimized
* hire/release based on need
* focus is on job assignment
* job/task specific training stressed
* blame for errors assigned
* rewards based on short-term results

ASSETS(5)
* ROI on HR maximized
* focus on career management
* value = human capital
* learning stressed
* rewards based on value
  created over long term

12. REWARDS ARE BASED ON:

(1)----------------------(2)------------------------(3)--------------------------(4)----------------------(5)

(1)INDIVIDUAL CHARACTERISTICS
* loyalty/seniority
* effort/ conformance to policies
* competencies possessed

OUTCOMES PRODUCED(5)
* performance in job/role
* results compared to goals
* relative contributions

13. HIGH LEVELS OF PERFORMANCE IN THE FUTURE WILL REQUIRE:

(1)----------------------(2)------------------------(3)--------------------------(4)----------------------(5)

**(1)INCREASED EFFICIENCY,
QUALITY & RELIABILITY**
* reliable delivery of high quality at
  reasonable cost is key to success
* doing things better is major concern
* heroes reliably execute & generate
  continuous improvement

**CONTINUOUS, DRAMATIC INNOVATION
AND REVISIONS TO MISSION(5)**
* mission is continually evolving
* culture must be continuously reshaped
* doing <u>new</u> things is critical
* heroes are those who invent new &
  re-invent existing products

Figure 5.1 Continued

14. DECISIONS SHOULD BE BASED ON:

(1)----------------------(2)------------------------(3)-----------------------(4)-----------------------(5)

(1) VERIFIED AND OBJECTIVE FACTS RELEVANT TO ISSUE	INTUITION AND PERSONAL KNOWLEDGE (5)
* all relevant data should be accumulated and analyzed to identify patterns	* decision-maker should "feel" the situation
* rational models should be employed	* feelings about what will work are applied
* decision should be based on analysis	* personal experience in similar situations should be considered
* most correct solution should be selected	* alternative approaches should be tried

15. THE RELATIVE EMPHASIS PLACED ON THE INTERESTS OF EACH OF THE MAJOR CONSTITUENCIES BELOW IS & SHOULD BE (RATE 1 - 5):

(1)----------------------(2)------------------------(3)-----------------------(4)----------------------(5)

(1) MINIMAL   VERY STRONG (5)

CONSTITUENCY	IS NOW	SHOULD BE
CUSTOMERS	_____	_____
EMPLOYEES	_____	_____
RATE PAYERS	_____	_____
SOCIETY/GOVERNMENT	_____	_____

Figure 5.1 Continued

And a democratic process may not be suitable for formulating the business strategy or shaping a culture that will facilitate execution of the strategy. But experience suggests that this process can provide management with an understanding of whether employee perceptions of what the culture is align well with reality. It also may suggest refinements that might not have occurred to them. And, finally, it can alert the organization to a lack of a clear and consistent understanding by employees.

Johnson & Johnson uses its credo to provide clarity about its values and priorities and spends significant resources to ensure the message is interpreted correctly and that it results in providing guidance. The Tylenol crisis (the appearance of a few poisoned tablets caused the company to pull all product out of circulation immediately) demonstrated how clear priorities can enable people to react immediately to crises. J & J acted quickly. and many think the action went beyond what was necessary. The credo provided guidance. Shortly after that crisis, Coca-Cola experienced a contaminated water supply impacting the quality of their beverages in Europe. They first denied it was their fault, but subsequently disclosed the cause, along with assurances it would not happen again. Their reaction suggested uncertainty about the values that drive management decisions and the priorities the organization set. This endangered their brand, which is one of the most valuable in the world. BP performed even more disastrously after the Gulf oil spill, and when the CEO complained about the reaction to the spill and asked for his life back it displayed how public relations can go wrong.

Each organization must shape its culture to provide an environment within which people will be successful and that convinces them that the organization is a good place for them to be. A primary cause of success or failure of any organization is the existence of "social capital," that serves as a glue to hold diverse constituencies together. The World Bank definition of social capital, which can be applied to countries, societies or organizations, is: "norms and social relations imbedded in social structures that enable people to coordinate actions and achieve desired goals." Social capital exists in the relationships between people. It requires mutual commitment, since if one party withdraws it disappears. Social capital and culture are different, albeit closely related. Culture is the software that enables an entity to create social capital and to apply it in a manner that produces value. Since social capital promotes shared values, aligned objectives, commitment, collaboration, engagement and loyalty, it sets the stage for a "citizen" mindset, rather than a "free agent" mindset. This makes social capital a necessary but not sufficient prerequisite for effectively using human resources (a.k.a. intellectual capital).

Organizations are appearing/disappearing, changing their names/identities, globalizing and forming alliances at an unprecedented rate. Much as with nations, organizations survive and prosper when there is something to align people's beliefs, values, priorities and goals. There are management theorists proposing the "virtual organization" as the model for success in today's kind of environment, particularly as organizations attempt to globalize. But many others are uneasy about this "film crew management" approach as a way to build organizational value and sustain it. When all of an organization's assets (its intellectual capital) go home on at the end of the day and are free not to come back the next day, investment analysts wonder what the organization really possesses that is of sustainable value. As organizations realize their market value is many times their "book" value they struggle to identify ways of effectively managing the intangibles that account for the majority of their value. Investment analysts currently base a significant portion of their valuation of organizations on intangible "assets" or "capital" that the accountants do not enter into their books. Current accounting rules that require investments in intangibles (e.g., R&D and employee training) to be treated as current expenses with no certain future value both discourage these investments and understate the value of organizations assets. That does not prevent treating intangibles as valued assets and investing in them.

Much of this "intangible" value of organizations is in the form of intellectual capital. It can be used to gain competitive advantage and many organizations find it is their only sustainable competitive advantage. In order for it to act as a sustainable advantage, however, an organization's intellectual capital must be of value to customers, be difficult to imitate, be superior to that of competitors, produce the needed products, be capable of being diffused throughout the organization and remain useful in the future. Those suggesting that intellectual capital is the only form of organizational capital that can produce a sustainable competitive advantage point out that the traditional forms of capital (financial, operational and customer) can be duplicated easily by competitors or be bypassed by strategies such as early emulation or being a low-cost provider.

Effective management of intellectual capital requires that the knowledge critical to organizational success be created or captured, organized and analyzed, disseminated and applied to produce the desired results, thereby enabling the organization to know what it needs to know in order to remain viable. And organizations must have the learning capacity to expand intellectual capital as required, as well as to use it in a manner that enables external adaptation and internal integration. The management of intellectual capital appears in the literature most frequently under the heading of "knowledge management." But there is confusion over the definition of "knowledge management," since most of the literature is focused on the technology used to transfer information. This probably is far too narrow a focus.

Intellectual capital encompasses both legally protected intellectual property and the knowledge, skills and behaviors that can be used to an organizations' advantage, but that can also be learned and used by other organizations, since they lack legal protection. Figure 5.2 shows the relationships of the types of capital.

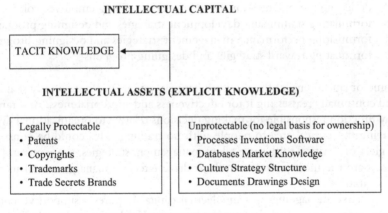

INTELLECTUAL CAPITAL

TACIT KNOWLEDGE

INTELLECTUAL ASSETS (EXPLICIT KNOWLEDGE)

Legally Protectable	Unprotectable (no legal basis for ownership)
• Patents	• Processes Inventions Software
• Copyrights	• Databases Market Knowledge
• Trademarks	• Culture Strategy Structure
• Trade Secrets Brands	• Documents Drawings Design

COMPLEMENTARY ASSETS
Production/service capabilities; Alliances; Infrastructure; Administrative capabilities; Learning Capabilities; Distribution networks; Customer Relationships; Related technologies

REALIZED VALUE/BENEFITS
Revenue Growth; Reduced Costs; Shareholder value; Reputation/Image; Litigation avoidance; Access to technology; Design freedom; Blocked competition; Customer loyalty; Licensing revenues; Tax benefits; Attractiveness as partner; Future opportunities

Figure 5.2 Intellectual Captial: Components and Value Chain.

Technology is a necessary but not sufficient prerequisite for the effective management of knowledge. Having technology available does not mean people will utilize it to build and leverage intellectual capital ... it only makes it possible. The critical challenges associated with effectively managing intellectual capital are:

- defining what the organization needs to know/be able to do and who needs to know it/be able to do it
- determining what the organization does know/can do and who knows it/ can do it
- identifying "need to know–do know" and "need to do–able to do" gaps
- formulating a strategy to close these gaps
- creating the vision/mission, culture, environment, strategy, structure and adopting talent management strategies/programs that will facilitate effectiveness in the short term and sustain it over the long term, through continuous learning

The appropriate strategies/programs must be in place to encourage people to produce the desired results. Effectively managing intellectual capital requires:

1. defining, evaluating and shaping culture
2. designing the organizational structure and defining employee roles
3. formulating staffing and development strategies and designing programs
4. formulating performance management strategies and designing programs
5. formulating reward strategies and designing programs

Some organizations let their culture happen, rather than consciously shaping it and continually reassessing it for effectiveness and appropriateness. And rarely is any function responsible for making decisions relative to organizational design, leaving this critical area to people with no training. This could be considered neglect of a critical tool, since talent management strategies, programs and processes are the most powerful tools to drive effective management of intellectual capital.

Effective management of intellectual capital requires a supportive culture. Knowledge is first and foremost cultural, and only then technological. The culture must be such that knowledge sharing is asked for and rewarded, people are given resources to facilitate it, people are trained in the skills required to do it and the structure, role design and staffing levels enable it to happen. Whether an organization views its people as costs or as assets will profoundly impact how extensively it will invest in ensuring its culture is supportive of building and leveraging intellectual capital.

Performing a cultural assessment is a critical step for an organization toward ensuring that its culture nurtures effective creation, dissemination and application of intellectual capital. A culture that facilitates widespread employee involvement is more apt to prompt widespread sharing of knowledge and more apt to instill the view that all employees, customers, suppliers and other constituencies are potential sources of valuable knowledge. And if managers consider the effect of their decisions and actions on overall organizational results, rather than only on their own unit, knowledge is more likely to be shared across units, maximizing its value to the organization. But if the culture encourages silence and conformity to minimize conflict and/or if management believes that decisions should be centralized at the upper levels of the organization, the flow of communication and the creation, dissemination and application of knowledge will be impeded. Tools such as the U.S. Army's After-Action Reviews and GE's Work Out promote sharing the organization's objectives and pooling knowledge gained by units to the benefit of the overall organization and its workforce. They also communicate a faith in the participants and their ability to resolve difficult issues.

An organization's culture can encourage a "share your knowledge for the common good" mindset or it can reinforce the "keep the best of what you have in order to look better relative to others" approach learned during school years. Few parents encourage their children to finish in the middle of their class rankings. Organizations that use hierarchical structures and career management principles predicated on competition at the individual level throw a significant cultural hurdle in the path to effective knowledge management. The prevailing business culture in the West is individualistic, especially after the downsizing and reengineering of the last decade, which left most people with a "survival of the fittest" mindset. Interpersonal skills are often not emphasized in training programs, at least not relative to analytical and problem-solving skills. Effective communicators can persuade others to accept their ideas. But if leaders act as if they are always "right" and criticize those who are "wrong" it is hard to convince people to pursue open dialogue that will make others as effective as they can be, to the betterment of the overall organization.

This kind of culture can result in managers being reluctant to hire people more capable than they are and can also lead to them to controlling the flow of critical information. Technology using databases and expert systems can increase access to information needed for effectiveness. But if managers control access to the knowledge through the use of hierarchy and rules, they negate the potential knowledge leveraging capabilities of the technology.[1] Another challenge facing many organizations is the existence of a strong "NIH" (not invented here) bias imbedded in the culture. This goes beyond the "we have always done it this way" mindset that works to oppose change. NIH thinking presents a real barrier to having new knowledge and approaches imported from the outside. This mindset can impede honest consideration of best practices discovered through benchmarking, and even impede transfer of practices and ideas from other parts of the same organization. In an attempt to provide an antidote to this malady, Raychem instituted an "NIH award" that goes to those using knowledge from within the organization ... and the source of the knowledge receives a certificate stating "I had a great idea and X is using it."

Additional challenges are created when organizations utilize cross-functional and cross-cultural teams to perform critical functions such as product design. Individualistic cultures such as in the United States or Australia will not be as friendly to knowledge dissemination as will collectivist cultures such as Japan and China.[2] Mixing people from different cultures raises issues concerning the appropriate team structure and culture. Occupational differences (e.g., specialized knowledge, different priorities and processes) also complicate the knowledge transfer process, as do generational differences.

As already stated, there typically is no position or function charged with defining, evaluating and shaping the organizations' culture. Human resources is the most logical function to assume this responsibility, guided and supported by executive management. Defining the culture, assessing its effectiveness and formulating strategies for reshaping it naturally fall within the purview of HR. Selecting, developing and rewarding people in a manner that facilitates the creation of the desired culture is the key to getting the job done well, and these strategies/programs are usually shaped by HR. Direction from executive management in the form of a clear vision and articulated values is needed, but it will be HR strategies/programs that will set the stage for developing and maintaining an appropriate and effective culture.

Effectively managing knowledge requires attention to the nature of the knowledge. Much knowledge is "tacit," which may be difficult for someone possessing it to externalize in specific terms. Tacit knowledge is acquired through socialization and practice (both cognitive and physical) and must be transmitted person-to-person (e.g., in a master-apprentice type of relationship), because it cannot be rendered "explicit" by writing it down. The other type of knowledge is "explicit," that can be conveyed through the written word (policies; procedures; algorithms). Expert systems have been limited by the extent to which the experts can codify the decision rules and techniques they use to do their work. Much of today's work requires exhibiting job-related behaviors that are the result of internalized learning, resulting in heuristics that cannot be expressed directly. Therefore, "slack" built into staffing levels may not be synonymous with waste, but a necessary condition for transferring tacit knowledge. Lean staffing is economically desirable, but it may result in people lacking the time to "swap stories" at the latte machine ... often a source of innovation. Some organizations formalize their commitment to allowing time for innovation and sharing. 3M has for decades encouraged employees to spend 15% of their time on something they believe may create value for the organization, even though it is not directly related to their current role.

Research has identified the chief inhibitors to the flow of knowledge to be: (1) the source and/or the recipient of knowledge do not know what the other knows or needs to know, (2) resources (time, budget) necessary for the transfer are not available, (3) there is a lack of an established relationship between the person with the knowledge and the person needing that knowledge, and (4) delays are caused by structural rigidity and poor processes. In addition to these factors a lack of mutual trust will inhibit the free flow of knowledge. The most powerful inhibitor is the lack of knowledge about who knows/does not know and who needs to know what someone else has to offer.

One of the tools that has been used to remedy this defect is an internal knowledge directory ... a sort of knowledge yellow pages. A wide range of knowledge types (knows about, knows how, knows why) can be included in an accessible database and individuals/groups possessing the required knowledge can be indexed to a topic list. Software tools can be utilized to facilitate searches and to make contacting appropriate parties less difficult. An example of this approach was a hundred-year-old utility with a wide variety of technologies, methods and processes that have been used. The utility found great value in identifying people who were competent to work with the older, rarely used equipment and systems. When a less experienced staff member needed to know "how this stuff really works," rather than what the operating manuals (when they existed) said, an inquiry could quickly and easily be directed to the appropriate party. In addition to increasing productivity and speed, the recognition associated with being listed as an "expert" was found to be a source of significant job satisfaction.

Organizations are outsourcing functions more frequently, using contractors and consultants to supplement their workforce and entering into alliances/ventures with other organizations. The structure used to accomplish work and assign roles to the various players will have a major impact on how effectively work is done. The free flow of knowledge to and from contractors is difficult to achieve, since contractors often view their knowledge as their "product" and sharing that knowledge can create competitors. Organizations are also often hesitant to share their intellectual capital (processes and technology) with outsiders, particularly if it is not possible to protect its value by turning it into intellectual property through patents and copyrights. Alliances and joint ventures therefore pose difficult integration issues, which are often overlooked until the desired results do not materialize and the cause is identified too late in the venturing/contracting process. A successful inter-organizational alliance will ensure both organizations are committed to identifying where relevant expertise resides within the two entities and to pooling intellectual capital across organizational boundaries.

Obstacles to the free flow of knowledge also exist when temporary and part-time personnel are used. Organizations often do not recognize the benefits of training these people and of informing them fully, particularly when it is felt that they are just passing through or that they have their heads and hearts somewhere else. But if these depictions are indeed true it argues for reconsidering the use of such personnel to serve customers or to perform important work. Yet even if their importance is recognized there must also be an economic justification for investing in training temporaries and part-timers, particularly considering today's mobility among skilled people. Organizations relying on knowledge management as a competitive advantage will be more likely to recognize these people as important participants in the workforce, since information will typically be broadly disseminated and everyone will be viewed as potential contributors of new knowledge and will be required to use knowledge effectively ... as long as both the culture and the structure support it.

A workforce capable of developing the required pool of intellectual capital can be built by staffing the organization with the right people and training them to act in a manner conducive to creating, disseminating and applying knowledge. Competencies that support effective intellectual capital management can be used to select personnel. People who share their ideas can be identified through a number of selection instruments and the interviewing process can incorporate criteria related to knowledge sharing. It is also possible to increase the range of personal approaches to problem-solving, through the use of focused staffing criteria. Mixing "left-brained" and "right-brained" people can produce a "whole-brained" workforce. Additionally, diversity relative to points of view, experience and training should be incorporated in staffing strategies, to ensure that sufficiently different viewpoints are inputted when the workforce engages in dialogue. Someone once observed that nothing new will be produced in a room full of like-minded and reasonable people.

Staffing levels should be evaluated to ensure there is sufficient knowledge overlap between people (horizontally and vertically) and that an appropriate amount of slack resources (time; budget) exists, to facilitate knowledge sharing. This runs counter to one of the cultural icons within Anglo-Saxon business culture - the principle of efficiency. The loathing of redundancy or overlap throws an obstacle in the path to knowledge sharing and the absence of overlap in organizations impedes knowledge flow. Many successful Asian companies find it easier to disseminate and even create the necessary knowledge, even though they might appear to be "over-staffed" in the eyes of North American management thinkers. To them, overlap and redundancy of knowledge are viewed as enablers for knowledge transfer, rather than sources of inefficiency.

Performance management and career management programs that recognize and reward those who do contribute to the effectiveness of others through knowledge sharing can be very effective in motivating behavioral change. Promotions accompanied with clear explanations as to why a promotion occurred can be used to celebrate the value of knowledge sharing and supportive behavior. Writing behavioral competencies into career ladder definitions can communicate to employees what it takes to be successful and can encourage them to exhibit the desired behaviors. If employees think success is looking better than others, rather than making others more effective, they will be likely to behave in a counter-productive, self-serving manner.

Recognizing contributions to creating intellectual capital and turning intellectual capital into intellectual property as a dimension of performance can encourage organizational citizenship. Most organizations underutilize their patents and other forms of intellectual property. There are numerous stories of organizations doing simple reviews of their intellectual property inventories and realizing millions by selling unused patents and reactivating the use of those having application to current or new products. It is rare however for organizations to do assessments of the full range of their intellectual capital that would enable them to determine what can be converted into intellectual property. Existing methods and processes often contain technology (e.g., equipment modifications or unique processes) that could be rendered explicit and protected, potentially making them salable or licensable products. In order to encourage this type of activity it should be made clear that this is an important value adder and that these contributions will be measured as a part of performance management and that they will be recognized through the rewards programs.

Contributions to creating new knowledge and/or more effectively disseminating and applying existing knowledge can be rewarded if compensation programs are designed appropriately. The most popular reward for performance in U.S. organizations is merit pay. Merit pay can potentially be effective in encouraging effective management of intellectual capital if the performance metrics related to making others effective are built into the performance appraisals and if the appraisals impact rewards. However, many merit pay programs are set up as a fixed sum game (e.g., each manager has 3% of payroll to use for salary increases). This has the unfortunate effect of putting individuals in competition with each other, thereby retarding the propensity to share knowledge and to make others effective. After all, why would anyone behave in a manner that made competitors more effective? The use of various forms of "person-focused" pay can encourage acquisition of skill and knowledge without putting employees in competition with each other and the prevalence of these programs has increased significantly for occupations that fit this approach.[3]

The use of individual, group and organization-wide variable compensation plans can also acknowledge and reward contributions and encourage future efforts. Funds for variable compensation plans tend to flex based on results, rather than being a fixed budgetary item.[4] That means that collective success may create a "we won" attitude, since the funds available for rewards are larger and everyone can share in success. Promoting a sense of "shared destiny" is typically one of the main objectives of profit-sharing, employee stock ownership and group incentive plans. These plans also increase alignment between individuals and groups, by creating shared performance criteria, standards and measures ... and by tying the size of reward funds available to realized performance. It has been argued that a weakness of aggregated measures is that they do not provide a "line of sight" between what an individual does and what the eventual outcomes are at the group/organization-wide level. But organizations have successfully linked performance measures at all levels together to ensure they are integrated. Individual merit pay has not been made obsolete by incentive programs; instead, merit-based base pay and variable pay are being used in conjunction with each other to elicit multiple behaviors through a balance between individual success and group/organizational success measures.

Recognition programs can also provide a source of valued rewards. If having a reputation of being an innovator, a mentor or a contributor to organizational effectiveness brings honor and prestige to the person there is an incentive to contribute. Money is usually not expected for all forms of contributions, such as making others more effective, and the satisfaction produced by sincere recognition and thanks can be even more potent.

Employee ownership programs seem to offer the ultimate incentive to create, disseminate and apply knowledge effectively, particularly as knowledge increasingly is becoming the key to sustained competitive advantage and increased organizational value. Equity-based programs have the advantage of aligning the economic interests of all the constituencies within the organization, specifically aligning employee interests with shareholder interests. Assuming that people share equally or proportionately in total shareholder return (price appreciation plus dividends) there is a common interest in creating the performance that will increase that return. Broad eligibility for equity-based programs does have its dangers, since many employees do not understand the equity markets or the implications of equity ownership. But most organizations willing to invest in at least the minimum amount of education required have found that these obstacles can be overcome. And equity programs do not require the organization to fund employee rewards out of operating earnings ... the equity markets provide that wealth through stock price appreciation.

It takes an entire organization to raise an idea. Creating knowledge is easier in a culture that communicates everyone is important and capable of contributing. Disseminating knowledge is facilitated when organizational structure and role design provide the necessary resources and the mechanisms for sharing knowledge. Disseminating and applying knowledge becomes a priority for employees when they are selected for, trained for and rewarded for doing so. Effectively managing intellectual capital means more than creating an intranet site and asking employees to post ideas and to learn what they need to know. A company I worked with put up a suggestion box and the only submission the first week was a suggestion to get rid of the stupid box. The approach was not a good fit to the existing culture. Technology can be an enabler, but in order for it to improve knowledge dissemination employees must both want and know how to share the knowledge they have. The primary mechanisms for providing the impetus lie within the organization's talent management strategies and programs.

Workforce Culture

Workforce culture is increasingly important because the cultural diversity in most multinational organization workforces has increased. The organization has some control over shaping its culture but attempting to influence the cultural orientation of employees presents challenges. The global mobility of talent has increased cultural diversity even in organizations operating in a single country. If the organization does not go "there" the talent will come "here." The United States has prided itself in having a population that has come from all over the world and historically has assumed the melting pot effect would lead to a homogenous citizenry. But even though employees may subscribe to the organizational culture to a degree what they learned from parents, friends and teachers during their socialization process does not leave them easily. There are cultural enclaves within the country that preserve the beliefs and values prevalent in other national/ethnic cultures and tensions are created when laws and regulations conflict with beliefs. A Muslim population in a city in Michigan demanded that the public swimming pools be gender segregated for periods during the day, conflicting with laws and mores prevailing in the United States.

Cultural orientation also impacts employee reactions to the way that organizations do business. Someone from a culture that is collectivist in nature may view pay being tied to individual performance as inappropriate, believing that pay rates should be more egalitarian and that performance be defined and measured at a group or organizational level.[5,6] So organizations with culturally diverse workforces attempting to convince employees that the way in which performance is defined, measured and rewarded is fair, competitive and appropriate may find there is no easy way to achieve that goal.[7]

Another dimension of cultural orientation is occupational culture. Some would question whether there is such a thing, but people trained in accounting and marketing may view stretching the truth a bit differently. A design engineer may want to continue to refine a design until it is good as it can be, while the controller may argue that "good enough" should be the rule. When I worked in the electronics industry, we always used the Bang & Olufsen example that demonstrated consumers were not willing to incur unlimited cost for "better" if the additional improvement was not of sufficient value to them. Equipment that is very expensive because it is capable of reproducing sound at frequencies that only dogs can hear will probably not be a big seller, although a few dog lovers may make the investment. The increased use of concurrent design processes to develop new products necessitates agreement between incumbents of a wide variety of occupations and the different perspectives can wreak havoc on the time it takes to arrive at mutually acceptable decisions. The controller and the design engineer must collaborate to find a commonly acceptable stance relative to cost. Diversity is valuable in promoting a wider view of alternatives but does not facilitate rapid consensus.

When doing presentations on the impact of occupation on people I use this slide as an illustration of possible effects, always acknowledging that it is an outrageous stereotype. But it can also provide insights into how occupation can influence orientation.

Ask Someone What 2 + 2 =
Differing Occupational Perspectives

- Accountant
- Actuary
- Purchasing Agent
- Marketing Rep
- IT Professional

- HR Professional

- 4
- 4.00000000
- 3
- Sky's the limit
- 1 year and $ 1 million to find out

- Employee survey needed

Both organization and workforce culture impact the effectiveness of strategies for selection, utilization and development. Lincoln Electric found that its pay system was not accepted in some cultures when it established foreign operations. The organization felt their pay philosophy was a necessary element of their management philosophy and their way of doing business, and rather than trying to force acceptance of their approach or to modify their approach they elected to exit the countries. It is very difficult to effectively utilize talent when the employee beliefs conflict with the organizational culture. After I spoke at a regional conference in Dubai an HR executive of a large Middle Eastern organization asked me how you can motivate someone to put forth their best effort when the person believes that all outcomes are Allah's will. This is an example of a situation where Western motivation theory does not provide guidance when faced with a fundamental belief. That was one of the most difficult questions I have been asked and my formal education in theory was not of much use. So organizational culture can contribute to or detract from an organization's ability to attract and retain the talent it needs and can impact the motivation to perform well. How it does business is an element of its value proposition and if it does not align with the talent it wishes to attract it will impede recruitment and retention.

Assigning Newly Hired Employees

The first 30 days as an employee have been cited as the most critical to shaping the employee's satisfaction with his or her decision in both the short and the long term. How they are treated, whether they are given the information they need immediately and what their experiences are like are all critical determinants of their satisfaction level. Employee satisfaction has been shown to impact attendance and turnover so that makes the case for investing in the things that will promote satisfaction among new hires. The need to create satisfaction also applies to employees transferring to different departments, although having been in the organization for a time will probably diminish the perception that everything is new and different. There has been a lot written about effective onboarding in the last few years and readers who wish to develop a process that is effective for them have access to a lot of advice.[8] A sound guiding principle is what works is what fits. And it is what fits the particular context at a particular point in time that has the best chance of working well.

One of the key factors impacting how an employee views his or her early days is the reaction of coworkers. It is human nature to employ equity theory to decide if the new person got a better deal relative to the person making the assessment. Professionals who have invested heavily in formal education to acquire their knowledge and skills unsurprisingly tend to be very concerned about their standing in their profession. This became clear to me when I was called in to undo the damage caused by organizations that adopted "broad banding" for scientific and engineering staff. This "new" approach collapsed four to six levels in classification models to one or two. The people advising organizations to do this must not have understood the importance professionals place on a system that acknowledges their growth in their profession, both through promotion and increased compensation potential. But the adopters of this approach probably read numerous articles about the broad banding programs that were adopted successfully and forgot that literature is biased ... who writes about their failures?

An engineer may start with an organization as a new graduate and retire 30 years later ... as an engineer. But that person inevitably is a different kind of engineer, capable of doing work of higher complexity. The failure to administratively celebrate the person's professional growth misses a chance to reinforce his or her development. Ignoring that professional growth is a recipe for maximizing dissatisfaction. The perception that the organization does not value the increased capabilities of the person can brand the organization as a poor place to grow professionally. Table 5.1 is an example of a model that can be used for both employee classification and career management. This example is designed for incumbents of STEM professional disciplines. Table 5.2 is an example that can be used for administrative professionals. Tables 5.3 and 5.4 can be used for technical support personnel and administrative support personnel, respectively. Using these frameworks an organization can customize them to fit their particular context and culture.

Given the importance of how employees are classified it is critical to ensure that new entrants are properly classified relative to experienced employees. It is possible that a new hire may be justifiably classified at the same, or even higher, level than someone with long service, if that person brings knowledge and skills that warrant that placement. But scrutiny will be exercised by current

Table 5.1 Career Planning and Progression Model for Scientists and Engineers

Level → Job Criteria ↓	Science/Engineering Intern	Associate S/E	S/E
Work Description (type, complexity, variety, difficulty)	• Understands concepts of codes and standards. • Learning codes and standards.	• Performs work of limited scope and basic complexity, generally in support of more senior S/Es. • Develops solutions to routine technical problems of limited scope. • Focus is on applying academic knowledge to the work environment and developing good work/team habits.	• Performs work of moderate scope and complexity. • Develops solutions to problems of well-defined scope. • Participates in developing field programs and designs. • Assists in researching and analyzing data.
Latitude Exercised/Direction Received (authority, autonomy, supervision received)	• Works under close supervision, directly with S/Es and other technical employees	• Assists in compiling and summarizing data. • Works under direct supervision with general guidance from more experienced S/Es. • Limited use and/or application of technical principles, theories, and concepts. • Follows specific established engineering and technical procedures and instructions. • Exercises discretion and judgment in collaboration with peers regarding how principles and methods are selected for and applied to work. • May serve as a member of work teams.	• Works under general supervision with limited guidance from more experienced S/Es. • Frequent use and application of technical standards, principles, theories, concepts, and techniques. • Often serves as a member of work teams. • Exercises discretion and independent judgment in how principles and methods are selected for and applied to work.
Potential Impact of Work	Work has minimal impact (due to level of oversight)	Work has limited impact on costs, schedules and results (lack of results can normally be overcome without serious effect).	Work impacts costs, schedules and results.
Internal Personal Contacts (type, level, purpose, frequency)	• Daily contact with S/Es and other technical employees	• Closely coordinates work efforts through interaction with peers, project leaders, and supervisor. • May seek information from other sources.	• Frequent coordination and communication with supervisor, project leads, and other organizations.
External Organizational Communications (type, level, purpose, frequency)	• Extremely rarely has contact with customers and vendors	• Minimal, occasional contacts with customers and vendors.	• Participates in customer and program meetings as a contributor and as a source of information. • May be active in technical community and may author or contribute to publications and presentations.

(Continued)

	Senior S/E	Principal S/E	Senior Principal S/E	Distinguished S/E
Responsibility for Work of Others (mentoring, teaching, assigning & directing work, providing technical & project direction)	None	May monitor the work of and provide guidance to technicians and other support personnel.	Mentors less experienced staff in related technical areas.	
Education and Experience	Working toward a Bachelor's degree in a technical (STEM) field, may have limited experience	Bachelors in technical (STEM) field plus 0–1 years relevant experience.	Bachelors in technical (STEM) field plus at least 2–4 years relevant experience. Masters in technical (STEM) field plus at least 0–2 years relevant experience.	

Level → / Job Criteria ↓	Senior S/E	Principal S/E	Senior Principal S/E	Distinguished S/E
Work Description: (type, complexity, variety, difficulty)	<ul><li>Performs work of well-defined scope and complexity.</li><li>Develops solutions for a range of complex problems and issues.</li><li>Conducts research, data compilation, and data analysis.</li><li>Develops field programs and designs. Selects and implements instrumentation systems.</li><li>Serves as a discipline-specific SME to other S/Es and management.</li><li>Participates in proposal preparation for business development</li><li>Participates in subcontract preparation and evaluation.</li></ul>	<ul><li>Performs work of broadly defined scope and significant complexity.</li><li>Develops solutions that may be new and unique.</li><li>Oversees research, data compilation and data analysis.</li><li>Oversees field programs, designs, and instrumentation systems.</li><li>Serves as SME to both internal and external parties.</li><li>Provides cross-disciplinary integration for complex projects.</li><li>Defines customer needs and develops technical proposals.</li></ul>	<ul><li>Focuses on the most complex projects with the broadest technical scope, requiring interdisciplinary and interagency coordination.</li><li>Devises entire courses of action of the broadest scope to solve multiple problems of very complex nature.</li><li>Assures solutions optimize state-of-the-art technology and minimizes programmatic constraints.</li><li>Sets priorities and standards for research, data compilation and data analysis. Conducts in-depth analyses considering multiple tangible and intangible factors.</li><li>Carries out special or unique studies requiring unconventional or novel approaches and techniques.</li><li>Serves as an expert resource, consultant, and advisor.</li><li>Develops new initiatives and technical capabilities</li></ul>	<ul><li>Defines cutting edge projects that have impact on the business.</li><li>Conceives, plans, and conducts pioneering work in heretofore unexplored areas.</li><li>Exercises recognized technical leadership, creativeness, and judgment to prove or disprove the feasibility of ideas and devices.</li><li>Develops, defines, and modifies strategic research objectives in the course of planning and conducting innovative work.</li></ul>

Table 5.1 Continued

Level → Job Criteria ↓	Senior S/E	Principal S/E	Senior Principal S/E	Distinguished S/E
Latitude Exercised/Direction Received (authority, autonomy, supervision received)	• Works under limited technical direction, exercising S/E judgment. • Executes work in a disciplined manner to demonstrate compliance with laws, codes, orders, and company policies and procedures. • May serve as lead on teams with well-defined scope of work.	• Exercises considerable latitude and judgment in determining best approaches to achieve objectives on an assignment. Tasks are broadly defined and often self-initiated. • Ensures team's processes and deliverables comply with laws, codes, orders, and company policies and procedures. • Interprets and adapts guidelines for specific cases. • Leads teams which require coordination with other teams.	• Independently plans, schedules and directs S/E projects, guided by accepted consensus approaches and national guidelines per established program objectives, budgets and schedules. • Ensures team processes and deliverables comply with laws, codes, orders, and company policies and procedures. • Establishes professional guidelines through participation in consensus committees, influences government guidance and authors company directives.	• Exercises a very high degree of originality and sound judgment in formulating, evaluating, and correlating broad engineering and scientific programs. • Recommendations and conclusions are considered authoritative. • Empowered to make independent decisions and to establish company positions.
Potential Impact of Work	Work typically has a significant impact on costs, schedules, performance and customer evaluations.	Work has an impact on company's technical capabilities and reputation, and a major impact on the success of large projects and programs.	Work has a major impact on critical projects, company's reputation and its ability to succeed in meeting organizational and customer goals.	Work has a long-term effect and impact on company's future in terms of building new capabilities and expertise.
Internal Personal Contacts (type, level, purpose, frequency)	• Frequently coordinates work with peers and regularly works with managers. • Routinely works closely with company's service organizations such as procurement, property, and facilities. • Develops relationships and identifies opportunities across organizational boundaries.	• Works with peers, other disciplines and other company organizations to coordinate project execution and compliance. • Develops and presents education or training in applicable discipline. • Represents organization as primary technical contact to other company organizations. • Fosters relationships and identifies opportunities across organizational boundaries.	• Advises management on technology utilization and development. • Reports project status, issues and results to management. • Identifies organizational and interdepartmental issues. • Frequently invited to serve on internal and external technical committees. • Provides guidance to senior management regarding strategic development opportunities for new technologies and capabilities.	• Provides strategic direction to senior management. • Serves as expert advisor and consultant to internal and external senior management. • Develops and communicates long-range technical positions and strategies within defined corporate goals.

| *External Organizational Communications (type, level, purpose, frequency)* | Engages with customers, program sponsors, external project partners and vendors to coordinate work planning and execution details.

Active in technical community, including publications, presentations, consensus bodies and professional committees. | Routinely engaged with customer or program sponsor and primary contact for external project partners and vendors to solicit customer requirements and for project planning and coordination.

Builds collaboration with existing and potential partners.

Highly visible in technical community. Known for contributions to the body of knowledge in their field.

May represent company or customer interests at conferences and meetings.

Viewed by customers as a leader in one or more areas important to the business. | Primary contact for the organization in which they work to solicit new work, redress customer concerns and build corporate image. May also collaborate with vendors.

Recognized nationally in technical community. Known for leadership in contributions to the body of knowledge in their field.

Routinely represents company or customer in conferences and meetings.

Develops relationships with leaders in customer community.

Participates in creating strategies for increasing company's technical capabilities, business opportunities and intellectual property.

Identifies and cultivates external relationships to secure new talent, technology, and partnerships. | Serves on expert review panels and committees concerned with planning and inter-organizational programs, as an authoritative expert in their specialty area(s).

Expert communication skills to advise customer decision makers.

Has extensive influence on customer management and technical experts. |

(Continued)

Table 5.1 Continued

Level → Job Criteria ↓	Senior S/E	Principal S/E	Senior Principal S/E	Distinguished S/E
Responsibility for Work of Others (mentoring, teaching, assigning & directing work, providing technical & project direction)	• Coordinates work of designers, technical staff, and S/Es working on their projects. • Leads small or short-term work team(s), labs, and projects, providing direction to technicians and other support personnel, plus less experienced S/Es. • Presents technical training (not limited to company personnel) in discipline applicable to work. • Coaches and mentors new S/E personnel and less experienced technical staff.	• Leads moderate-size projects/labs. • Coordinates efforts with peers, other disciplines, and organizations as well as with contractors and suppliers. • Leads work team(s), providing direction to less experienced S/Es, technicians and other support personnel • Defines training needs and prepares and conducts technical training (not limited to company personnel). • Mentors less experienced S/Es and technical staff in defined areas.	• Leads large/complex projects/ labs, directing the work of S/ Es, contractors, and suppliers in multiple locations and/or on joint or multiple teams by ensuring their efforts are integrated and focused on established objectives. • Leads collaboration to achieve project and mission execution. • Identifies, plans, prepares and conducts specialized technical training (not limited to company personnel). • Advises S/E staff and technical management on advanced methods, processes, and best practices. • Encourages development of intellectual property and publishing in refereed journals.	• Guides others in analyzing and solving unique problems. • Leads the work of teams that cross-functional engineering and scientific boundaries.
Education and Experience	• Bachelors in technical (STEM) field plus at least 5–8 years relevant experience, OR • Masters in technical (STEM) field plus at least 3–6 years relevant experience, OR • PhD in technical (STEM) field plus 0–3 years relevant experience.	• Bachelors in technical (STEM) field plus at least 9–13 years relevant experience, OR • Masters in technical (STEM) field plus at least 7–11 years relevant experience, OR • PhD in technical (STEM) field plus at least 4–8 years relevant experience.	• Bachelors in technical (STEM) field plus at least 14–19 years relevant experience, OR • Masters in technical (STEM) field plus at least 12–17 years relevant experience, OR • PhD in technical (STEM) field plus at least 9–14 years relevant experience.	• Bachelors in technical (STEM) field plus at least 20 years relevant experience, OR • Masters in technical (STEM) field plus at least 18 years relevant experience, OR • PhD in technical (STEM) field plus at least 15 years relevant experience. • Recognized by a selection (gating) committee as being in the top echelon (upper 0.5%) of technical workforce.

Table 5.2 Classification Standards

Administrative Professionals	
Job Criteria	*Associate Business Process Administrator*
Nature of Work Performed (type; complexity; variety; difficulty)	Performs administrative activities of limited scope, related to business and technical operations, processes, programs and projects. Conducts analyses of administrative processes and makes suggestions for improving effectiveness.
Skill/Knowledge Required	Applies knowledge of principles, concepts and theory related to a professional administrative discipline/field and employs a systems approach to address issues and to define and resolve problems.
Latitude Exercised/ Direction Received (authority; creativity; autonomy; nature & frequency of supervision received)	Works under general supervision, receiving closer supervision on issues new to incumbent or on more complex assignments. Exercises discretion and judgment in performing work and assists with implementing improvements to existing processes as appropriate.
Responsibility for Interpersonal Contacts (type; level; frequency; expected results; potential impact)	Exchanges information and works with peers, both within unit and from other units. May work with outside agencies, customers/sponsors and suppliers when directed to do so. May coordinate work of own unit with that of others.
Responsibility for Work of Others (mentoring, assigning/ directing work, providing technical direction)	May provide guidance and training to administrative support personnel, students, interns, contractors and other support personnel as required to complete assignments.
Potential Impact (cost; customer/ supplier relations; unit performance)	Quality of work can have a limited impact on project quality, costs and results.
Education	BA or BS degree in related field
Experience	0–2 years of experience in related work

(Continued)

Table 5.2 Continued

Administrative Professionals

Job Criteria	Business Process Administrator	Senior Business Process Administrator
Nature of Work Performed (type; complexity; variety; difficulty)	Performs administrative activities of broad scope, related to business and technical operations, processes, programs and projects. Conducts analyses to determine how well administrative processes are functioning and contributes ideas for solving problems/ addressing issues and for improving unit effectiveness.	Performs a wide variety of administrative activities of broad scope, related to key business and technical operations, processes, programs and projects. Evaluates administrative effectiveness for programs and processes and formulates recommendations for solving problems/addressing issues and for improving unit effectiveness.
Skill/Knowledge Required	Applies knowledge of principles, concepts and theory related to a professional administrative discipline/ field and employs a systems approach to address issues and to define and resolve problems.	Applies knowledge of principles, concepts and theory related to a professional administrative discipline/field and employs a systems approach to address issues and to define and resolve problems. Uses experience with administering projects and programs to apply knowledge.
Latitude Exercised/ Direction Received (authority; creativity; autonomy; nature & frequency of supervision received)	Works independently, with general direction, receiving more specific direction on issues new to incumbent or on more complex assignments. Exercises discretion and judgment in performing work and contributes recommendations for improving operations/ processes. Assists in implementing improvements to existing processes as appropriate.	Works independently, receiving direction as required to ensure project/ program objectives are met and that administrative policies and strategies are appropriate. Exercises considerable discretion and judgment in performing work and conducting evaluations of operation/ process effectiveness. Initiates changes required to implement improvements.

Table 5.2 Continued

Administrative Professionals

Job Criteria	Business Process Administrator	Senior Business Process Administrator
Responsibility for Interpersonal Contacts (type; level; frequency; expected results; potential impact)	Exchanges information and works with peers, both within unit and from other units. Works with outside agencies, customers/sponsors and suppliers as assigned and coordinates work of own unit with that of others.	Works with other units and outside agencies, customers/sponsors, suppliers as required to effectively administer projects and programs. Develops relationships as needed to perform work effectively.
Responsibility for Work of Others (mentoring, assigning/directing work, providing technical direction)	May provide guidance and training to administrative support personnel, students, interns, contractors and other support personnel as required to complete assignments.	Provides guidance to administrative support personnel, students, interns, contractors and other support personnel, as a mentor or as a team/project leader.
Potential Impact (cost; customer/ supplier relations; unit performance)	Quality of work can have a significant impact on project quality, costs and overall results and impact the effectiveness of the unit.	Quality of work can have a major impact on project/ program results and substantially impact the effectiveness of the unit.
Education	BA or BS degree in related field	BA or BS degree in related field
Experience	2–4 years of professional level work	5–8 years of professional level work

Job Criteria	Principal Business Process Administrator	Senior Principal Business Process Administrator
Nature of Work Performed (type; complexity; variety; difficulty)	Performs the full range of administrative activities required to support large and complex projects and programs. Participates in formulating policies and develops methods for effectively managing business and technical operations, processes, programs and projects. Evaluates major programs, processes and operations and formulates recommendations for improving administrative effectiveness.	Performs the full range of administrative activities required to support large and complex projects and programs. Participates in formulating policies and develops methods for effectively managing business and technical operations, processes, programs and projects. Evaluates major programs, processes and operations and works with executive management to formulate strategies for improving overall administrative effectiveness.

(Continued)

Table 5.2 Continued

Administrative Professionals

Job Criteria	Principal Business Process Administrator	Senior Principal Business Process Administrator
Skill/Knowledge Required	Applies expert knowledge of advanced principles, concepts and theory related to professional administrative discipline(s)/field(s) and employs a systems approach to address issues and to define and resolve the most difficult and challenging problems. Utilizes broad scope of understanding about organizational processes and operations.	Applies expert knowledge of advanced principles, concepts and theory related to professional administrative discipline(s)/field(s) and employs a systems approach to address issues and to define and resolve the most difficult and challenging problems. Utilizes understanding of organization-wide operations and its objectives to act as an authority on key administrative matters.
Latitude Exercised/ Direction Received (authority; creativity; autonomy; nature & frequency of supervision received)	Works independently, receiving direction on project/program objectives and strategies. Makes decisions on how to perform own work and formulates strategies for improving operations/processes. Directs initiatives to implement improvement strategies.	Work is guided by consultation with management, based on project/program objectives and strategies. Makes decisions on behalf of management, within prescribed scope of authority. Utilizes organization-wide perspective to identify possible improvements to key business processes.
Responsibility for Interpersonal Contacts (type; level; frequency; expected results; potential impact)	Develops and maintains relationships with customers/sponsors, suppliers, outside agencies and with other units within the organization as needed to facilitate meeting project/program and unit objectives. May act as principal representative of the organization.	Responsible for creating and developing relationships with key parties-at-interest relative to long-term issues and initiatives. Acts as principal representative of the organization and assists in negotiating the terms of critical administrative relationships.

Table 5.2 Continued

Administrative Professionals

Job Criteria	Principal Business Process Administrator	Senior Principal Business Process Administrator
Responsibility for Work of Others (mentoring, assigning/ directing work, providing technical direction)	Directs the work of administrative support personnel, students, interns, contractors and other less experienced personnel, either as a mentor or as a team/ project leader. Serves as a role model and source of expert knowledge.	Provides overall administrative direction on long-term and critical programs and projects. Establishes organization-wide standards and participates in developing/ applying new technologies to administrative management.
Potential Impact (costs; customer/ supplier relations; unit performance)	Quality of work directly and significantly impacts the quality of project, program and/or unit administration.	Quality of work directly and significantly impacts the performance of major projects and programs.
Education Required	BA or BS degree in related field; Master's degree desirable	BA or BS degree in related field; Master's degree preferable
Experience Required	8–12 years of professional level work	12–15 years of professional level work

employees and it is very important to convince them classification is done equitably. One of the areas of contention is whether education counts for more, less or about the same as experience. Knowledge and skills can be acquired from both sources and qualifications for entering a classification must be defined in a manner that provides appropriate weights to them. For example, the entry-level engineer classification may require a BS in engineering but no experience. Entering the next level in the career model may require a BS and 2–3 years of experience *or* an MS with no experience. The next level may require a BS and 4–7 years of experience *or* an MS with 2–3 years of experience, and so on. Many research organizations also hire PhDs, so it is possible that a new PhD graduate could enter into an organization's third level. However, if it took someone with a BS 8–10 years to reach that level and if the majority of the work draws on practical experience rather than theory the incumbents of that level may resent the classification of a new PhD and consider it inequitable. This perception would be due to a belief that experience should be given more weight than graduate education, especially if the work does not draw heavily on knowledge gained through taking courses in school. The organization must create a method for valuing both education and experience in a manner that is viewed as equitable and appropriate.

Equitable treatment is equally important when employees progress through the levels in the career model. This action typically constitutes a promotion and

Table 5.3 Technicians/Technologists

	Technician	Senior Technician
Work Description (type, complexity, variety, difficulty)	• Performs work of very limited complexity and scope with specific direction and oversight. • Collects data with specific task direction.	• Performs work of limited complexity and scope, generally in support of scientists and engineers. • Uses established technical standards, practices and procedures as well as technical knowledge to address problems and complete tasks. • Completes data collection problems of limited scope when established procedures exist. • Possesses basic knowledge of operating principles, measurement standards, practices and procedures.
Latitude Exercised/Direction Received (authority, autonomy, supervision received)	• Works with specific task direction and supervision from scientists, engineers and technical staff. • Learns basic S/E technical procedures for data collection and measurement. • Performs routine work with supervision. • Work is reviewed by supervisor for overall quality and adherence to procedures.	• Works under direct supervision from scientists, engineers and more experienced technical staff. • Follows established basic S/E technical procedures for data collection and measurement. • May perform routine work with minimal supervision and follows standard protocols when performing more complex tasks. • Work is reviewed by supervisor for overall quality and adherence to procedures.
Potential Impact of Work	• Quality of work generally has negligible impact on project schedules or results. • Contributions are limited to task assignments.	• Quality of work will have a limited impact on project costs, schedules and results. • Contributions are usually limited to assignment-related activities.

	Technologist	Senior Technologist
Internal Personal Contacts (type, level, purpose, frequency)	Internal contacts are primarily with direct supervisor and others in the group or department.	• Coordinates work through contacts with peers and S/E personnel, generally for purpose of reviewing results or receiving technical direction. • Internal contacts are primarily with direct supervisor and others in the group or department.
External Organizational Communications (type, level, purpose, frequency)	• May attend project and staff meetings as an observer or to provide clerical support while learning about project evolution.	• Participates in project and staff meetings as a contributor and as a source of technical information. • May seek information from external sources to accomplish task objectives.
Responsibility for Work of Others (mentoring, teaching, assigning & directing work, providing technical & project direction)	• No direct responsibility for work of others.	No direct responsibility for work of others.
Minimum Education and Experience	High School with coursework in math and science	Associate's degree in technical field
Work Description (type, complexity, variety, difficulty)	• Performs work of moderate complexity, generally in support of scientists and engineers. • Assists in compiling and analyzing measurement data. • Participates in field operations, data collection, and report generation.	• Develops solutions to a wide range of measurement tasks and problems. • Assists in researching, compiling and analyzing measurement data. • Participates in developing field operations and reports, designs, approaches, and proposals. • Implements computer applications used in S/E measurement work. • Drafts, revises or reviews technical procedures and documentation.

(Continued)

Table 5.3 Continued

	Technologist	Senior Technologist
Latitude Exercised/Direction Received (authority, autonomy, supervision received)	• Works under general supervision with technical direction provided. • Executes work in a disciplined manner to demonstrate compliance with NSTec policies and procedures. • Identifies work processes needing improvement. • Independent work is reviewed for technical adequacy and accuracy. • Acts appropriately in response to constructive criticism and feedback. • May serve as a technical support person on teams with well-defined scope of work.	• Works under general supervision with limited technical direction. • Executes work in a disciplined manner to demonstrate compliance with NSTec policies and procedures and laws, codes, and orders directly applicable to task execution. • Performs work of moderate complexity independently and makes recommendations on issues and problem solutions. • Identifies areas needing improvement and provides approaches to solutions. • Independent work is reviewed for technical judgment and accuracy. • Acts appropriately in response to constructive criticism and feedback. • May serve as lead technical support person on teams with well-defined scope of work.
Potential Impact of Work	• Quality of work can have an impact on project costs, schedules and results. • Contributes to the overall success of project task objectives.	• Quality of work can have a moderate impact on project costs, schedules and results. • Contributes to the success of overall organizational and project task objectives.
Internal Personal Contacts (type, level, purpose, frequency)	• Periodically coordinates work with peers and S/E personnel and supervisor. • Periodically interfaces with other functions such as property and facilities. • Develops process improvement relationships and opportunities within organizational boundaries.	• Frequently coordinates work with peers and regularly with senior S/E personnel and supervisor. • Routinely interfaces with other functions such as procurement, property, and facilities. • Develops process improvement relationships.

	Principal Technologist	Master Technologist
External Organizational Communications (type, level, purpose, frequency)	• Participates in customer and project meetings as a contributor and as a source of technical information. • Engages with peers and colleagues to facilitate task planning and execution details.	• Participates in customer and project meetings as a technical resource and as a source of specialized technical information. • Engages with peers, colleagues, and vendors to complete task planning and facilitate execution.
Responsibility for Work of Others (mentoring, teaching, assigning & directing work, providing technical & project direction)	• May have limited responsibility for work of others. • May provide direction to less experienced S/E technicians and monitors the work of support personnel.	• Has defined responsibility for work of others. • Provides direction to less experienced S/E technicians and monitors the work of technicians and support personnel. • Mentors junior staff in selected area(s) of specialty.
Minimum Education and Experience	Associate's + 4 years of related experience	Associate's + 8 years of related experience
	Principal Technologist	Master Technologist
Work Description (type, complexity, variety, difficulty)	• Resolves conflicting design requirements, utilizing unconventional materials and complex coordination. • Participates in developing field operations and finalizing designs, approaches, reports and proposals. • Creates innovative approaches through application of emerging technical developments, processes and standards. • Develops equipment or work specifications, evaluates bids and makes recommendation for awards of purchase contracts. • Contributes to development of technical solutions employing new approaches, concepts, or techniques.	• Devises solutions to significant technical problems of broad scope. • Applies engineering technologies to perform scope of work similar to that for degreed scientists or engineers, work contributes directly to engineering performance. • Serves as an advisor to other S/E personnel and management on difficult and critical technical issues. • Participates in business development, by defining customer requirements, developing proposed approaches and planning projects that will produce results meeting customer needs. • Applies technical concepts and techniques for practical purposes.

(Continued)

Table 5.3 Continued

	Principal Technologist	Master Technologist
Latitude Exercised/Direction Received (authority, autonomy, supervision received)	• Works with minimal supervision. • Assignments may be self-initiated, pursuing courses of action based on broadly defined project requirements. • Viewed by colleagues as an accomplished technical performer and lead. • Exercises considerable latitude and judgment in determining best approaches to achieve technical objectives on an assignment. • Work is reviewed for judgment exercised on approaches to goals.	• Independently plans, schedules and leads technical tasks/projects. • Focuses on projects of substantial complexity and broad scope, requiring interdisciplinary coordination. • Often works independently to uncover and resolve problems. • Advises and demonstrates leadership to senior staff and management in providing solutions to technical issues. • Viewed by customer as a technical leader in one or more functions that are critical to our business.
Potential Impact of Work	• May lead technical teams of 2–3 people. • Quality of work has a significant impact on project costs, schedules and performance. • Contributes to the success of specific organizational goals and objectives.	• Quality of work has a direct impact on the S/E capabilities and a major impact on the success of larger projects and programs. • Serves as technical resource to engineers and scientists, providing practical advice on implementation of technical solutions.
Internal Personal Contacts (type, level, purpose, frequency)	• Works with peers and other disciplines to coordinate project execution and compliance. • Provides technical guidance to solve operational issues.	• Ensures the work of S/E support personnel, contractors and suppliers are integrated and focused on established objectives. • Provides technical expertise to solve operational problems and issues.

External Organizational Communications (type, level, purpose, frequency)	• Routinely engages with customer and serves as primary contact for external project partners and vendors to define customer requirements and facilitate project planning and coordination. • Viewed by management and customers as a technical resource in one or more areas important to the business.	• Routinely engages with customer and primary contact for external project partners and vendors to integrate customer requirements and for project planning and execution. • Works with customer personnel to ensure their needs are clearly defined and works with others to meet customer objectives.
Responsibility for Work of Others (mentoring, teaching, assigning & directing work, providing technical)	• Provides technical direction to less experienced personnel and reviews their results. • Trains and mentors less experienced staff. • Advisor on technical work of junior staff.	• Provides technical direction to support personnel. • Assists with training and mentoring personnel. • Advises senior staff and management on solutions in technical areas. • Integrates and directs work of specialized personnel to produce desired results.
Minimum Education and Experience	Associate's + 13 years of related experience	Associate's + 18 years of related experience

Table 5.4 Administrative Support Personnel

Job Criteria	Administrative Associate	Senior Administrative Associate	Administrative Specialist	Senior Administrative Specialist
Nature of Work (type; complexity; variety; difficulty)	Provides administrative support to assigned organizational unit. Develops understanding of policies and procedures and performs a variety of activities as assigned.	Performs varied administrative duties with relatively broad scope. Develops knowledge of specialized functions. Applies knowledge of how unit activities integrate with each other and with activities performed outside the unit. Collects and organizes information required to perform assigned work.	Performs varied and complex administrative duties with broad scope. Applies knowledge of a broad range of specialized functions and assists in coordinating unit activities with those of other units. Researches topics, conducts analyses and presents options based on findings. May lead and guide activities of others.	Directs varied and complex administrative tasks with broad scope. Has full command of a broad range of specialized functions and coordinates unit activities with those of other units. Conducts analyses, prepares options, and recommends action for management consideration. Leads activities of extended duration.
Latitude/Direction Received (authority; creativity; nature & frequency of supervision received)	Exercises discretion and judgment in performing work with prescribed routines. Receives close supervision for more complex work. Manager sets priorities for performing assigned work.	Exercises discretion and judgment in performing work. Works under general direction. Sets priorities for self in doing work and manages time to ensure that deadlines and objectives are met. Seeks guidance for more complex work.	Works independently, reporting upon completion of assigned duties/projects. Guidance is in terms of results expected. The work of other administrative support personnel may be directed and coordinated to meet objectives. Expected to demonstrate creativity in how work is performed and in addressing work processes.	Works independently, reporting upon completion of assigned duties/projects. Guidance is in terms of overall objectives. The work of other administrative support personnel is directed and coordinated to meet objectives. Expected to recommend creative solutions to complex problems.

Responsibility for Interpersonal Contacts (type; level; frequency)	Exchanges information with others as directed, typically within own group/unit.	Exchanges information with other units and outside entities that is required in order to be able to perform work.	Exchanges information with other units and outside entities and may be responsible for integrating the activities of own unit with others.	Exchanges information with other units and outside entities and takes responsibility for integrating the activities of own unit with others.
Responsibility for Work of Others	None.	May provide guidance and training to other administrative support personnel as needed.	May provide guidance and training to other administrative support personnel as needed.	May provide guidance and training to other administrative support personnel. Expected to act as a resource and a role model.
Potential Impact on Unit (quality; customer satisfaction; cost; responsiveness)	Quality of work impacts unit's costs and efficiency and may impact customer satisfaction.	Quality of work directly impacts unit performance and may significantly impact costs, efficiency or customer satisfaction.	Quality of work may have significant impact unit performance and on customer satisfaction, the costs of doing business and the degree to which unit objectives are met.	Quality of work significantly impacts unit performance and can have a major effect on customer satisfaction, the costs of doing business and whether unit objectives are met.
Education/ Training	High School	High School	High School, with course work in analytical techniques preferred.	High School, with equivalent of Associates degree preferred.
Experience & Special Skills	No experience required. Able to use basic office software.	1–2 years of office experience. Command of full range of office software.	3–5 years of office experience. Command of full range of office software.	5 or more years of office experience. Command of full range of office software.

even if there is no immediate pay adjustment the person will be classified in a grade that has a higher pay range, increasing future pay potential. And progression is also a form of recognition that the person has increased his or her ability to perform a wider range of work and/or to cope with a higher level of difficulty and variety of work. Given what is at stake it is not surprising that incumbents evaluate whether promotions are done equitably and consistently across the organization. It is difficult to get managers to share a common perspective and if the specifications that are built into the career model are not sufficiently rigorous there will be inconsistent interpretations by different managers. For that reason, it is common to have a review board approve progressions, at least at higher levels. Chapter 7 will treat career progression in more detail.

People who feel they have been undervalued or inequitably treated will not be satisfied or engaged. When new entrants are onboarded, it is critically imperative to ensure they are classified correctly, as well as being paid equitably. This applies to progressions as well. Feelings about classification inequities may be strong but pay inequities can result in equally intense emotional reactions. Equity theory sheds light on how people decide on what is equitable and what is not. The party making the determination selects a "referent other" (a person, a category) to compare to. Then an assessment is made of both the inputs parties offer the organization and the outcomes they experience. The "input–output" ratio of the evaluator is compared to the ratio of the referent other. In theory, if one finds the ratios to be equivalent, they should feel equitably treated. If they feel inequitably underrewarded, they will be motivated to complain, to exit the situation or remain and be dissatisfied with their treatment. Ed Lawler has contended that if someone feels inequitably overrewarded, they will do a new computation or work harder to deserve the largesse. But people seem to have the ability to make feelings of overpayment disappear in nanoseconds.

Assuming classification and compensation conflicts do not exist or are reconciled the next concern is how work is allocated to individuals. It is not uncommon for the new person to be assigned the work no one else wants to do, especially if incumbents have a say in who does what. But if a manager selects a new hire based on specific capabilities that person may be assigned work that more senior people would like to do. Even though the senior employees may not be as competent to do the work as the new entrant is if it is the type of work that is in demand in the labor market, they may feel they have right to develop their competence.

It is important as well to ensure a new hire is supported if their assignments are going to stretch their capabilities. One of the benefits of doing knowledge management well is that employees know that showing others how to do what they know how to do is valued, and in some cases rewarded. If an employee is transferred internally from another part of the organization things may be done somewhat differently from where they came, and it is usually peers that can point the new arrival in the right direction. A person who is used to being encouraged to try new things even if they result in failure may have to reorient their thinking if they move to another part of the organization and find they are expected to do things in a specified way. Given that managers set the tone in their area of responsibility what seems like an easy transfer on the surface may turn out to be a very substantial change in what the employee is expected to do and how. Whether the human resources function assumes some oversight responsibility for matching employees to roles may make a difference in how well potential issues are anticipated and dealt with.

The new employee orientation process differs across organizations, from a "hello, here is your workplace" to extensive grounding in all matters relating to the person's employment. One of the national research laboratories I consulted with developed a multi-day orientation, including a two-hour in-depth module on performance management and another two-hour module on rewards management. These two systems had been redesigned and the organization wanted to be sure everyone understood what was expected of them, how their contribution would be evaluated and what impact their performance had on their compensation. They also focused on how individuals were classified into the career management ladders, to facilitate acceptance that the methodology was sound.

Many organizations leave new hires free to figure out how things work and then are startled when word-of-mouth communication does not lead to an accurate understanding of how these critical processes are supposed to work. There are topics that probably can wait to be explained. If someone does not vest in any benefit in a retirement plan for five years, the subject should not be a part of the tsunami of information that comes at the new hire at orientation. However, if there is a waiting period before some elements of health insurance coverage kick in a simple statement that this will happen at a specified future time should dispel anxiety over why the plan provisions were not covered in detail. The danger is providing too much information in a new employee orientation that nothing is remembered with clarity.

Many organizations believe in assigning sponsors, coaches or mentors to new employees. Ensuring everyone has defined responsibilities and clear marching orders can promote consistency. When a new hire finds out peers have more resources made available to them it can breed discontent. More discussion of how an organization invests in employee development will occur in Chapter 7, but there may be types of support that occur only during the onboarding process. Intranet websites can fill some of the needs of new people. Being able to find the information needed without having to go to someone increases the likelihood the employee will make the effort. But questions should not go unanswered and wrong information can cause an employee to make mistakes or behave in a manner that is not sanctioned. Part of the orientation process may consist of passing an online course with an associated test, all done on the intranet. It is common for people to take courses available on the internet, to fill in knowledge gaps or to develop new skills. Requiring employees to pass tests that follow intranet courses on things like HR policy can ensure they get the correct information and understand it. This is especially important if the employee is expected to do things that have not been done before or done in the manner that is expected.

How well the role an employee is assigned to play is defined is a vitally important pre-condition for successful integration. Even though the characteristics of well-designed roles have been extensively researched the findings are too often not utilized. Defining a job that no one wants creates challenges relative to keeping people in the job and having them be satisfied with it. The Job Characteristics Index is a model that has been heavily supported by research.[9] The characteristics that lead to satisfaction are:

Skill variety: the role requires a range of skills to perform the tasks. This enables the person to avoid the boredom and fatigue associated with performing simple tasks in the same manner repeatedly. It also enables the person to use their skills. Increasing variety is called job enlargement in the academic literature, while adding work at a higher complexity level is called job enrichment.

Task significance: Why the role is meaningful to someone or how it contributes to a result that has an impact. Intensive quality control requirements when developing navigation software for airplanes is more understandable when the employee knows it can have an impact on safety in the air.

Autonomy: Incumbents are allowed an appropriate amount of latitude as to *how* tasks are performed. What has to be done may be specified but the "how" can in many instances left to the employee.

Feedback: Results can be measured according to a standard and the incumbent is continuously provided with adequate knowledge that enables him or her to know how well (s)he is performing.

Different roles will possess these characteristics to a differing degree. A person arming an explosive device may be required to put the black wire on post A and the red wire on post B. Although there is little autonomy the nature of the responsibility is such that latitude could be costly. Henry Ford used auto assembly lines consisting of simple and repetitive tasks, while Volvo used teams to assemble major components of a car. The differences in the roles are significant and there is no clear answer to which is "better." They are different. And they will appeal to different people. Whether someone prefers to do their work while thinking about something else (like what time they get off) or whether they would rather use their ingenuity to create the best way to achieve an outcome will certainly impact what they view as a desirable role. And if they are promised something different than what they experience once they are on the job it is not surprising that it might result in dissatisfaction. A person assigned a structured and repetitive task may surprise everyone and invent a new and better way of doing things. But if they are censored for doing so that behavior will probably be extinguished via social pressure.

The importance of knowledge management has already been discussed. Once employees are onboarded, placed in roles they are competent to perform and encouraged to contribute to meeting organizational objectives it is important to communicate the importance of sharing knowledge. Although a free flow of knowledge is more important in contexts where work is interdependent it is always beneficial to have employees willing to share their best ideas and techniques. Some people are more inclined to share, rather than hoard, what they know and, when possible, it is prudent to attempt to evaluate candidates on this aspect of personality. Past behavior interviewing can be used to find out what a candidate's inclination is, based on how they have behaved in the past. Once on board, employees should be informed of the importance of sharing.

Knowledge can be explicit or tacit. When it is explicit it can be accessed and used by anyone knowing where to find it. Formal education and training conveys explicit knowledge and open communication can also transmit it from one person to another. But when it is tacit it is difficult to transmit ... people often know more than they can articulate or demonstrate. Through repeated emulation, the knowledge can become tacit within the learner. Coaches, mentors and trainers can transmit tacit knowledge, but the organization must identify the right parties, define their role, provide the necessary resources and reinforce the desired behavior to facilitate success.

There are informal groups commonly called "communities of practice" that are formed by people with common interests. Even though there is no formal recognition of these groups by the organization employees will sometimes form them as a way to grow their competence or just for the satisfaction of sharing common interests. COPs are a type of shadow organization, since the interaction within them can produce new knowledge and/or increase the dissemination of existing knowledge. Knowledge management is a powerful engine for making employees more effective and decreasing the amount of learning that is done by time-consuming and often expensive trial and error experimentation. Organizations need to identify these networks and provide an appropriate amount of resources as well as encouragement to maximize their value.

Authority in COPs goes to people who have the expertise and knowledge, rather than someone who has a title that supposedly accords authority to the holder. Often COPs will connect to resources outside the organization ... suppliers, past employees, academic researchers, regulators and even employees of competitor organizations. This could be a concern if there is a fear that intellectual capital could be lost, particularly capital that cannot be turned into intellectual property by legal protection. Yet the expansion of the firm's knowledge may be sufficiently attractive to make investing in COPs a wise decision. In order to ensure that valuable knowledge is exchanged the organization may need to staff at levels that enable employees to engage in this activity. "Lean and mean" staffing can appeal to those focused on efficiency but can preclude interactions that might increase effectiveness.

The explosion of social media has also created networks that nowhere appear on organization charts. Their creation presents both opportunities and challenges. A new employee who is left to wander aimlessly in a new wilderness may vent frustration on Glassdoor, suggesting to outsiders that working for the organization does not feel like a recreational activity. Unfortunately, frustration sometimes breeds inaccurate descriptions of what occurred or in an overstatement of abuses. Since employers have difficulty undoing negative postings even when they are inaccurate this has created public relations challenges and damage to employer brands. The only cure seems to be satisfying every employee. Given the low probability of that being achieved, the best strategy is to get as close to that optimal result as possible.

The potential for social media and other communication technology can have positive benefits. Graduates of educational institutions may stay in contact with faculty and have access to new developments they otherwise may not be aware of. Online courses can also provide growth opportunities that do not require organizational support. But if the organization views individual study as an enhancement of its talent pool it may take the initiative and encourage employees to pursue courses relevant to their work ... or to what they might do in the future. Tuition reimbursement programs send the message that the organization values employee growth and that it is willing to support further education. An engineering technician with an Associate's degree can become a future engineer for the organization if further education results in a BS degree. And given the shortage of STEM graduates in the United States, this can be an answer to a serious talent shortage for an organization. More about continuing education will be discussed in Chapter 7.

Where the Work Is Performed

Technology has made it possible for people to do their jobs when they are not colocated with others. Telecommuting is an option that many organizations have utilized for a number of reasons:

1. It reduces office space requirements. Especially in high space cost areas having more employees in the office increases the square footage required and consequently the budget for purchasing or leasing space.
2. It reduces or eliminates commuting time. When employees are commuting to and from their offices they often cannot be as productive as they would be if they were in a home office location. Law enforcement has increased scrutiny of cell phone use, especially text messaging. Using phones to stay in touch with others while driving can raise safety issues. Some organizations use outlying satellite locations rather than having everyone commute to a central location. This can make face-to-face interaction possible and provide access to expensive equipment that would not be available at a home location. In congested and expensive areas like Silicon Valley, people may have to live some distance from work and some of the

technology companies provide van service, which may allow employees to be productive during long commutes.

3. It tends to reduce absences and breaks. An employee who has a medical condition that precludes commuting can still "attend" if they can work from home. There are jokes about how much time a telecommuter will spend accessing the refrigerator, but research has indicated that this is not a major issue ... the distance to the refrigerator is probably shorter than the distance to the break room at the central office anyway.
4. Employees who are care providers may still be able to fulfil those responsibilities while working full time.
5. Employees generally believe they have fewer extraneous distractions, since latte machine trips do not result in being drawn into conversations about sports or looking at baby pictures.

Telecommuting does have potential drawbacks, however:

1. Social interaction and idea sharing may be more difficult when not co-located. Impromptu discoveries can occur as a result of an inquiry such as "what are you working on?" Firms that rely on innovation go to great lengths to combine the ideas that employees have, using techniques such as brainstorming. Although idea sharing can occur at a distance it is generally easier in face-to-face interactions.
2. Employees may begin to disconnect and be less engaged in addressing issues the organization is dealing with. When not prompted by others it is easy to focus on one's activities to the exclusion of other things that are going on in the workplace. Having a peer ask for help with an issue can not only enable knowledge to be disseminated but may also be gratifying to an employee because it reflects on the perceptions of others about their competence.
3. Managers often find it more difficult to measure and evaluate employee performance when they are unable to physically observe their employees. Although some think this can be overcome by focusing on results, it is difficult to assess how an employee interacts with peers and customers and how the results are generated.
4. The organization may have to make a significant investment in equipment necessary to perform the work and it is less possible to share things like printers when people are working remotely.
5. Employees may not want to be "out of the loop." Much like the concern that employees on expatriate assignments have about being forgotten, due to their not being onsite, working remotely can make it difficult to ensure that others are aware of what the employee is contributing.

There have been instances where organizations pull people back into the office after allowing employees to telecommute. Yahoo was in the press several times ... first as an extensive user of telecommuting ... then pulling people back in ... then re-instating telecommuting options for some. The re-instatement of the option was an attempt to avert losing critical talent but also a recognition that some roles were better suited to remote working than others.

Global Workforces

Employees who are on international assignments or who work remotely across national borders present a somewhat different challenge than those who are located in the headquarters country. They are at least to some degree out of sight of corporate management. Although the assignee may be expected to report to and take direction from local management this may have undesirable consequences. Some assignees "go native" and not only take local direction but see the way things are done in the host country as the right way, even when it conflicts with corporate philosophy. When the local manager evaluates performance of subordinates who are on assignment, as well as determining rewards, there is a tendency to take direction from that manager. Expatriates or third-country nationals sent into a location to change the way things are done may over time begin to see the local way as the best way and fail to accomplish the changes.

Another danger for assignees who are in professional fields is that how something is done locally (i.e., accounting, human resources, rewards management) may be viewed as a good fit to the context, irrespective of its variation from corporate and professional standards. This is problematic when there is a danger of deviating from what is accepted as sound practice. When an expatriate from corporate is the only one who finds practices to be unprofessional or even unethical it is difficult for that person to stand their ground and enforce policies. The key to avoiding illegal and unwanted practices is for the organization to provide the training and the support the expatriate will require to resist local management directives. Although similar dangers exist even within a headquarters country the physical and cultural distance between corporate and foreign locations makes close attention to monitoring how business is done everywhere mandatory. Working employees six ten-hour days may be acceptable locally but this can be considered to be unacceptable practice elsewhere and can damage the brand of the organization. Nike and Apple have had to deal with these issues in their offshored manufacturing facilities, which even though out of sight cannot be out of mind.

Performance Management

When employees have been onboarded, assigned to well-designed and defined roles, and given the resources necessary to succeed the last critical requirement is to define expectations clearly. The key to effective performance management is ensuring an employee knows what is expected and how they are doing on a continuous basis. In order for an employee to be motivated to perform well (to do what is expected) there are four prerequisites: They have to (1) be able to do it (and believe they are), (2) be allowed to do it, (3) know what it is and (4) want to do it.

In order for them to be able to do it, they must be given the time, budget, staff and other resources, which include possessing the necessary skills and knowledge. If an employee does not believe they are capable of doing it or if they believe the expectations are unobtainable their motivation to try will be diminished. They may still attempt to do it just to save their job for a time but a sense of futility will extinguish effort.

In order for them to be allowed to do it, they must be given an appropriate amount of autonomy to decide how to do what is required. If they feel overly constricted this too will diminish motivation.

In order for them to know what it is, there must be clear performance criteria and standards provided prior to performing and must be updated if things change. This specification of expectations must also include relative importance weights assigned to the goals, so priorities can be set when what is to be done exceeds what can be done at the moment.

Finally, in order to want to extend the required effort and focus that effort on the established goals, employees must believe that their performance will be accurately evaluated and that the consequences associated with success and failure are known and believed to be equitable. If a high performing employee is rewarded in the same way and amount as those performing at lower levels equity theory suggests the willingness to extend one's best efforts in the future will be diminished.[10]

Goal setting is a powerful motivational tool if done well. But employees must accept the goals as reasonable and be willing to commit to achieving them if possible. They must also believe goals set for other employees are equally difficult to achieve. One way to "level the playing field" is to use an evaluation system similar to the way that Olympic diving is scored. The score is the product of the difficulty of the dive and the quality of execution and divers know that attempting a more difficult dive that has a lesser chance of perfect execution may still be their best choice.

An organization's human resource management policies impact the way work is assigned and done. Work schedules, where work is performed, and controls governing what is permitted and how it is done are all elements of policies. When employees assess the attractiveness of an employer, they will be influenced by the organization's willingness to accommodate their specific needs and wants. Someone who wants to work under a different schedule, work at a different location or negotiate other conditions of work may find that policies prohibit accommodation or that managers decide that variations are not acceptable. Often individual managers make decisions that differ from what other managers do. This happens because managers don't know what the policies are, disagree with them, think operational needs override them or believe that certain employees deserve special accommodation.

Figure 5.3 is a model that can guide policy interpretation and decisions about variations for individual employees.[11] The questions posed can guide both good decisions and consistency across managers. Some organizations think policies should be rigid rules, to be followed for everyone under all circumstances.

Figure 5.3 Evaluating Idiosyncratic Deals.

Others think they are guidelines, subject to interpretation if conditions warrant it. Yet others think them to be noble aspirations and humor the human resources department by pretending to abide by them. But failure to interpret and enforce policies consistently can cause perceptions of inequity and potentially lawsuits related to discrimination.

Notes

1   Zuboff, S. *In the Age of the Smart Machine* (New York: Basic Books, 1989).
2   Trompenaars, F. & Greene, R. *Rewarding Performance Globally* (New York: Routledge, 2017).
3   Greene, R. *Rewarding Performance, 2nd ed.* (New York: Routledge, 2019).
4   Greene, R. *Rewarding Performance, 2nd ed.* (New York: Routledge, 2019).
5   Greene, R. *Rewarding Performance, 2nd ed.* (New York: Routledge, 2019).
6   Trompenaars, F. & Greene, R. *Rewarding Performance Globally* (New York: Routledge, 2017).
7   Greene, R. *Rewarding Performance, 2nd ed.* (New York: Routledge, 2019).
8   Cascio, W. *Managing Human Resources* (New York: McGraw-Hill, 2015).
9   Hackman, J. & Oldham, G. *Job Redesign* (Reading, MA:Addison-Wesley, 1980).
10 Greene, R. *Rewarding Performance, 2nd ed.* (New York: Routledge, 2019).
11 Rousseau, D. *I-deals* (New York: Routledge, 2015).

Chapter 6

Utilizing Talent from Outside Sources

There is a decided trend toward having more work done by outsiders. Contractors, consulting firms and freelancers are a source of talent that an organization might find more cost-effective or capable of doing things the organization cannot do with its own talent pool. The rapid development of technology in many fields may result in the knowledge and skills of its work-force to be inadequate to effectively utilize new resources. This was illustrated when the Y2K event caused many organizations to contract out the development of new IT systems to replace their legacy systems which would not work in 2000 without major redevelopment. Their workforce did not have the required skills and knowledge to create network-based systems, so they elected to contract out the work to other firms, to individuals who were not employees or to technology.

Outsourcing to Technology

The emergence of technology opens the door to utilizing software or robots to do work. Using an algorithm to find information, analyze data, execute defined processes and make decisions can reduce the workload of employees. Researching legal precedents with software that contains search criteria is faster and less costly than using attorneys or paralegals, and it may reduce errors. Anything that can be fully prescribed is a candidate for automation.

Using robots or software requires that some type of algorithm is available that can control their actions. One of the concerns when robots share work-places with humans is safety. If a robot is instructed to move an arm in a circular fashion and a human happens to occupy the same space through which the arm travels accidents are likely. In 2019 airplane crashes have been caused by soft-ware that prescribed bringing the nose of the plane down when the pilots knew the nose should go up. The interaction between automated actions and human actions needs to be controlled and contradicting actions must be reconciled. This requires a command hierarchy that allocates authority in a way that will result in correct actions.

The potential difficulties presented by using algorithms and robots lies in their nature. They do not consider consequences or alter routines when what is prescribed does not make sense.

Human decisions can also project a false intent if the basis upon which they are made does not include consideration of such things as what people might conclude from the results produced. Automating any type of analysis runs the additional risk of capturing cognitive biases that humans are prone to and often unaware of. One approach to preventing bias is having more than one person involved in developing an algorithm. Although this goes against the tendency of technical professionals to want to create their own tools it may be necessary to ensure bias does not influence analysis. But the team involved in creation must be diverse, so premature decisions are not reached without the appropriate amount of debate. A group of like-minded people will often not result in considering a broad range of ideas.

When analyzing alternative sources for having work done by outsider resources it is necessary to ensure the measures used to make the selection decision are not deficient or contaminated. A decision algorithm is deficient if it does not include all the factors that should be considered. Rewarding a production employee for high levels of physical output without considering the quality of what is produced is an example. A decision algorithm is contaminated if it includes measures that are not relevant or that should not be considered. But even when the criteria used are appropriate sound decisions about workforce management often require incorporating other considerations.

A multinational organization that has only headquarters country incumbents in key roles but is trying to understand global markets and persuade consumers to purchase their wares may consciously prefer adding new decision makers who come from the culture of the customers. Diversity for diversity's sake can unnecessary or even lead to bad decision making. But if there is value in understanding the customer it may alter the factors used to select people who understand that culture, no matter where they are currently located.

Outsource to Firms or Individuals?

Even though technological development has been dramatic most work is performed by people. Outside resources may be freelancers, employees of consulting firms or volunteers. As has been discussed earlier one of the challenges when having work done by outside parties is integrating their work with that of employees.

Another challenge is ensuring that employees do not feel the decision to outsource work harms them. By factoring these concerns into decisions about allocating work the organization can make better decisions. One of the most difficult aspects of managing work done by outsiders is ensuring the desired results are produced without damaging employee morale. Employees often suspect that the outsiders are getting the "good" work. Work that requires the most up-to-date technology and skills will be attractive to employees because it gives employees an opportunity to remain marketable. If the use of outsiders deprives them of a learning opportunity it could result in dissatisfaction.

Decisions relating to the type of outsider to be used will almost inevitably involve a consideration of cost. If a project would require an organization to add staff in order to get the job done it will be possible to project the cost of doing so. That cost can then be compared to the cost associated with using alternative sources of outsiders. It is helpful to understand how contractors/consulting firms cost out their resources. A simple rule of thumb is charging three to four times an employee's hourly salary/wage for each hour they work. This enables the contractor/consulting firm to cover the cost of employing people, the benefits they provide them, the office space they maintain and the equipment and technology they must have. There is also a built-in profit margin.

If a contracting firm assigns one of their employees at $100 per hour and the client organization could hire someone to do the same work for a salary of $50,000 it is tempting to think the charge-out rate of the contractor to be excessive. But since the organization would typically incur benefits costs of approximately 40% of an employee's salary and would have to provide them with office space and their work tools the rate seems a little less daunting. However, the most important consideration is whether a newly hired employee could be kept busy full time. When comparing based on cost it must be remembered that the contractor only bills for the time spent on the project. Vacations, sick days and idle time are on the contractor. It is also necessary to consider is whether an employee can do the work as well as the contractor and be as productive. If an employee would have to be trained or go through a learning curve this might make him or her less productive than the contractor.

The difference between outsourcing work to another organization or to an individual is significant. A contracting firm will generally have a pool of talent, which makes it possible to align the qualifications of the people to the requirements of the work. The contracting firm will also manage the work of individuals assigned to a project, subject to direction from the customer. Inadequate performers can be immediately removed by a contracting firm and be replaced by someone who can meet expectations, assuming their staff is adequate. Organizations using contracting firms should ensure the depth and breadth of those firms are adequate to perform the work required, both in the short and long term.

There needs to be an advance understanding between the customer and a contractor about whether the customer can hire one of the contracting firm's employees after the person has done work for the customer. It has been common for temporary help firms to write a provision into the contract to exact a fee if a customer hires one of their employees. Consulting firms must bear the risk of losing an employee who impresses the customer too much. Given the mobility of talent today the risk of losing employees who are contracted out seems to go with the territory.

When there is no intermediary between the organization outsourcing the work and the individuals who will perform the work the charge rate issue is quite different. An individual is free to set the charge rate at any level deemed appropriate, assuming the customer accepts that rate. Someone who is employed full time by another organization and who views the work as a source of additional income may use a different rate-setting equation than someone who relies totally on contracted work for their income. Some free-lancers will charge a set rate for their work while others will vary the rate based on the nature of the work and the skills required to do it. The rate charged will be what the individual believes their talent is worth as well as what they think a customer will pay. During times of high unemployment, the rate may be lowered, although some skills seem always to be in short supply and command a high rate. The customer will consider the value of the work when deciding what they are willing to pay.

One of the concerns in the United States related to contracting work out to individuals is whether they will be considered employees under the law. If the customer directs the work of the person performing the work, both the what and the how, there is a danger that regulations will mandate treating the person as an employee. Uber and Lyft have been struggling with regulators about classifying their drivers, as to whether they are contractors or employees. To date, they have been successful in convincing authorities that they are only digital intermediaries but have struggled to maintain that status in countries outside the United States. A freelancer that derives virtually all income from one customer over a long period of time is a candidate for examination by regulators. The state of California has adopted new regulations that may force people now treated as contractors to be reclassified as employees and other countries have been addressing this issue.

Perhaps the most difficult perception to alter is the belief by employees that outsiders have a better deal. If an employee finds out what the hourly rate is for an outsider, they might multiply that by 2,080 and compare that to their salary. This is an invalid comparison, but perception is reality and care should be taken to clarify the reasons for the different rate for outsiders. Just saying "they don't get benefits" might prompt the employees to offer to sell back their benefits for one-half of the difference they have computed. The most important reality to convey is that outsiders only are paid at that rate for every hour they work directly on the project. Another fact that is useful to convey is that the individuals working for contracting/consulting firms only receive a small share of what is paid to the outside firm. Freelancers must also find enough work to support themselves and can be subject to long gaps between assignments. But they do get to keep all that they bill, except for what is paid in taxes.

Resolving conflicts arising when outsiders and employees are sharing the work is critical. Who sets the direction must be determined and clearly communicated. When outsiders are brought in to provide technical direction and to do work the employees are not capable of doing it seems reasonable that they would have a say in setting the course. But if the approach they recommend is inconsistent with the way employees have done work there can be contentious debates that must be settled. If employees feel they do not receive appropriate credit for having the necessary knowledge and skills deferring to outsiders may be difficult. And if managers within the organization begin to set the direction (the what and the how) it raises issues about whether contractors should be classified as employees. These potential conflicts should be considered before outsourcing decisions are made.

It is in the interests of an organization to make outsiders as productive as possible. It is also helpful to make outsiders feel they are respected and treated appropriately, since this will impact their satisfaction. When using individuals who have skill sets that are in short supply the organization using them benefits if it is seen by outsiders as being an attractive place for them to work. This is especially true if their services will be needed over a longer period of time. Decision scientists are in short supply today, principally because so many organizations have decided they need their skills at the same time. This is a replay of the scenario that occurred in the late 1990s when the small number of qualified network software people were needed by so many organizations. The dramatic increase in AI and machine learning tool usage has made the skill shortage for decision scientists obvious and organizations are struggling to close the supply–demand gap. Regrettably there has been a shortage of people in STEM fields in the United States for some time, so there is a limited supply of people who could be brought up to the required competence level in areas like workforce analytics in a short period of time.

Attempting to get heavily into the analytics game at a fast pace is going to exacerbate skill shortages in some fields. As discussed in Chapter 1, workforce planning can anticipate supply–demand imbalances if organizations are doing continuous environmental scanning and are reassessing their priorities quickly enough to develop ways to meet talent needs. There will be instances when there are too few people qualified to do what organizations want to do. This will make the competition for talent more intensive and will generally increase the price of short supply skills. And it will frustrate the attempts by organizations to upgrade their workforce quickly enough and at a tolerable cost. This will likely increase the need to augment the talent pool by accessing outside sources. Managing the outside resources effectively will be a challenge that organizations should prepare themselves to meet.

There are similarities between using employees to do work and using outside firms or individuals. But there are also differences that should not be overlooked. If employment becomes less attractive to a significant number of people, it will impact the supply of candidates aspiring to work as employees. In the United States, one of the obstacles to operating as a freelancer has been the availability and cost of health care for people purchasing insurance as an individual. This is one of the consequences of having the type of health care system that relies on organizations to provide insurance. There are talent platforms that have begun to offer insurance coverage on group rates, which may increase the number of people willing and able to operate as independents. Organizations might find that freelancers who are citizens of other countries have their health care coverage provided by their government and this might increase the number of foreigners utilized in foreign locations.

By doing a thorough analysis of the comparative benefits and costs associated with using employees' or outsiders' organizations can make good decisions about distributing work. Doing environmental scanning and workforce planning continuously enables organizations to assess changing labor market decisions and to make the right decisions. It is also important to determine whether the organization's managers will be able to effectively direct and control work and to integrate outsider and employee efforts to produce the desired results.

Chapter 7

Developing Talent

Once the right workforce is created, its viability must be sustained. A dynamic environment creates a need for new knowledge and skills and organizations often find that the change is so rapid that it outpaces the ability of current employees to adapt. There are several approaches to development, and which is appropriate for an employee or occupational group at a specific point in time will depend on the type of development required and the timeframe within which it needs to occur.

Development can be aimed at increasing skill/knowledge depth or breadth. An apprentice electrician can be prepared for advancement to journey electrician by increasing the individual's depth of knowledge and skills. A programmer can be prepared for advancement to analyst/programmer by developing the breadth of the individual's knowledge and skills. The development of either of these individuals can be facilitated by training that increases depth or exposure to a broader range of skills and knowledge, using developmental assignments or by training that increases breadth.

Training is the most commonly used development tool. Training can come in the form of specific instruction in how to execute procedures or in the form of educational programs that provide concepts and principles that broaden a person's perspective. Often education is considered a developmental activity and not as training. On the job training can be done while the person is actively performing his or her job in the workplace or can be done in a "vestibule" setting that is offline. Simulation technology and computer-based instruction can be utilized at any time and often at any location. The advantage of simulation is that it does not disrupt operations, which can be very important when the work is a part of a process. Pilots train in simulators so their mistakes do not result in equipment replacement costs or endangering the well-being of crew members and passengers. And game-based training software can reduce the drudgery associated with many training programs. People tend to do more of something they enjoy, as opposed to reading a textbook or operating manual.

Most organizations invest in some type of training, that may vary across occupations and the nature of the skill/knowledge employees are being trained for. One of the most effective ways to ensure the right type of training is being designed and used is to evaluate its effectiveness. There are four levels at which effectiveness can be evaluated.[1] The first level, which is the most common, is to assess trainee satisfaction. Asking those participating whether the material was relevant to the objective and effective in transmitting the required knowledge or increasing skill level seems reasonable. But all that is measured at this level is satisfaction. The second level is to assess whether the desired learning occurred. This can be done by using a pre-test/post-test method, which measures the increase in skill/knowledge associated with the training. The third level is whether the training had the desired effect on trainee behavior. The degree to which the learned skill/knowledge is actually used when back on the job is an important measure. Often the training is never applied due to a resistance on the part of co-workers to changing how things are done, meaning that competence was increased but the value of that increase does not result in a tangible benefit for the organization. The fourth, and most critical level of assessment, is to measure the impact of the training on efficiency, effectiveness or other desired outcomes. If the training resulted in learning and changed behavior, but not in an improvement in the way work is performed it may indicate the design of the training did not address the operational needs.

Education and training can keep the knowledge and skills of workers current, as well as helping them to maintain their competence in dealing with changing requirements. Supporting continuing education through tuition reimbursement and even sponsoring extended programs that occur away from the workplace can encourage employees to both remain current in their work and to expand their capabilities to perform a wider variety of work. Tuition reimbursement programs are very common in the United States, but research indicates fewer than 10% of employees of organizations with these programs use the benefit annually. This is surprising, since an organization can provide $5,250 of educational assistance annually to each employee on a tax-free basis. Although the employee typically has to pay when registering for a program and wait for reimbursement upon course completion the time between payment and reimbursement is fairly short, which means it is unlikely that a student loan would be necessary.

Some organizations limit their tuition assistance programs to courses that lead to degrees in a field related to the employee's work or occupation. Others do not restrict program selection. Expanding the knowledge and skill of employees can increase the supply of candidates for work that they are not currently doing, which assists in sourcing talent, as described in Chapter 3. But supporting education has a financial cost and may reduce the time the employee is on the job. And even if courses are scheduled outside work hours, they use up employee energy. Completing a two-year evening MBA program while working full-time made me aware of just how much studying on weekends and attending class after a full workday can drain the pool of energy one has available. Conversely, doing both resulted in me being able to apply what I was learning to what I was doing on the job and to apply work experience to my studies.

Organizations must realize that employees with young families also have additional demands on their time. So even though all expenses are reimbursed, the employee must contribute time and energy.

Online training/education programs are proliferating. They are developed and offered by educational institutions, professional societies, foundations and organizations themselves. Many "corporate universities" have developed catalogs of courses that are similar to those offered by traditional universities. Using intranet access, an organization can create career progression models that specify the credentials necessary to move from one job to another, and even from one occupation to another. The shortage of engineering and IT professionals has made it prudent to increase the qualifications of employees, particularly when they are competent to do work that supports technical professionals. The distinction between an engineer and an engineering technician is often related to education. Technicians may know a lot because they have experienced a lot, but they may lack the formal education that provides them with the conceptual knowledge necessary to address issues outside their specific experience. Dealing with issues that are unique requires the application of a conceptual understanding of principles.

There has been a dramatic increase in course offerings in coding, which has become a skill required in a broader range of occupations. Coding is an activity that is more like a skilled trades qualification than something requiring a technical degree. People trained to do coding are often candidates for expanding the variety and depth of their knowledge, which equips them to perform more complex work. But the different requirements for coding and designing software are so great that there is often a gap like the one between the Engineering Technicians and the Engineers.

Some knowledge and skills can be transferred from experienced people to "apprentices," and this can be accomplished in a variety of ways. Working side by side can enable transfer, as can having experienced people convey knowledge in formal training sessions. Developing "internal yellow pages" can provide people engaging in self-directed training with access to those competent to assist them when needed. Formal mentoring programs can also be used to assign responsibility to designated people for ensuring trainees learn what they need to learn. Re-defining the role of highly qualified people nearing retirement can provide a faculty for directing learning. Phasing into retirement has become increasingly popular and those going through that process may welcome part-time or full-time duty as trainers, mentors or coaches. The desire to share what one has accumulated during their career can provide the motivation to delay full retirement until one's tacit knowledge has been transmitted to successors.

Communities of practice are other sources of knowledge transfer and development. COPs are much like professional associations, since they connect people with common interests and capabilities. However, they tend to be less formal and may not even be known to organizations within which they exist. Silicon Valley is known for the "coding clubs" that bring together people from different organizations and have contributed to the increase in the supply of skilled people. People involve themselves for different reasons. Some are willing to share what they know to increase their reputation and their standing in the field. Others may believe that sharing can be a two-way street, and even though they may be a teacher one day they may become a student the next. Incubator facilities are being created to bring together people to share resources, knowledge, equipment and imagination, and many start-ups spent their early days utilizing them. Organizations may consider contributing some of their employee's time to this kind of activity, which can give them access to talent that might be candidates for future employment or utilization on project work. Supporting internal COPs is another way to disseminate knowledge and to identify capabilities in current employees.

Governmental support for occupational training in the United States has existed since the late 1940s. The amount of resources available has varied, based on the priorities of each administration. The U.S. Department of Labor publishes an occupational demand study annually that projects the growth or decline in a wide variety of occupations ten years in the future. Although projecting that far into the future with any accuracy is difficult the projections are updated each year by using continuous environmental scanning and information received about the national workforce. This information can be useful for organizations as well as national, state and local governments. Many local governments have provided support for incubator organizations that enable entrepreneurs to share resources that they might not have been able to afford on their own. This investment is generally aimed at improving the local economy by creating new businesses, but it also can upgrade the quality of the local workforce and attract business to establish operations there. I served on the board of Operation Able in Chicago, an organization that pooled federal, state and local funds to provide retraining to economically displaced workers and older workers requiring reskilling. This support enabled people to receive up to two years of training in skills and knowledge that increased their probability of gainful employment. Governmental assistance can be a valuable approach to retraining people rather than placing them in unemployment lines.

One type of qualification that is becoming increasingly required in many occupations is technical certifications. Cyber security is a field that relies on specific technical certifications to ensure people can do what is required. Not only are multiple certifications typically required at a given time, but new certifications are being created in response to new types of threats to security. To incumbents being qualified must seem like running full speed on a treadmill but only holding one's position. And not wanting to "go back to school" can destine someone to obsolescence. The rapid replacement of skills is not only a concern of the incumbents in the disciplines affected but also a critical concern for the organizations relying on them to do the work. The choice organizations must make is whether to support the acquisition of these certifications or to recruit people holding them. Since the demand far exceeds the supply in many technical professions investing in development rather than in recruitment may be the most effective strategy.

There are occupations that require licenses for people performing certain types of work. Surgeons must be Board-certified, attorneys must have passed the bar exams and many accountants need CPAs. But there are some licenses and certifications that only apply to members of an occupation who perform specific work. A professional engineer (PE) certification is required for those signing off on certain types of projects (e.g., bridge designs) and an organization may need at least one person in the unit holding that qualification, unless they choose to pay an outsider to do sign off on the project. It is common for organizations to require a PE for engineers who are promoted into roles that involve approvals. But it is important to determine whether formal certifications or licenses are required. Requiring qualifications when they are not a necessity can not only make recruitment and retention more challenging but will also raise the price of people holding them.

One example of addressing a skill shortage by reallocating work would be for an organization to relieve engineers of administrative responsibilities when they are directing projects and to assign this work to specialists in project administration. The Project Management Institute (pmi.org) has created several certifications in this area and educational institutions have developed programs to prepare people for the certification exams. The net effect is to reduce the required number of engineers, who are in short supply, by having the administrative work done by qualified people who are less expensive.

Figure 7.1 is an example of a career management structure for engineering that incorporates a third "ladder" for project administration. There may be opportunities to develop the skills and knowledge of these specialists by having them work side by side with engineers. They might also be good candidates for working towards a degree that would enable them to be future candidates for engineering roles.

Increasingly, organizations are viewing career models as lattices, rather than ladders. Horizontal or diagonal moves are viewed as both possible and beneficial when this perspective exists. But mobility across occupations and specialties generally is not feasible unless there is an investment in development.

Developmental assignments are a way to expand the capabilities of people. Temporary assignments can increase exposure to different types of work and different ways of doing things, as well as providing assignees with a broader understanding of the organization's business. If an employee is working in a unit that designs products time spent in the unit that has to actually make the product can not only increase one's understanding of the entire process from idea to shipping, but it may also help the person understand that how something is designed can impact the work of those who have to make it. Supporting a sales representative on a customer call may provide an understanding of how well the product design meets the needs of the customers. Sending an employee on an international assignment may broaden the person's understanding of what works in different contexts.

Concurrent development is an approach that does not require individuals to transfer from one unit to another. Instead, employees from design, production,

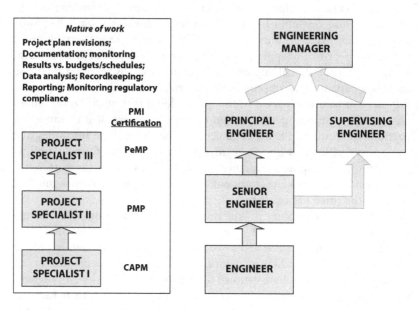

Figure 7.1 Engineering Career Management Structure.

sales and finance may be assigned to a product development team. This tends to minimize production finding a design is difficult to make and having to send the plans back for rework. It also can minimize the creation of products that potential customers find inadequate for meeting their needs. Filling warehouses with products that cannot be sold is not a path to success. Like any type of team those participating in concurrent development must possess competencies beyond their technical expertise in their own field. They must be able to handle conflict resolution and be capable of working towards a consensus. But the payback is providing employees with a wider and deeper understanding of what is required for success.

One of the most difficult types of career move to make is going from doing the work to managing the work. In organizations where going into management is perceived to be (and may be) the only way for employees to increase their compensation employees may attempt to make that transition even if they are not suited to the new role and do not really prefer it to what they have been doing as an individual contributor. Decades of experience consulting with national research laboratories has provided me with experiences where an exceptional scientist moves into a managerial role and becomes a mediocre or even poor manager.

Table 7.1 is a model that was used for leadership development in a research organization. It was based on a model created to help organizations define expectations for managers at all levels.[2] It illustrates the nature of managerial

Table 7.1 Exhibit 2: Leadership Practices Matrix: By Level

MANAGEMENT LEVELS: RESPONSIBILITY FOR FIVE LEADERSHIP PRACTICES

LEVEL	Inspire a Shared Vision	Model the Way	Challenge the Process	Enable Others to Act	Encourage the Heart
CEO/COO	Develop a vision for the lab's long-term future. Imagine new and exciting missions for the lab. Engage others through shared values and aspirations.	Define the core values that will serve the lab well over the long-term. Articulate the values and live them daily. Align and engage others to ensure everyone abides by the values	Seek innovative ways to change, grow and improve the lab, as well as to provide maximum value to the constituencies. Experiment/take risks in order to identify new directions and processes.	Strengthen the workforce of the lab by sharing power and discretion. Foster collaboration by promoting cooperative goals and by building trust.	Celebrate victories and those who create them. Recognize contributions of individuals and groups and create a community rich in social capital.
Vice President	Develop a mission for the division that is consistent with the lab's vision. Oversee the missions developed for units within the division to ensure they contribute to fulfilling the lab's mission.	Develop a strategy that fits the organization's values and ensure the division's values are integrated with the lab's core values. Live the values/engage others to behave in a manner supporting the values.	Seek innovative ways to change, grow and improve the division, as well as to provide maximum value to the constituencies. Experiment/take risks in order to identify new directions and processes within the Division and across the lab.	Strengthen the workforce managed by sharing power and discretion. Foster collaboration by promoting cooperative goals and by building trust.	Celebrate victories and those who create them. Recognize contributions of individuals and groups and create a community rich in social capital.

(Continued)

Table 7.1 Continued

| LEVEL | MANAGEMENT LEVELS: RESPONSIBILITY FOR FIVE LEADERSHIP PRACTICES | | | | |
	Inspire a Shared Vision	Model the Way	Challenge the Process	Enable Others to Act	Encourage the Heart
Director	Develop a mission for the center that aligns with the lab's mission and contributes to other units and the lab fulfilling their mission.	Develop a strategy that fits the organization's values and ensure the unit's values are integrated the lab's core values. Live the values/engage others to behave in a manner supporting the values.	Seek innovative ways to change, grow and improve the unit managed, as well as to provide maximum value to the constituencies. Experiment/take risks in order to identify new directions and processes within the unit and across the lab.	Strengthen the workforce managed by sharing power and discretion. Foster collaboration by promoting cooperative goals and by building trust.	Celebrate victories and those who create them. Recognize contributions of individuals and groups and create a community rich in social capital.
Level II Manager	Develop a mission for the departments/ subfunctions managed that aligns with the center's mission and contributes to other units and the lab fulfilling their mission	Develop a strategy that fits the organizational values and ensure the unit's values are integrated with those of the lab. Live the values and engage others to ensure they behave in a manner consistent with values.	Seek innovative ways to change, grow and improve the unit managed, as well as to provide maximum value to the constituencies. Experiment/take risks in order to identify new directions and processes within the unit and across the lab.	Strengthen the workforce managed by sharing power and discretion. Foster collaboration by promoting cooperative goals and by building trust.	Celebrate victories and those who create them. Recognize contributions of individuals and groups and create a community rich in social capital.

Manager	Develop a mission for the department/programs managed that aligns with the mission of the center, the division and the lab.	Develop a strategy that fits the organizational values and ensure the unit's values are integrated with those of the lab. Live the values and engage others to ensure they behave in a manner consistent with values.	Seek innovative ways to change, grow and improve the unit managed, as well as to provide maximum value to the constituencies. Experiment/take risks in order to identify new directions and processes within the unit and across the lab.	Strengthen the workforce managed by sharing power and discretion. Foster collaboration by promoting cooperative goals and by building trust.	Celebrate victories and those who create them. Recognize contributions of individuals and groups and create a community rich in social capital.

work other than command and control. There will typically be a limit on how much an individual contributor can earn compared to people in management roles. But in an organization like a national research laboratory where new knowledge is created individual contributor levels can be justified that provide significant career and compensation progression. A research fellow in an organization like this can often have a pay range that is equivalent to second or third level management positions, which lessens the pressure to transition into management by people who are better at individual contributor work. Forcing the best scientist into a management role can result in losing a great contributor and creating a poor manager.

International developmental assignments are used for several purposes. Some are designed to have headquarters personnel guide and train personnel in foreign operations. Others are used to broaden an employee's understanding of cultural differences across the globe. When one attempts to sell to diverse markets it is necessary to understand the beliefs and wants of potential customers. Managers dealing with a culturally diverse workforce need to have an understanding of what the differences are and how they impact the work. A manager might read about how Chinese workers tend to be more collectivist than U.S. workers and how they defer to authority, but the implications of those differences must be understood if that manager is going to be successful. In cultures in which hierarchy is respected, a manager who is used to brainstorming ideas with subordinates may find the silence deafening during the first attempt to engage them in debate. My own experience teaching in Indonesia taught me that students deferred to the "authority" at the podium and would not challenge what was said, even though they thought some of the material was not useful or even wrong. Having engaged in this frustrating experience made it clear that the research predicting deference to authority was sound. In some cultures, a manager is expected to have all the answers and to provide direction to others, even if the manager lacks sufficient knowledge or is unsure of how to act. An American manager who responds to a question with "I don't know ... let's figure it out" when working with people from a different culture is in danger of losing the subordinate's respect.

In order for a developmental assignment to be considered successful both the organization and the individual must believe it to be so. Often the perspective of the person is overlooked, and this can result in dissatisfaction on the part of the person. One of the biggest mistakes made on international assignments is that when an employee finishes the assignment it is considered successful. But the repatriated employee may evaluate the experience and believe that it did not advance his or her career and, in some cases, it may be thought to be a setback. Research has demonstrated that the weakest part of the international assignment process is repatriation.[3] In the United States, there is a significant amount of voluntary turnover within the first one to two years of return from completed international assignments. Much of that turnover is due to the perception that the person lost ground relative to peers who stayed home. Failure to adequately plan for repatriation can result in there being no job available that utilizes what the employee learned on the assignment. This deprives the organization of the learning that should be available from the returnee.

Even though training and development that will increase a person's capabilities are made available, the person must be willing to make the effort to take advantage of it. As mentioned earlier development generally comes with a cost to the individual, in the form of effort and time. Some are content to do what they are doing at the level they are doing it for the rest of their career. They might work to live, rather than living to work. Having a competent and stable cadre of workers enables an organization to operate effectively. But if there is a need to continuously expand and upgrade the knowledge and skills of the workforce the organization must sustain the viability of that workforce into the future. It is often necessary to offer inducements to employees to make the investment in development that go beyond threatening those with capabilities becoming of less value with the loss of their employment.

One of the inducements offered employees for extending the effort to increase the depth or breadth of their knowledge and skills is to offer financial rewards for doing so. Often called "skill-based pay" one approach is to tie base pay rates to what employees are capable of doing, rather than on the job they currently are doing. If a machine operator is more valuable when he or she is able to perform routine maintenance in addition to operating machines the organization may be willing to pay that person more once competence is demonstrated on the additional skills. As the employee's skill level in machine operation increases there may also be additional pay for increasing depth. Skilled trades personnel have traditionally been classified into ladders based on skill level (apprentice–journey–master). But when skill variety is increased it may make the person more valuable. Whether or not the additional cost to the organization by increasing pay levels is offset by the benefits of having more skilled employees must be determined. The additional cost would also include lost work time while training and the cost of training in addition to the increased pay level. This must be offset by increased operational efficiency that will result. Organizations that have used skill-based pay have generally found that average pay rates tend to increase, attributable to the financial motivation to expand one's skills. But having a multi-skilled workforce often enables staffing levels to be reduced, since employees are able to address variations in what needs to be done currently using their broader and deeper level of capabilities.

Conclusion

Developing talent is one way to deal with talent shortages. It is also a way to provide career opportunities to people, which may influence one's decision to join an organization, to contribute one's best efforts and to remain an employee. The decision to invest in development should be based on a cost-benefit analysis. There will be instances where it is more effective to replace current employees lacking the skills and knowledge that will be needed in the future. But there will also be instances when the costs of replacing current employees will exceed the benefits. The brand of an employer known for investing in employee development can result in attracting and retaining high-quality talent. There will also be instances when it is more effective to augment the current workforce with outside resources. If the rate at which the talent needs change outpaces the rate at which current employees can develop the newly required competence, there may be no choice but to outsource the work or retain outsiders to do the work.

Development can consist of training, education or reassignment and an organization needs to choose between the alternatives based on the short and long-term costs and benefits. As a larger share of employment in the United States is in smaller and startup organizations the large investment in education and training required may be out of reach of individual organizations. Doing it themselves, rather than relying on governmental agencies, may be a choice that organizations may prefer. But it may not be feasible. This can require local or national governments to invest in upgrading the capabilities of the citizenry.

Valuing its human capital will motivate an organization to place a high priority on investing appropriately in that capital. Treating talent as an asset rather than viewing it as a cost will increase the willingness to invest. Despite the fact that accepted accounting practice demands that training expenses be booked as a short-term cost, with no certain future benefits that would justify the costs, organizations must recognize that assets often require current investment to retain or even increase their value. Investment analysts have increasingly recognized such things as sound management, a competent workforce and appropriate talent management systems can be considered as assets, even though their value does not appear in financial statements. Developing talent can lead to that unique source of sustainable competitive advantage: a competent workforce committed to organizational success.

Notes

1 Kirkpatric, D. "Great Ideas Revisited." *Training and Development* 50, 1996.
2 Kouzes, J. & Pozner, B. *The Leadership Challenge* (Hoboken, NJ: Wiley, 2017).
3 Briscoe, D., Schuler, R., & Tarique, I. *International Human Resource Management* (New York: Routledge, 2012).

Chapter 8

Talent Management in the Public and Non-profit Sectors

It has been contended that there is little difference between private and public/ non-profit sector organizations, at least with regard to what constitutes sound talent management. Others believe they are two separate universes. There are many similarities in the strategies and programs commonly used in the two sectors to create workforces and manage them.[1] People have expectations that are shaped in the employment market and they seek many of the same employer attributes when job hunting. And all organizations want their employees to perform at high levels, however they define performance. But how exactly do private sector organizations' talent management practices fit non-profit and governmental organizations?

Comparing Organizational Contexts

Human resource practitioners should recognize that there are significant differences between the public and the private sector. Public sector organizations answer to different constituencies than do private sector organizations. In addition, elected officials impact how a public sector organization can pay its employees, accomplishing this through the budgeting process. Also, public sector organizations often make decisions based on political considerations, rather than on the impact to the organization or the ability to fund obligations in the future. The needs and the perceptions of the public may not be weighed appropriately when making decisions.

Organizations that operate in the public and non-profit sectors generally measure organizational effectiveness differently than do private-sector organizations. Many private sector organizations use profitability, growth, return on investment (ROI) and total shareholder return (TSR) as the only legitimate measures of their success. Shareholders often balk at letting non-financial measures, such as citizenship in the community, dilute the focus of management. Conversely, concerns about profit and TSR do not exist in the public/ non-profit organization and growth may or may not be considered a legitimate objective.

There may also be uncertainties in public sector entities about the financial resources that will be made available through the political process. This difference can have a profound impact on an organization's ability to fund programs on a long-term basis and to pay employees at fully competitive levels. Although it can be argued that the private sector is also full of financial uncertainties, there is at least some ability to fund current shortfalls through assuming debt or using discretion to reduce profits in order to ensure compensation levels remain adequate for attracting and retaining critical employees. Perhaps as an offset to that uncertainty, it is commonly believed that job security is greater in the public sector and that economic turbulence will not have profound effects on staffing levels.

Finally, the governance of the sectors is very different. Private sector organizations answer to boards or to owners if the organization is privately held. Boards are generally concerned about workforce costs only as they impact profitability ... that is, they are often willing to compensate employees generously if the financial performance of the organization seems to warrant premium rewards. Legislatures or city councils on the other hand must be sensitive to the opinions of taxpayers and voters. If these constituencies believe compensation costs are excessive, they will put pressure on those responsible for oversight, either through the media or the voting booth. Yet the employee benefits provided in the public sector are not limited by the same fiscal discipline that exists in the private sector. Pension liabilities and other benefits costs are not subject to the same accounting mandates, since unfunded pension liabilities can be made to seem smaller by making unrealistically high investment return assumptions (e.g., teacher pension funds assuming an 8% investment return when 2–3% is realistic for funds that are conservatively managed). This enables legislatures and councils to "kick the can down the road," leaving future regulators to worry about serious underfunding of plans with certain liabilities. It is largely due to this reality that has enabled public sector benefits to be significantly more generous than those existing in the private sector. The ability to attract and retain the required talent is certainly impacted by factors other than pay and both benefits and job security are considered by those desiring employment. There is also often a concern about whether performance expectations are reasonable. Whether or not it is valid, there is a widely held belief that less is expected of employees in the public sector.

As a result of the differences in the employment value propositions, there is a widespread belief that different types of people gravitate to the public and private sectors. Those seeking stable employment and generous benefits might be inclined to prefer the public sector compensation packages to those in the private sector. But the underlying preference for the public sector may also be due to a desire to do something meaningful that impacts the lives of others, rather than making anonymous investors wealthy. Too often stereotypes about public versus private sector employees lead people to make assumptions about what influences employment choices, given that there is little solid evidence to determine what considerations are given the most weight.

It is important to be aware of public opinion, since everyone funds the cost of public sector workforces through taxation, and the economic downturn that began in 2007 increased criticism of the "safe harbor" public sector employees are thought to have. In 2010 the *Economist* magazine reported that public sector employees are paid 17% more than private-sector employees if the actual time worked is considered ... and that the benefits in the public sector are 30% more generous than in the private sector. Taxpayers who believe the public sector employees they pay for are enjoying 47% more in total rewards than private-sector employees are certain to view this as unacceptable. The 47% does not have to be true, only believed to be so.

Public/non-profit organizations are increasingly adopting strategies that have historically been used in the private sector, principally to attempt to generate higher levels of performance and to better control workforce costs. The most recent economic crisis decimated the revenue sources in many cities, counties and states and the necessity to reconcile revenue-cost gaps put pressure on legislatures and councils to get the job done with fewer resources. But since most direct compensation is in the form of base pay and benefits, which are commitments, total compensation costs are difficult to adjust in response to swings in revenue, making downsizing the only way to cut costs during economic downturns. Yet downsizing can have detrimental effects, since public sector organizations must still provide services. And there are social and political factors that may result in a reluctance to reduce staff because of the impact on the economy of the community. In some countries there are laws that strictly limit staffing reductions and the costs associated with doing so can make even permitted headcount cuts uneconomical.

Organizational Differences and Performance Measures

There are differences in the occupations existing in the two sectors. Some employee groups, such as direct sales personnel, do not exist in the public/non-profit sector. Uniformed service (police and fire) occupations tend to be limited to the public sector. And some occupations have different functions between the two sectors, such as marketing, public relations and finance personnel. In addition, executives generally have a completely different set of performance criteria. Yet the balanced scorecard concept that is popular in the private sector has increasingly become accepted in governmental agencies as well. For example, the U.S. Department of Energy bases the fees of many of the contractors operating the national research laboratories on their "scores," using a balanced scorecard approach. Similarly, some non-profit organizations have adopted performance models that include multiple criteria.

The U.S. government has, for decades, used a step-rate system that advances employee base pay rates on a specified time schedule. This type of system is still common in state, county and city governments, but there has been movement towards using performance-based pay systems. Although the general schedule

(GS) system still exists for about half of the federal workforce, many agencies have found it to be ineffective in getting and keeping the workforce they need. As a result, they have exited the system by developing "excepted service" programs. These programs most commonly utilize open pay ranges, merit pay and performance management systems that differentiate based on contribution, and that look more like systems prevalent in the private sector. And the Office of Personnel Management has experimented with variable pay programs as well. These programs have not had widespread success, due in part to the difficulty in objectively measuring contribution and results. Many more state, county and city governments still utilize the time-based approach, as do quasi-governmental organizations. But that is changing in some types of public sector organizations. About one-third of water utilities still use step-rate systems, according to the American Water Works Association's annual Water Utility Compensation Survey. The trend, however, is moving away from basing rewards on longevity, evidenced by the fact that over two-thirds of the utilities used step systems ten years ago. But water utilities often operate with separate boards, since there is a strong argument for running a utility like a business, enabling them to employ different strategies than the counties and cities they serve.

Governmental and non-profit organizations may need to fully consider the implications of using private-sector talent management programs, since some practices could potentially have a socio-political impact. For example, if a governmental entity uses merit pay, an employee receiving a smaller increase than a peer often has seemingly endless appeal mechanisms that can be used to "wear down" managers who do differentiate based on performance. A common argument is that there are no clear, quantifiable metrics upon which to appraise performance, at least at an individual level, so differentiation is unwarranted. However, this is a weak argument. Subjective criteria are broadly used in private sector organizations to appraise performance and to make decisions about pay increases. But despite this reality, it has proven to be very difficult for many public sector organizations to move from time-based pay to performance-based pay and to adopt variable pay programs.

Unions are much more common in the U.S. public sector than in the private sector, and the existence of a union can have an impact on the employer's freedom to manage its people. Pay systems that use single-rate or step-rate approaches are often favored by unions, because they remove management from the individual pay determination process and ensure that the union can bargain for pay increases rather than allowing the employer to get the credit. Variable compensation plans are more difficult to implement for collective bargaining units party because the lack of hard metrics to use in determining the available rewards makes unions reluctant to accept this approach. Even performance management systems are often resisted by unions, due to a lack of trust in management to administer these systems fairly.

There is a belief in a significant number of non-profit organizations that employees "should not be in it for the money," given the charitable or noble mission of the organization. It is not clear if those who believe this have a plan for employees that would enable them to maintain a decent standard of living. A charitable/religious organization may find that employees are willing to work for less than they would in the private sector, but it is not clear whether hiring standards can be maintained at high levels if the compensation package is not competitive. Many non-profits rely heavily on volunteers to do much of the work and may still be able to pay selected occupations at reasonably competitive levels. For example, fundraisers are so critical to the typical non-profit that they may be given a direct compensation package that is competitive, although much of it is in the form of contingent results-based incentives. Since these entities can "do good" only if they "do well" on the fund-raising side, the risk of being criticized for paying fundraisers like sales personnel may be overcome by necessity.

As "reinvented" governmental agencies reshape themselves to look in many ways more like private sector organizations, it is reasonable to anticipate that their talent management strategies may also change. For example, city/county water utilities generally conformed to the pay system used by their parent organization up until a decade or so ago. However, many of them have realized that for-profit competitors are offering to operate the utilities on an outsourced basis and the pressure created by this new reality has increased the need to at least consider how the workforce can be made more productive and how to control people costs more effectively. The search for talent management strategies that could accomplish this may lead to more emphasis on performance-based compensation.

There has been an increased level of scrutiny in the benefits packages offered in the public sector, particularly by citizens who pay for them. Defined benefit pension plans have all but disappeared in the private sector, due to the difficulty in administering them in a manner consistent with the extensive and restrictive regulations that apply to them. Another problem is the future liability that accrues when pension plans are used. The private sector has largely replaced defined benefit plans with defined contribution plans, for a number of reasons. First, they can control the buildup of future liabilities for which they are responsible. Organizations are drastically modifying the way they do business in order to remain viable in the volatile competitive environment. Second, mobility of talent becomes more valuable as they change their focus. Having an employee join the organization right out of school and staying 30 years until retirement has become a very rare occurrence. This increasingly unlikely scenario has contributed to the use of pension plans, but changing realities make defined benefit plans a questionable practice.

Defined benefit pension plans are still prevalent in the public sector. And they have resulted in enormous unfunded liabilities being created, due to an unwillingness of legislatures and city/county boards to address how these liabilities will be funded in the future. It is surprising that citizens tolerate this lack of responsibility, but it is difficult to exert enough pressure politically to force change. The time off (vacation and sick leave) policies in the public sector are also much more generous than they are in the private sector, resulting in larger staffing levels and the subsequent costs.

Given the changing talent needs the supposed benefits of having public sector employees remain with an organization for their entire career may cease to be valid. Talent mobility has not only increased because people want a different type of career. It is also due to the temporal nature of demand for skills that have evolved due to changing technology. For example, IT personnel are valuable only when their knowledge and skills fit the current needs of the organization. The Y2K event illustrated that the qualifications of long service employees may be inadequate for upgrading technology. And unless workforce planning has been done well and there is adequate time to retrain existing employees the implementation of new technology may make past service of limited value.

One of the biggest obstacles to adopting strategies that are similar to private sector practices is culture. Employees may resist change, since what is being proposed is radically different than what they "signed up for" and what they have been accustomed to. People plan their lives based on what they expect will be their future reality, particularly when it comes to their income stream while working and in retirement. Pay that is suddenly contingent, rather than certain, can create anxiety. And it is more difficult for managers to do honest performance appraisals when they suddenly have significant economic consequences. Although convincing employees that the external realities make changes such as these mandatory in order to survive, the implementation may be difficult.

Boards, legislatures and councils must justify how much and how public sector workforces are compensated and whether staffing levels are warranted. The appropriate talent management strategies for public/non-profit sector organizations should be determined based on external and internal realities, culture and what the organization is charged with going forward. If the competition for critical skills escalates to the point that the entity is unable to get and keep the people necessary for continued viability, then change is no longer optional.

Talent management strategies may need to change in the public sector. Pay and benefits are not the only components of the employment relationship that require evaluation. The last three cohorts entering the employment arena have different expectations than the baby boomers cohort. Due to longer average service the public sector workforce has different age demographics than the private sector and this impacts the willingness of employees to accept radical restructuring of their conditions of employment just because the context has changed. So even though a different talent management philosophy might be needed translating that into strategies and programs will be likely to face considerable resistance. Laws limiting the ability of public sector organizations to "take back" anything given also can be impediments to implementing change. Whether talent management becomes more similar between the public and private sectors will depend on both the environment and the political priorities.

Note

1 Buford, J. & Lindner, J. *Human Resource Management in Local Government* (New York: Southwestern, 2002).

Chapter 9

Talent Strategies for Different Occupational Groups

Organizations have a variety of occupational groups in their workforce. They all have management personnel, technical and administrative professionals and technical and administrative support personnel. Some have direct sales personnel and others have international personnel. Employees working in teams often bridge occupations when each member is expected to be able to do anything that is required. Whether a single talent management strategy will be effective for all occupational groups is a question that each organization must answer.

Both the nature of the incumbents of each occupational group and the nature of the work performed by each group can vary widely. As noted in earlier chapters what an organization decides to do using employees and what it uses outsiders for will impact both the nature of the work and what type of people it requires. For example, the legal department may litigate cases in one organization, while another retains outside counsel for litigation. They will require different skill sets in their legal departments as a result. A national research laboratory will employ scientists with the most advanced knowledge while another organization may only need for its employees to apply research, outsourcing pure research that involves the creation of new knowledge. Apple creates new technology while other organizations use existing technology in their products. Again, this impacts the type of talent required by each organization.

This chapter will address the differences across occupational groups and explore the impact of those differences on the type of talent required and how that talent is managed.

Executives and Managers

There are unique characteristics of executive and managerial roles that should be considered when developing talent management strategies. Executives are the top decision makers that set the strategic direction of the organization, or a significant part of the organization, whether that part be a strategic business unit or a corporate function. The performance of executives is generally measured in terms of overall organization or business unit performance, and the measurement periods used tend to be longer range than they are for other employees.

Since executives are responsible for the strategic direction of an organization, as well as formulating policies, it is reasonable to define their performance in organization-wide terms. Certainly, the CEO and COO can legitimately be measured solely on overall organizational results. Top functional or business unit executives, the second tier of executive management, also tend to have their performance evaluation based at least partially on organizational performance, although functional or business unit performance is usually considered as well. Performance metrics such as profit, return on investment, return on equity, revenue growth, market share, economic value added and total shareholder return are commonly used in performance models used to evaluate and reward executives. These organization-wide measures are tangible and are routinely computed via the accounting systems.

In corporations and in most other private sector organizations the board of directors is directly responsible for establishing the criteria and standards used to select executives and to measure and reward their performance. The board is accountable principally to the shareholders and as a result is charged with determining what is reasonable from the perspective of the investors and the investment community. In the case of not-for-profit and public sector organizations the board represents the constituencies (e.g., the public, contributors or the government).

Since key executive positions usually have only one incumbent selecting, directing and evaluating executives can become, or at least appear to be, personal. For that reason, it is common for emotions to play a role in the governance process and for personalities and relationships to make the process contentious. Board members fear being criticized for being too generous by stakeholders but at the same time want to attract and retain the best available talent for the key positions. The human resource function, which is generally charged with designing and administering performance and rewards management systems, is often less involved in executive compensation than it is with compensation programs for other employees. When it is involved there is always a concern about neutrality, since the HR executive is accountable to top management. Selecting a new CEO or senior executive is directed by the Board, even though the members may not have training in human capital management.

In the book *Good To Great*, Collins reports on the extensive research into the impact of leadership on organizational effectiveness: "great organizations have level 5 leaders – individuals who have extreme personal humility, modesty and a ferocious hope and resolve to do whatever it takes to make a great company."[1] In order for an organization to effectively use its intellectual capital it must have adequate social capital. Since social capital is built on trust and requires that all constituencies believe there is equity in the organization it can be assumed that how executives are treated will significantly impact social capital.

The 1990s and the first two decades of the 21st century have been a tumultuous time for executive compensation in the United States. Since compensation is expressed in numerical terms it appears that objective assessment of compensation levels can be made. It is much more difficult to "objectively" measure the quality of leadershiip an executive provides and that person's ability to align the efforts of everyone. The media reports of accounting irregularities and executive compensation arrangements that seem out of touch with reality have created widespread public anger aimed at how executives comport themselves. Believing they were performing well and that they should be richly rewarded was easy for many executives throughout the ten years of uninterrupted prosperity the United States enjoyed during the 1990s. It was much like the post–World War II era (1945–1970), when American managers convinced themselves of their brilliance, forgetting that it is easy to compete when everyone else's factories have been destroyed and when demand is far in excess of supply. But the optimism of the 1990s, caused by the economic boom, resulted in the compensation gap between top management and the rest of the organization widening at an increasing rate.

As reported in *The New American Workplace*, CEOs of Fortune 100 companies earned about 39 times what the average worker in their organizations earned in the 1970s.[2] In 2000 the multiple had grown to about 400 times. The multiples existing today seem absurd to many when they are compared to any standard of fairness or to the typical gap existing in other countries. The 2008 financial system crisis caused a public outcry over the earnings of Wall Street managers and bankers, the very people who seemed to have created the crisis. Many of the financial institutions shown to be in poor condition had been rewarding executives handsomely, raising doubts about the system governing executive compensation. Since compensation is expressed in numbers it is easy to measure. And organizational performance can also be measured, at least partially, in numbers. If compensation is high and performance low stakeholders are bound to question the compensation. Even though an executive is wisely investing in the future well-being of the organization, and consequently is negatively impacting profits by investing in that future, judging that strategy is difficult and shareholders typically are focused on their short-term ROI.

When a few people are treated as if they alone make the organization successful it can create a culture that results in "everyone else" feeling underappreciated and under-rewarded. As more and more employees view the widening gap between executives and themselves as unwarranted the social tension has escalated. Employees through the prosperous 1990s wondered "If I do not benefit now, with all of this sustained prosperity, then when?" The most destructive fallout has been the erosion of trust and the increase in cynicism on the part of the parties with a stake in the well-being of organizations: employees, shareholders, customers, suppliers and the general public.

There are dramatically different perspectives about how much executives actually contribute to organizational success or failure. Different constituencies tend to believe their perspective is the appropriate one. Since in Western cultures there is a widespread belief that rewards should be based on contribuion to results compensation becomes the metric for determining relative "worth." If the other employees prosper, the investors receive above expected returns and the organization does not damage the environment or indulge in criminal or unethical behavior most people will accept that those who contribute the most to those results are performing well and should be well rewarded. In other countries the more collectivist cultural orientation leads to a belief that it takes everyone, not just a few, to do well. Comparing CEO – average employee multiples across countries makes it clear that in the United States there is a greater acceptance of the notion that the CEO significantly drives results.

As with the views about the real contribution made by executives there will also be different perspectives about how appropriate rewards should be determined. Executives compare their earnings primarily to those of other executives with similar roles in similar organizations. Graef Crystal, one of the most prominent executive compensation experts, has long suggested that these comparisons serve to escalate average levels if not carefully done and if not related to performance.[3]

It has become apparent that other employees have a different perspective when it comes to evaluating the executive pay levels of late. They often compare executive pay with their pay. It could be argued that this is a poor metric for determining equity, but emotion enters into these comparisons and both unions and the press have made the multiple of their pay the metric that is talked about. Employees who value working for an ethical organization that contributes to societal well-being may feel that a hard–edged capitalistic approach to doing business needs to be managed carefully. Making big profits by exploiting labor or by damaging the environment may be deemed unacceptable. And people are most inclined to follow leaders who seem to share their beliefs and values.

The degree of resentment among employees is greatly impacted by how they feel about their treatment by the organization. If they enjoy relatively competitive pay and benefit levels and have a reasonable amount of employment security the amount of angst they might feel when they see comparative data is apt to be lessened. When their organization is facing a crisis the executives are typically blamed for the situation, and as the confidence that their employment is secure wanes, the employees become even more critical. Like coaches of sports teams, executives tend to get too much credit for success and too much blame for poor performance.

The board is charged with selecting, directing, evaluating and rewarding executives. To minimize conflicts of interest in determining how executives are treated there must be a compensation committee in the United States, which is required to develop and articulate a management philosophy and to demonstrate that the programs they approved were consistent with that philosophy. And the committee members must be "outsiders," rather than company executives.

Investors may have a different perspective than either employees or the board. The people who provide the capital for publicly traded organizations are very diverse and are large in number if vested stakeholders in pension funds are included. As a result, their interests are varied and their perspectives relative to how executives should be treated are hard to characterize. Since most are not involved in the management of the organizations they own a piece of the prevailing viewpoint is typically focused on total shareholder return (dividends plus stock price appreciation). If the return is better than they believe they can get anywhere else at an equivalent level of risk they will tend to hold the stock. And since they are also free to divest themselves if they believe otherwise, there is less pressure for them to complain about pay levels.

Most investor interests are represented by professionally managed funds, and individuals may not even know which companies they own stock in. Some institutional investors have holdings that are so large that they prefer to take concerted action rather than sell stock. They press on issues relating to corporate governance and "suggest" guidelines to be followed if an organization wants them to purchase and hold their stock. Those guidelines are dominated by the theme of paying only for performance and limiting the conditions under which stock programs operate. But issues such as divesting operations or growing through acquisition are considered by large investors to be things they have a right to have an opinion on, so executive decision-making may not be something done by a one-person edict.

It is predictable that each constituency believes the perspective it holds is correct. Given the multiple parties at interest and the diversity in their perspectives about executive performance and the treatment of executives it is difficult to decide who reconciles them and how. Members of the key board committees are typically conversant in the business issues but not highly skilled in the technical aspects of executive selection, evaluation and compensation. Many boards retain outside advisors to provide that expertise, but any such consultant will lack the benefit of working within the organization and knowing its context intimately. HR may be viewed as biased, given that the CEO and other senior executives outrank the top HR executive and make decisions impacting the employment and compensation of that executive. Still, it is critical that HR demonstrate its ability to consider all perspectives and to advise the board on how the differences can be reconciled.

The strategies for selecting, directing and evaluating other management personnel should be appropriately integrated with the strategies used for executives. Since directors, managers and supervisors make up the cohort that may produce the future executives, organizations should ensure that career management structures and the rewards associated with each level are in proper relationship to each other. And investments in management development can be critical in determining if there is a solid "bench" equipped with replacements for departing executives. Designing the management structure is a critical step in making effective management possible. If there are too many levels in the reporting structure, defining responsibilities for purposes of measuring performance becomes difficult. In addition, compensation levels will be compressed relative to each other, diminishing the attractiveness of assuming higher levels of responsibility. If there are too few levels, the compensation potential may be adequate but the jump from one level to another may be too large, resulting in under-qualified personnel filling key slots.

Another issue is the span of control associated with any structure. The author worked with a national research laboratory that had "flattened" its structure, leaving vice presidents with 15 or more directors reporting to them, making it difficult for those directing major programs to see their VP within a reasonable time. This created practical difficulties related to communication, but also made it difficult for a VP to do a credible performance assessment of that many people – and, in fact, even know how well each of them was doing. But "flat is better" as a concept has its limits, although the management literature has been dominated by recommendations to move in this direction. Having too few levels can make moving up the "pyramid" harder, since more people are competing for fewer slots.

A major issue is defining performance at each management level. As mentioned earlier, senior executives are typically measured based on overall organization performance, while functional and business unit heads may be measured based on a mixture of organizational and business or function/business unit performance. At the lower levels of management, employees may feel they have less control over organizational performance and more over their unit's performance, as well as their individual performance. As a result, they may be measured using organizational, unit and individual measures, with the balance between them moving from organization-wide to unit and then to individual from the top to the lower levels.

How performance is defined can of course vary across individuals at the same level. For example, a business unit that operates independently may evaluate managers based largely or totally on unit performance, while another that is highly interdependent with other parts of the overall organization may base a significant amount of the performance rating on overall organization performance. Too many organizations fail to create an overall performance model and define in advance the level(s) at which performance will be measured and rewarded for all types of managers.

A necessary prerequisite for deciding on what constitutes performance is the clear definition of the responsibilities of managers. Table 9.1 is an example of how the expectations for incumbents at each level are defined in a large organization, as well as the impact they may have in that capacity. Having management levels defined is useful for defining performance expectations and communicating to managers the changing role requirements as one advances through the levels. There is a need to define levels in such a way that they fit the individual organization and emulating other organizations should be done carefully, since the nature of the organization, its culture and its strategy will determine what kind of structure is ideal for it. An organization whose prime concern is reliability and safety, such as a utility, may justifiably have more

Table 9.1 Management Career Model

| | OPERATING RESPONSIBILITY
Responsibility for decisions affecting operations and impacting success in meeting mission/objectives. | FUNCTIONAL RESPONSIBILITY
Responsibility for creating and managing the organizations infrastructure, i.e., people, functional processes and systems. | ORGANIZATIONAL RELATIONSHIPS
Responsibility for integrating work of organizational units and for managing interfaces with entities outside the organization. | POTENTIAL IMPACT ON ORGANIZATION
The scope and magnitude of impact of decisions on the performance of organization and its constituent units. |
|---|---|---|---|---|
| Vice President/ Top Functional Executive Provides Leadership and Direction to a Laboratory Division | Responsible for developing a mission and long-range objectives for a major division/function that are aligned with and support meeting the laboratory's objectives. Scan the environment and ensure trends that may impact the lab and the division are identified and that scenarios are developed to respond to change. Create strategies and structures that facilitate meeting objectives and changing environmental conditions. Accountable for ensuring that the core capabilities of the division remain viable and that the performance of the division/ function contributes to the success of the laboratory. | Responsible for organizing, selecting, developing, and directing division/function staff. Ensure division/function and constituent units integrate their strategies, tactical plans, and policies. Ensure the human resource management philosophy is adhered to and develop divisional/ functional policies to ensure employees are fairly treated and effectively utilized. Monitor adherence to core laboratory values and direct the continuous evaluation and refinement of these values and of the laboratory's s culture. Anticipate future staffing/functional process needs. | Represent the division/function and the laboratory to outside entities. Coordinate division/function activities with the rest of the laboratory to ensure integration. Oversee the development of programs and manage the interface with existing sponsors/stakeholders and represent the division and the laboratory to potential customers, sponsors and stakeholders. Direct negotiation with customers and stakeholders to produce agreements that fit the lab's mission and meets customer/stakeholder objectives. Develop new sources of revenue as appropriate. Serve on internal and external advisory groups that may impact the future of the lab and its work. | Has a direct and significant impact on the short and long-range performance of the division/SMU/ laboratory and direct and significant impact on laboratory's reputation among customers, sponsors and stakeholders. |

Director **(equiv to** **SIRS Level** **4 Mgmt)** **(equiv to** **Generally** **provides** **leadership** **and** **direction to** **a Division** **Center**	Develop strategy, structure, and operating plans for a center that significantly impacts /division/ SMU/laboratory performance. Responsible for the long-term performance of the center and for integrating its operations with the rest of the division/SMU/laboratory.	Responsible for organizing, staffing, and directing the staff of the unit. Ensure the center's human resource management philosophy and divisional policies are adhered to and directly manages performance of management team. Anticipate future staffing/functional process needs.	Represent center to outside entities as appropriate. Coordinate center activities with the rest of the division/SMU/laboratory and ensure their integration. Oversee the development of programs and manage the interface with customers sponsors and stakeholders. Develop new sources of revenue as appropriate. Participate in negotiating agreements with customers and stakeholders in establishing mutual goals. Responsible for ensuring customer and stakeholder needs are met. May serve on internal and external advisory groups that may impact the future of the lab and its work.	Center performance has a direct and significant impact on organization's reputation among customers, sponsors and stakeholders, as well as significantly impacting the performance of the division/SMU/laboratory.

(Continued)

Table 9.1 Continued

Management Level Chart

	OPERATING RESPONSIBILITY *Responsibility for decisions affecting operations and impacting success in meeting mission/objectives.*	FUNCTIONAL RESPONSIBILITY *Responsibility for creating and managing the infrastructure, i.e., people, functional processes and systems.*	ORGANIZATIONAL RELATIONSHIPS *Responsibility for integrating work of organizational units and for managing interfaces with entities outside the organization.*	POTENTIAL IMPACT ON ORGANIZATION *The scope and magnitude of impact of decisions on the performance of organization and its constituent units.*
Group Manager **Generally provides leadership and direction to several departments**	Manage multiple departments encompassing a broad scope and significant variety/ complexity or directs major programs/ projects. Ensure department operating plans are integrated with function/ center/division/SMU/ laboratory operating and strategic plans. Participate in formulating function/ center/division/SMU/ laboratory policies and strategy.	Responsible for organizing, selecting, developing and directing subordinate staff, or directing program/project staff. Assist subordinate managers with development of their subordinates. Works with direct reports to project future staffing and functional process needs.	Represent departments with outside entities as appropriate. Ensure the integration of departments managed with those of the center/division/ SMU/laboratory. Lead and/or participate in cross-functional teams to facilitate integration. Participate in negotiations with customers and stakeholders in establishing mutual goals. Accountable for meeting customer and stakeholder needs. May lead or develop others to identify new funding opportunities and/or direct program development activities.	Performance of departments managed has direct and significant impact on the unit's reputation among customers, sponsors and, other stakeholders as well as impacting the financial and operational performance of the function/center/division/ SMU/laboratory.

Department Manager *Generally provides leadership and direction to a Department*	Develop operating plans and strategies for organizational unit managed that integrate into an overall center/division/SMU/laboratory operating plan. Organize to effectively and efficiently utilize department/center/division/SMU/laboratory resources to optimize performance goals. Manage the organization's operations.	Responsible for organizing, selecting, developing, leading, identifying, coaching, mentoring and directing subordinate staff and managing their performance through a variety of mechanisms. Project future staffing needs for a viable workforce. Project future functional process needs.	Represent department to outside entities as appropriate. Ensure that organization activities are integrated with those of other departments/center/division/SMU/laboratory and that customer and stakeholder needs are met. Manage customer and stakeholder relationships and resolve conflicts by optimally allocating available resources. May identify new funding opportunities and/or engage in program development.	Department/unit performance has direct and significant impact on department's reputation among customers, sponsors and other stakeholders, as well as impacting the financial and operational performance of the function/center/division/SMU/laboratory

(Continued)

Table 9.1 Continued

	OPERATING RESPONSIBILITY *Responsibility for decisions affecting operations and impacting success in meeting mission/objectives.*	FUNCTIONAL RESPONSIBILITY *Responsibility for creating and managing the infrastructure, i.e., people, functional processes and systems.*	ORGANIZATIONAL RELATIONSHIPS *Responsibility for integrating work of organizational units and for managing interfaces with entities outside the organization.*	POTENTIAL IMPACT ON ORGANIZATION *The scope and magnitude of impact of decisions on the performance of organization and its constituent units.*
Supervisor **(equiv to SIRS** **Provides** **leadership and** **direction to a** **team of employees**	Organize section and manage day-to-day operations. Monitor performance against established goals, taking corrective action as needed. Responsible for meeting established unit budgets and plans.	Responsible for organizing, selecting, developing and directing subordinate staff (typically exempt and nonexempt) and managing their performance. Perform human resource activities for staff (e.g., appraisal, discipline, career planning, etc.)	Represent section on routine matters or specific program/project phases to outside entities as required. Coordinate unit activities with rest of the organization.	Section performance is measured in terms of meeting schedules, operating within budget and meeting established goals. Section performance significantly impacts the performance of the department and may impact other departments and the center or division.
Team Leader/ **Supervisor** **Provides leadership** **and direction to a** **team of employees**	Organize section and supervise daily activities. Perform tasks related to unit work as required or in training staff.	Provide direct supervision to primarily nonexempt staff. Perform human resource management activities for staff (e.g., appraisal, discipline, career planning, etc.)	Coordinate section activities with rest of the organization.	Section performance is measured in terms of meeting schedules, operating within budget and meeting established goals. Unit performance impacts the performance of the department and may impact other departments and the Center.

levels of management, to ensure all decisions are subject to adequate review. A software design firm might have very few reporting levels, using multiple project teams extensively. What works is what fits. The structure certainly should also impact how performance at each level is defined and measured. The structure should also impact how performance is rewarded. It will also influence the characteristics of good-fit candidates.

Culture also has a major role in defining responsibilities for all types and levels of management personnel. In a national laboratory, managers may be expected to be thought leaders, operating at the leading edge of technical competence. In a utility, managers may be expected to manage the work processes and the people, ensuring they operate within established policy. A software design firm may have varying expectations, depending on what a manager is expected to manage (e.g., creating new technology or keeping the books).

There are significant differences across national cultures, relative to the role of managers. These differences have had a major impact on organizations operating globally. In some cultures, the manager is expected to know the answer to any question asked by a subordinate, while in others it is permissible for the manager to admit they need to find the answer, or even to ask the subordinate to research the issue and make recommendations.

Leadership is a topic with a huge literature and is generally accepted to be a part of a manager's responsibility. Every year brings numerous offerings that suggest the ideal style is X (e.g., emulate Attila the Hun), accompanied on the bookstore shelves by other authors suggesting it is Y (e.g., become more like St. Anthony). The concept that the best leadership style depends on the organizational and environmental context is widely accepted. Globalization has complicated the search for the appropriate leadership styles. Trompenaars, in *Twenty-One Leaders for the Twenty-First Century*, presented structured analyses of CEOs who succeeded in very different operational, economic and cultural contexts.[4] Rather than merely telling stories he used a cross-cultural framework developed in earlier research, which provided insights into why a particular style worked well in a specific context. Although difficult to do, each organization must decide how much and what kind of leadership its managers should exhibit and how this aspect of their role will be evaluated when judging their performance.

The GLOBE project was a very large research project examining which leadership styles seem to best fit specific types of cultures.[5] The national and regional cultures defined in the GLOBE study are matched to leadership styles that work well or poorly in each. Research such as this must be used cautiously, however, because national and regional cultures are difficult to define in global organizations where expatriates, inpatriates, local nationals and third-country nationals are mixed into their managerial cadres in all of their locations. But the research at least alerts organizations to the issues raised by cultural diversity. Trompenaars has put forth his "3 Rs" to address culture: *recognize* when cultural differences exist, *respect* people's rights to hold different beliefs and to have different values and *reconcile* the issues that are raised by the cultural differences.[6]

Leadership will almost certainly be a part of the definition of managerial performance. But it is much more challenging to measure objectively than hard financial metrics, so organizations struggle with using leadership effectiveness as a driver of rewards.

Management personnel are a critical part of any organization's workforce. The effectiveness of management personnel will almost certainly have a major impact on organizational performance in the short run and its viability in the long run.

Professionals

There has been a rapid increase in the number of employees who are called "professionals" over the last several decades, owing in large part to the transition to a knowledge-based society. Included in this category are scientists and engineers and a broad range of formally trained specialists in finance, information systems, legal, marketing and human resources. This evolution raises questions about the continued appropriateness and effectiveness of the talent management strategies most commonly used for professionals.

Professionals rely on their mastery of a defined body of knowledge in a particular field and require extensive formal education and/or training in that field. There are a number of characteristics of professional personnel that may warrant different human resource management strategies than those used for other personnel:

1. *They perform knowledge-intensive work.* Because of the technical nature of the work it is necessary for incumbents to have deep levels of understanding of concepts, theories and principles, rather than relying on general knowledge. Few would retain a surgeon not possessing board certification, and most construction firms would be reluctant to have a bridge designed by a self-taught person lacking the necessary education and required licensing in civil engineering. The formal education and training required often mean these people do not enter their field until they have demonstrated their mastery of the fundamental theories and concepts underlying practice.

2. *They often work relatively interdependently.* A professional in a specific discipline may be the only one with knowledge of that discipline. But since professionals often have highly specialized knowledge they often need practitioners from related fields to support them when facing complex, interdisciplinary challenges. For example, if creating a new ethical drug requires an advanced level of knowledge in chemistry, biology, statistics, IT, pharmacology and patent law, no one is likely to possess all of the necessary knowledge to independently produce the desired result. Consequently, cross-disciplinary project teams are the accepted way to organize work involving these requirements. Technical failures are often caused by people with a specialized discipline who act as if they were

islands unto themselves and who operate under their own set of rules, without regard to the impact on others and/or without counseling others with knowledge that is needed.

3. *Their work is predominantly project-oriented.* Engineers and systems analysts rarely have traditional "jobs," consisting of a stable set of specific tasks. Rather, they move from project to project, changing roles frequently. This reality often results in them being classified through the use of occupational career ladders. Their work may also be performed on cycles that often do not coincide with the administrative schedules that are used for appraising performance.

4. *Their orientation tends to be towards producing the very best, rather than what is good enough.* Any organization employing scientists will be familiar with the tendency of their people to want to achieve the very best (drug, system, idea), irrespective of developmental costs and the actual requirements. This largely results from the nature of their education and their professional pride. It also is the product of the need to work with the newest and best technology, in order to keep their knowledge and skills current and marketable. This tendency is often in conflict with the organizational standard, which is "good enough." The different perspectives make it difficult to keep the very best professionals satisfied with the way they are expected to function, how their performance is measured and how they are rewarded, particularly when resources are scarce.

5. *Their orientation is to progressing within their field.* When someone has invested 16–20 years in formal education to learn the body of knowledge in their field it is natural that they will be focused on that field, rather than on their current employer. This is particularly true in today's "free agent" market, where professionals are expected to be mobile. Professionals also rely on others in their field to keep them up to date, and therefore their networks often extend outside their employing organization. This may result in a focus on becoming a better professional, rather than rising through the ranks in the organization currently employing them.

   Professionals also tend to recognize authority based on expertise, rather than who has the highest position in the management hierarchy or an impressive title. This can create challenges relative to organizing and managing units consisting of professional personnel. With the increased use of freelancers, contractors and people screened through talent platforms their options for making a living have broadened outside traditional employment with a single employer. This means the organization must recognize the ability of those with scarce talent to augment their job with outside work or to request an alteration to their current status with the organization.

The first step toward deciding how an organization manages professionals is to define the roles played by incumbents of a particular occupation or function and to value them from the organization's perspective. Engineering personnel are a good example for illustrating the decision process. The role of engineers is most often that of working on projects, usually as a member of a team. They enter their field after an extended period of formal education and they tend to remain oriented to their profession, since it is more likely they will work for other organizations as engineers rather than working for their current organization outside of their field. Given the long duration of study required to become an engineer they may not aspire to retrain or to go into general management roles, although they certainly might choose to pursue engineering management roles.

Since most engineers are project-oriented, rather than having a specific set of duties they are often classified into occupational ladders, which has been discussed in an earlier chapter. Given the competitiveness in the labor markets for many professional disciplines, organizations are forced to classify them and to pay incumbents based on their attained level of expertise, rather than what they happen to be doing at a given point in time. Professionals should be progressed through the levels in the ladder as they grow in knowledge, skill and the ability to take on more responsibility for producing results. Their classification should be based on what they are capable of, rather than what they are currently doing. Movement from one level to another within the ladder is viewed by professionals as being just as much a promotion as it would be if they were to become a supervisor, and for many a preferred form of progress.

The process used to regulate the movement of professionals through a technical ladder is critical in determining how appropriately people are advanced. Although level criteria help to classify individuals, the process used must be viewed as appropriate and equitable by incumbents. If each of the direct supervisors makes decisions about progressions for their people there is a danger of uneven application of the standards. Some managers may be more aggressive in moving their people up than others, either because they interpret the standards differently or because they feel they must be advocates for their subordinates. On the other hand, it can be argued that attempting to control progressions on a centralized basis may result in decisions being made by people not intimately familiar with the qualifications of individuals.

A balance must be struck, and most organizations do so by having the supervisor make the original recommendation, supported by formal documentation, and then having a higher-level review of the nominations for consistency across supervisors. As the number of people in the function becomes large this balancing act becomes very difficult and often requires review by a panel of professionals representing a cross-section of the population. Progression into the highest levels in the ladder may also require the participation of experts from outside the organization, particularly if the candidate possesses knowledge that is beyond that possessed by anyone else in the organization. Senior members of university faculties and experts from other organizations or professional associations often are used as resources when a person's work involves the discovery of new knowledge.

A similar approach is increasingly being used for administrative profession-als. Career management models are often used to progress people. They are often supplemented by occupational definitions that define the specific fields in which incumbents are trained. For example, there might be separate models for finance, legal, HR, procurement and logistics management, even though the criteria used to define each level are similar. An advantage of having a common method for defining levels within ladders is that it sends the message of equiva-lent treatment, since progression is related to common standards. An advantage of having occupational disciplines defined and treated differently relative to compensation is that each occupation can be separately measured against com-pensation levels prevailing in the relevant labor markets and pay ranges can be set at competitive levels, differing across occupations as appropriate.

It is critical to recognize that the career model serves as a way for organiza-tions to administratively celebrate the growth of professionals in their field. By providing standards that act as score-keeping metrics the organization conveys the criteria and standards that will be used to recognize career progression. When an associate engineer is "promoted" to engineer it does not mean the person was radically transformed on the effective date of the progression. The reclassification is an administrative acknowledgement that the person better fits the standards for the higher level – a reality that emerged gradually over time. It is important for the organization always to remember that career progressions are for many professionals the only tangible evidence that they have grown in their field. Many professionals start their careers classified as accountants or systems analysts or engineers and end their careers in the same category, albeit more capable than when they started. Failure to recognize growth in compe-tence exposes the organization to losing valued talent to competitors who are more attentive to acknowledging the capabilities of professionals.

A confidential benchmark study conducted by a U.S. national research labo-ratory found that premier research organizations typically used formal ladders that had from three to six levels of expertise defined. Many of these organiza-tions considered it acceptable to have professionals peak at levels one to two levels below the top level. In other words, ending one's 30-year career as a sen-ior engineer did not constitute a failure, even though there were levels above senior in the ladder. In fact, moving someone to the highest levels based only on longevity is often considered an administrative failure, since it dilutes the meaning of the achievement to those who warranted the classification based on their capabilities and their contributions.

Another consideration in defining the roles of professionals is whether "competencies" will be used for purposes of selection, classification and career progression. Competencies were a popular topic in the HR literature in the mid- and late 1990s, and the notion of "competency-based pay" was proposed by many of the consultancies, particularly for professionals whose roles did not consist of well-defined duties and responsibilities. But competency models are more useful for selection and career management than for performance and rewards management, since defining potential as performance and paying for it may leave the organization without the results that would warrant rewards. What the resurgence of competency-based strategies did accomplish is that it recognized behaviors as being important things to define and measure. As many professionals operate in a service capacity, responding to customer or user needs, *how* they perform their work is important. The focus on behaviors also acknowledged that professionals often cannot control outcomes and therefore their performance should be measured using criteria that they can control: how appropriately they behaved, given the circumstances.

There is a tendency on the part of many managers of professional or technical work to employ the very best people available, even though their qualifications may exceed the nature of the work. This temptation becomes great during economic slowdowns, when the supply of people exceeds the demand. But people overqualified for their roles will become bored and anxious that their knowledge is not keeping up with the state of the art. Throughout the 1990s IT personnel were very focused on keeping their skills marketable, since the movement from mainframe systems to network-based technology was rapid, partly owing to the pressure put on by the impending requirement for Y2K compatibility. Those asked to keep the legacy systems running felt left out of the mainstream and were concerned that they would be less valuable when the new technology was in place. And it was also expensive to maintain a highly qualified workforce, particularly since they were mobile and oriented to their field. The organizations found that they had to pay them their market worth in order to keep them, and the high costs often impacted the competitiveness of the business. Developing qualification standards based on the nature of the work performed and staffing the technical functions with the appropriate mix of expertise are challenges that must be met.

A critical issue related to both role definition and career management is the definition of managerial roles within professional and technical functions and how managers are compensated relative to the people they manage. From a career management perspective the best tool for providing opportunity is a "dual ladder." The objective of a dual ladder is to provide a choice to incumbents of technical positions as to whether their career growth should be through technical progression or through the assumption of managerial responsibility. The best path will depend on the individual in each case, since eventual satisfaction will depend on whether the role the person plays is consistent with their competencies and with their preferences.

Again using engineers as an example, the new entrant to the field would typically start as an individual contributor at the associate level. That person would then progress through the engineer and senior engineer levels. At some point the person may experience a fork in the road: continue to specialize in the technical aspects of the work or begin to assume managerial responsibility. This decision should not be final and irrevocable. And Yogi Berra's advice ("When you come to a fork in the road, take it") might not be nonsense. An incumbent who decides to pursue management roles does not stop learning or stop being an engineer. Effectively managing professional or technical personnel requires substantial expertise in the field. To repeat an earlier point, real authority often follows expertise, rather than formal rank. So those aspiring to managerial roles find themselves with a wide variety of competencies to develop. And those making a choice of direction might also consider retaining the skills necessary to change paths if circumstances or preferences change in the future.

Not all professional or technical personnel are well suited to management. Promoting the best systems analyst to supervisor based on their technical performance can result in the wrong person managing projects or units. Some of the competencies differ between the two orientations, and a professional who both likes and is good at working alone to develop ideas and solve problems is a questionable candidate for management. It may also be a waste to put a brilliant technical person into a managerial role, particularly if the administrative work takes them away from what they do best. And the standards that a Nobel Prize candidate would use to judge subordinates might be totally unrealistic, thereby making them a questionable choice to do performance appraisals.

The career management strategy should incorporate principles relating to movement between the technical and managerial branches of the ladder, to ensure that choices are not irrevocable. People change their aspirations over time and sometimes discover they are limiting themselves by sticking to an earlier choice. A financial analyst may realize that they will never be able to operate effectively at the highest level of technical expertise and that management is not as bad as it seemed earlier. By providing reasonable flexibility relative to horizontal movement the organization can maximize the effectiveness and satisfaction of a valued employee. Career ladders can be replaced by career lattices. On the other hand the ability to change classifications should be limited by the person's ability to operate effectively in the other capacity. Too many organizations have disillusioned senior technical people by placing failed managers in a technical level they do not warrant just so their pay can be kept at the current level. As mentioned earlier, professionals view the prestige associated with being classified in a level based on who populates that level.

Research-focused organizations employ significant numbers of people expected to create new knowledge and to generate technical innovations. These people can be candidates for an extended technical ladder. It is not unusual for a technical level to be accorded similar status to a vice president or director, to whom they report administratively. This would mean that veteran technical personnel could be paid more than the person they report to, which in some corporate cultures would be heresy. However, the direct report manager may be incapable of supervising the actual work of a person at that level of technical expertise. The reality is that the manager is only responsible for the person administratively. As previously discussed organizations are recognizing the need for an occupation that includes project administration professionals.

This can add a third ladder to the career model and provide a role for those who have competencies that fit such a role but do not fit the line management role.

Defining and evaluating performance is often a challenge when professional personnel are concerned. The metrics that are appropriate to use to define performance may be qualitative in nature, and evaluating performance often requires a subjective judgment by another technical person. A quip about doing performance appraisals for scientists performing pure research in a leading R&D institution was heard recently: "What do we measure – ergs of original thought?" Another familiar refrain is "My people do creative work and you cannot measure that." A manager of technical personnel may dread making performance judgments based solely on how intently their people stare into space for extended periods when they are attacking problems that may be insoluble. But such instances are the exception. Subjective assessments can be acceptable criteria for appraising performance, as long as the method and process used are appropriate and all parties understand and accept the basis for appraisal and who does the appraisal.

Performance is defined by establishing criteria and standards. The criteria that will be relevant to the professional tend to include the standard productivity, quality and dependability dimensions, but since so many incumbents work on projects rather than performing recurring duties the definition of performance needs to be tailored to their work. Cross-functional work teams are being used increasingly to develop new products and to create new technologies.

An example would be a software design firm, where software engineers contribute by providing the design expertise, finance professionals by providing economic analysis and marketing professionals by creating the strategy for going to market. This type of design process presents two challenges relative to appraising performance at the individual level. Since it takes everyone involved to produce the result it makes better sense to measure performance at the team level, since relative contribution by individuals is hard to measure. The second challenge is that project work may be tied to project milestones, and the time-frames will almost certainly not coincide with the annual administrative cycle prevalent in most organizations. It is difficult for a manager to evaluate the performance of a systems engineer who is 5 months into a 14-month project segment. This raises the question of whether it is better to do the best appraisal possible at the end of the year or to appraise when results are clear, whenever that falls relative to the annual cycle.

It is of course possible to prorate the salary adjustment for someone who has to wait for more than 12 months until a project milestone is reached. There is no natural law that says everyone must have a performance appraisal and a salary adjustment every 12 months. Yet if performance appraisal is a continuous process, rather than a once-a-year event, appraising a professional at year-end should be possible. Most organizations appraise performance and determine pay actions on a single (focal) date, and they tend to do this for all personnel. If this approach is used for professionals focused on project work it is critical that some provision for periodic, if not continuous, performance measurement and feedback be built into the performance management system. Some organizations have separated personal performance from project performance and tie salary actions to the former and project incentives to the latter, which helps to reconcile the timing dilemma.

Another consideration relative to the performance of a professional is who should have input into the appraisal process. The professional's manager may have a narrow view of that person's performance, since it is not unusual for work to be performed for several project managers, out of sight of the manager having administrative responsibility for the person. This type of working arrangement argues for multi-party input to the appraisal, which can provide the manager ultimately responsible for doing the appraisal with a broader perspective. Project managers, peers, support staff and even customers may have differing perspectives about a professional's performance. But it is the responsibility of the appraising manager to decide whose views should legitimately be considered and to take them into account when doing the appraisal. It is advisable to ensure project managers are responsible for providing formal written feedback on the performance of each of the staff members to the direct report manager when the staff members' work is complete. Otherwise, it may be difficult for the direct report manager to get reliable input at a later date, since the passage of time blurs memory. The direct report manager can then create a performance "diary" that can be used when the formal administrative appraisal is conducted.

It is conceivable that professionals will be appraised on both their individual performance and their contribution to a team or unit. It is also possible that they will be appraised on a timetable that fits the cycle of their work, as opposed to an annual administrative cycle. And although the direct supervisor will be responsible for the performance appraisal it may be based on multiple perspectives to appropriately reflect the consensus of relevant parties about the person's performance.

Although professionals are oriented to their profession and place high value on both interesting, challenging work and career progression they will almost certainly want some money as well. Although there are those who argue that extrinsic rewards might destroy intrinsic motivation, there is no credible research evidence to support this contention.[7] Few professionals are independently wealthy, so compensation is a necessity. Since professionals are inclined to keep score, they will be likely to use their grade level and their salary as metrics for determining how they are doing and how the organization values them.

It is important that the salary potential (salary range) for a professional be both internally equitable and externally competitive. The career ladders discussed earlier can be used to establish and maintain internal equity. Job evaluation plans can also be used to evaluate the levels, enabling the organization to incorporate professional ladders into the job grade structures used for other employees. External competitiveness is achieved utilizing data on prevailing compensation levels in the appropriate labor market(s). For example, market data on engineers is most often accumulated and reported using surveys that employ ladders. The survey ladder acts as a "Rosetta Stone," enabling organizations to match their people to survey levels, thereby enabling sound comparisons to be made by the survey participants, even though their ladders are constructed somewhat differently. The market data can then be used to develop ranges of pay opportunity that are appropriately competitive for people with specific levels of expertise.

Although a generic classification matrix may be used for all professional personnel, an organization can differentiate between specific disciplines when creating pay structures. Using engineering as an example again, there can be significant differences between market pay levels for the various disciplines within engineering (e.g., mechanical, electrical, nuclear, chemical, civil, facility and software). Organizations with large and diverse populations will often have different salary ranges for different disciplines, or at least different targets within a range. This enables them to be competitive with market levels but yet at the same time maintain internal equity by having grade levels decided on that basis. The worst approach is to let temporary market variations trigger changes to grade levels. This will erode internal equity over time, since the disciplines tend to take turns being "hot" and then cooling down. Frequent grade changes are also difficult to explain to incumbents, particularly when they are in a downward direction.

Assuming the performance appraisal challenges described earlier are overcome, the prevailing approach to salary administration for professional or technical personnel is merit pay. Many organizations treat professionals somewhat differently within their merit pay systems. It can be argued that performance should be the sole driver of pay. But pay adjustments based on the degree to which someone has mastered the knowledge and skills critical to their work also are an appropriate basis for evaluating the position of a pay rate within a pay range. A systems analyst newly promoted from associate to analyst is typically paid in the lower part of the range for the new classification, while a seasoned analyst (assuming acceptable performance) would tend to be paid in the middle part of the range. A concern is that this pattern could be interpreted as paying for seniority rather than strictly for performance.

But it must be recognized that increasing knowledge and skill in their field makes an employee more valuable, particularly when there are long learning curves in the path to expertise. Therefore, the base pay rate must reflect both performance and competence for professionals, with more emphasis on the latter than is usually the case for other types of employees. And since performance of professionals is often difficult to measure objectively in concrete terms, as pointed out earlier, considering the rate at which employees increase their level of expertise when evaluating performance and adjusting pay makes a great deal of sense. It is prudent to ensure pay rates remain competitive, considering the mobility of professionals and their weak attachment to the organization.

Technical and Administrative Support Personnel

The discussion to this point has been focused primarily on professionals with university-level education in a field, and who are often paid as much as or more than employees in management capacities. In many organizations there are technical and administrative people who learn their skills on the job and/ or through training programs. For example, a manufacturer of semiconductors will typically have highly skilled technicians who perform electrical and mechanical work critical to the functioning of the production process, as well as lab people who contribute to the quality control and research functions. Some of these technical employees are skilled tradespeople and may belong to unions that train them, place them and even provide them with their benefits. Other technicians will have learned their craft through extensive work experience. For example, the IT department may utilize people who are experts in creating and servicing networks. Although these employees are typically not classified as "professionals" their skill levels may warrant very high pay and their performance may be critical.

There are also administrative support personnel who relieve administrative professionals of more detailed work that does not require university-level training. As with technical support personnel, extensive experieince may enable these employees to do things professionals would be too expensive to do or be unable to do as efficiently.

Organizations are wise to develop career management structures for support personnel. In the skilled trades, the "Apprentice–Journey–Master" ladder is well recognized and there may be formal criteria that are used to classify and progress individuals. If no career path is defined and communicated to employees they are more likely to go somewhere that recognizes that their knowledge and skills are becoming more advanced.

Support personnel are perhaps the most vulnerable to being replaced by automation. If the work they do is fully prescribed algorithms can be developed to do the same work, but do it faster and more accurately. Yet work that requires face to face contact may not be as easy to automate. There can still be careers for employees who function in a support capacity, due to the frequent need of human consideratons. Empathizing with a customer is not something algorithms do well and for some types of transactions working with the customer to find an agreeable solution to an issue may be a necessity.

Sales Personnel

Employees who have sales responsibilities vary in the nature of their work and the impact they have. A sales representative who is assigned a territory or a product line and who handles all aspects of a sale from initial contact to completion independently requires a different set of competencies than an employee who services customers or conducts promotional activities. Pharmaceutical firm representatives who introduce a drug to doctors by dropping off samples and describing the characteristics of the drug may have an impact on sales, albeit indirect and delayed. But they are more influencing sales than closing sales and their skill set will differ from the indpendent representative who makes sales. When selecting sales representatives the criteria used will depend on what they will be expected to do. The often-used "hunter (find new business) – farmer (manage customer relationships)" metaphor is useful for illustrating the contrast between the different types of sales personnel. The nature of the product will also influence the required capabilities for those involved in the sales process. Selling a complex enterprise-wide software system may require considerable techical knowledge in addition to selling skills. Diagnosing the needs of the potential customer and determining what will be required to meet them requires an understanding of customer processes. The representative may also need to have the ability to appeal to emotions and to create a sense of urgency on the part of the customer.

Developing competency models for sales personnel requires an understanding of the knowledge, skills, abilities and behaviors required for a specific role. Different competencies may be more necessary for someone who prospects for potential customers than for someone who closes sales. Sales support activities may require the ability to develop a proposal that includes an understanding of what a customer needs and the costs that would be incurred to meet those needs. And sales management roles may require some of the capabilities of an athletic coach at halftime when the team is down by two touchdowns.

Sales organizations often function more independently than most other functions. The direct selling may be contracted out, through agents or alliances. And even though the function is performed internally those managing sales often believe talent management is something they should do, with little or no assistance from the organizaiton's HR function. When sales executives have performance criteria and rewards packages that differ from those for other executives this increases the feeling of independence. Since the selling staff is usually compensated differently than other employees, based on quantitative measures, it may be difficult for the organization to remind sales management that their staff are employees and how they are managed will be scrutinized by others. Whether sales personnel believe career progression is important will depend on who is hired, how they are oriented and how their performance is measured and rewarded. The way the representatives relate to the rest of the organization will influence how they view their job ... as a temporary gig until something better comes along or as a longer-term relationship. High turnover rates among sales personnel can be highly disruptive if they develop relationships with customers and also if it takes a long time for someone new to become knowledgeable about the products and the target market.

Developing sales personnel can be challenging if a considerable portion of their compensation is directly tied to sales volume. Taking time out of field work for training or company meetings can impact their earnings so their resistance is understandable. It may also be difficult to encourage them to do "missionary work," such as promoting the organization at conferences or helping customers learn how to properly use the product. When working with one of the first organizations that provided computer timesharing services I found that different behaviors were required for different segments of the sales process. The first step in creating a customer was to get the organization to agree to take the necessary actions to enable them to access the software. This took considerable effort working with the customer's IT staff so the representatives were paid a bonus for connecting a new customer. But the sales volume that would be realized was dependent on the customer using connection time. This necessitated convincing engineering management that there was value in relying on the vendor's systems rather than developing them internally. And by instructing the engineers in how to best use the software it increased the lieklihood that it would be used frequently. Commissions were based on sales volume so the representative had an interest in ensuring an appropriate amount of attention was paid to those who controlled usage. The two different phases of the sales process made consideration of a "hunter–farmer" split, with different sales personnel attending to the phases. The organization also used its own engineers to work with the customer to address the technical challenges. This raised two questions: (1) are the engineers doing sales work? and (2) should they be compensated in some way for that work? Paying some of the engineers to provide counsel to the customer while other engineers did not have the opportunity to realize increased income could raise equity issues, but also may be the most appropriate strategy.

Talent management for sales personnel is challenging due to the diversity of roles that they might play and their potential impact on outcomes. Selecting the right people will require finding candidates that fit each role. How they are developed will depend on the nature of their work and also on their engagement with the organization. Some organizations use external agents so they do not have to concern themselves with developing them or managing their own sales personnel. The talent management strategy should possess the same characteristic as any strategy … be a good fit to the specific context, defined by the nature of the role and the nature of the incumbents.

Team Members

The use of work teams is most common when work requires a variety of knowledge and skill sets to perform work. Technology has enabled teams to be staffed virtually and asynchronously, which can create a global talent pool. Project teams may involve some members on a part-time basis and others on a full-time basis for a specific duration. This argues for consideration of specific competencies when selecting team members. Although a finance member may do all the finance work and an IT member all the IT work their work must still be done in a manner that makes their approaches compatible. Playing well with others may not be required behavior for someone doing independent work but team members generally must be able to effectively communicate and to reconcile differences of opinion. Competency models are useful for evaluating potential team members since they can define the need for working with others.

Teams that include members having different cultural orientations present unique challenges. How contributions are evaluated and rewarded becomes a concern if members come from both individualistic and collectivist cultures.[8] Cultural orientation may also impact how members view formal authority structures. Those believing that direction should be top-down will tend to defer to authority while others may believe they are expected to make decisions about how work should be done and to fight for their point of view.

The different types of team member will impact the type of talent members should possess. In process teams where everyone is expected to be competent to perform all aspects of the team's work each employee may require knowledge that spans occupational categories. Cell manufactuting requires multi-skilled individuals, making sourcing talent more difficult. If the organization cannot find candidates with the required variety of capabilities it will be necessary to develop those skills through on the job learning and/or training. Since career progression within a specific occupation may be limited it is common to provide income progression by using skill-based pay systems. These systems can reward acquisition of a wider variety of skills or a higher level of expertise within a specific skill. Although these systems will often result in members being paid at higher rates the efficiency gained by having flexible staffing to meet the workflow can result in lower staffing levels due to efficiency gains.

When employees are expected to move in and out of teams or across different types of teams yet another set of competencies may be required. Willingness and ability to learn, playing well with others, capacity to innovate and problem solve … all of these competencies may be required for an employee to be fully mobile across assignments. Whether an employee will serve on a work team full-time and for extended periods or to move in and out of team assignments will prescribe personal characteristics that are required for success. If this type of flexibility is required selection and development must be based on what is needed. Expecting more, particulary if it necessitates a rare skill set, may shrink the available talent pool, as well as increasing the price of talent.

Conclusion

Different occupations may require different talent management strategies and systems. Attempting to manage using one approach can result in a failure to recognize important differences in the nature of the worker and the nature of the work. Taking an average of different things produces a meaningless result. Trying to attract, retain and develop everyone in the same way may result in mediocre results for all occupations.

Notes

1 Collins, J. *Good to Great* (New York: Harper Business, 2001).
2 Lawler, E. & O'Toole, J. *The New American Workplace* (New York: Palgrave Macmillan, 2006).
3 Crystal, G. *In Search of Excess* (New York: W. W. Norton, 1991).
4 Trompenaars, F. & Hampden-Turner, C. *Twenty-One Leaders for the Twenty-First Century* (Oxford: Capstone, 2001).
5 House, R., Ed. *Culture, Leadership and Organizations* (Thousand Oaks, CA: Sage, 2004); Chhokar, J., Brodbeck, F., & House, R., Eds. *Culture and Leadership Across the World* (Mahwah, NJ: Lawrence Erlbaum, 2008).
6 Trompenaars, F. *Riding the Waves of Culture* (Burr Ridge, IL: Irwin, 1994).
7 Rynes, S., Gerhart, B., & Parks, L. "Performance Evaluation and Pay for Performance." *Journal of Applied Psychology* 56, 2005, 571–600.
8 Trompenaars, F. & Greene, R. *Rewarding Performance Globally* (London: Routledge, 2017).

Chapter 10

Talent Management in the Future

Predicting which talent management strategies will be successful in the future is challenging if the environment makes it the equivalent of navigating permanent whitewater. Workforce planning is a critical component of any talent management strategy, as discussed in Chapter 1. Environmental scanning must be a continuous activity, since it enables organizations to identify trends and track change. Scenario-based planning is an approach that prepares an organization for a range of alternative futures. Selecting a single strategy that is based on a specific future makes it rigid, when agility is a key characteristic. Agility is critical since technology can surprise even those following trends. The emergence of tools like artificial intelligence can be a source of continual surprises. AI has been expected to "come of age" for several decades and evolution has occurred in advances, followed by pauses, followed by advances … leading to optimistic predictions that at the time they were made seemed prescient but in retrospect seemed absurd. This is a period of optimism and many believe that AI is coming of age, but … who knows.

Some things are well known … Boomers will be retiring … Gen Z entrants will face a different environment than have Xers, Yers and Millenials. Technology is altering the nature of work in many ways. And human nature will not fundamentally change so understanding it enhances the ability to project people's reactions to things like artificial intelligence and the use of robots. If a development does not threaten one's livelihood it is less likely to be resisted. If technology produces tools that makes work less tedious it will probably receive a warm reception. And many people will misread the tea leaves and react in unwarranted ways.

What is certain is that the fundamental concepts underlying sound talent management have not been completely obsoleted. Whether the prevailing form of organization will change or remain the same depends on economic, technological and human factors. If people find being employed by a single organization is less attractive than being a solo operator or an entrepreneur, then organizations will have to use outsiders more to perform more of the work. If the educational system does not keep up with technological change in some countries the organizations in those countries will find it difficult to compete globally. More work will be outsourced and offshored if technical developments make doing work anywhere by anyone more effective than having colocated employees.

Technology needs to be managed if it is to be of value. And the intellectual capital required to manage it will continue to be the primary determinant of the impact it will have on work. The concept of sociotechnical systems developed decades ago made it clear that the interface between technology and people must be designed and managed effectively. Total quality management, Six Sigma, reengineering and other tools have come on the scene noisily. Though heralded as the next best thing they often failed to live up to the hype. The disappointment was not due to the concepts being fundamentally flawed, but rather due to inadequate consideration of the need for the right talent to make them work well.

The two authors of the best-selling book on reengineering had to subsequently write other books that included confessions they had forgotten about the people issues. Redesigning key business processes to make them more efficient was a sound idea but the authors failed to consider that if not carefully implemented the outcome might be downsizing followed by the need to deal with an overworked, stressed and dissatisfied workforce. Total quality management is based on sound principles, but the people needed to make it work must have both the required skills and the right mindset to make it work.

Few futurists doubt that AI and other advanced technology will become a critical contributor to organizational effectiveness. But the path to success needs to be paved with the right building blocks. The most critical prerequisite will be possessing the only sustainable competitive advantage: a competent workforce committed to the organization's success. Competence will require mastery of the tools that technology is creating. But in order for the workforce to be motivated to put forth maximum effort and to focus that effort on the things that will contribute to the organization's success the talent management strategies and programs must be appropriate and effective.

The competency models that will be used to select talent in the future are likely to emphasize some competencies differently. In an environment that is rapidly changing hiring for a specific job is likely to be ill-advised in many cases. Rather, there is a need to hire people with the required native intelligence and who have both a willingness and a desire to learn continuously. What constitutes competence in specific roles will change if the demands of those roles change. Employment security will be earned by those who commit to acquiring the knowledge and skill required currently. And if the demands change rapidly so must the person. When organizations have used skill-based pay systems and skill demands have changed rapidly one of the frustrations that incumbents experience is the sense that they are on a treadmill, running at full speed to stay in the same place. But if this is the new reality then that is what must be accepted. Organization must be able to recognize that when skill demands are outpacing the ability of current employees to re-skill then training programs cannot be the only answer. Alternative strategies for having the right workforce at all times must be considered.

If the educational system in the United States adequately equips graduates with the knowledge required to utilize technology, there will be fewer shortages of qualified candidates among those entering the workforce. But if more students do not select STEM fields of study the shortage of occupations demanding technical knowledge will be even more pronounced. Immigration policies across the globe can facilitate the movement of the required talent to where it is needed, or they can frustrate it. If the U.S. government does not support the continuing education and development needed to sustain the competence of workers, then work will go offshore to places where an adequate supply of people with the currently required qualifications are.

Those developing new technology must broaden their perspective to include consideration of how the tools will be used by people and what those people need to know and be able to do in order to employ them. Having repetitive and fully defined routines performed by technology will free up people to do other things. But people must be able to successfully perform higher level and more complex work. Given the low unemployment rates and the persistent shortages of some skills significant numbers of people cannot be ejected from the employment arena without dire consequences. This means that there must be a strategy for reskilling current workers so they are competent to do what will need to be done. Machine learning must be augmented by people learning. Analytical tools can improve prediction of who will be successful in a specific role so selection of talent can be a more scientific process. But those utilizing these tools must also rely on human judgment and ingenuity to find talent management strategies that will be successful in a different kind of world.

Talent management strategies in the future will in some ways still be based on the same principles that have been successful but there will be changes required. What works is what fits, and if the context is changing, so must the strategies.

Appendix: Applying Analytics to Talent Management

Understanding the concepts and techniques that can be used for acquiring and applying quantitative data and research findings is a critical area of competence for those responsible for managing talent. This appendix provides a basic understanding of the types of measures and how they can be acquired, analyzed and applied when making decisions. Data scientists and others doing the data analysis are an integral part of the interpretive process. And all people are subjected to cognitive bias that may distort their interpretation. Even though sophisticated tools employing AI, machine learning and advanced statistical processes can identify correlation and causation patterns how the results of the analysis are applied to talent management strategies and programs will require human intervention. Being aware of cognitive bias can help an interpreter attempt to control the bias, but it cannot remove it from human thought processes. After discussing the technical aspects of talent analytics, a summary of cognitive biases and their implications will be addressed.

Talent Analytics: The Process

Analytics are used to find answers to questions and approaches for dealing with issues. Turnover that is deemed excessive and damaging … difficulty in attracting the right kind of talent … expressed dissatisfaction by employees … these are all issues that organizations struggle to resolve. The role of analytics is to find a path to the best solution, using the principles underlying the scientific method. The process used typically involves the following steps:

1. Asking the right question
2. Evaluating alternative methods to find the answer and select the best one
3. Creating a database consisting of all relevant data and other forms of evidence
4. Analyzing the data to identify correlations and casual relationships
5. Deciding what the data analysis shows and attempting to uncover the "why"

6. Developing practical experiments to test the preliminary conclusions
7. Formulating recommendations for actions to be taken based on the results
8. Evaluating the impact of the actions and deciding if further action is required
9. Imbedding intelligence-gathering tools to monitor future environmental change
10. Reassessing the effectiveness of strategies to ensure they continue to be aligned with the environment and the objectives of the organization

The key to effective talent analytics is identifying the right measures to use for assessing what is currently happening and that can be used to predict future effectiveness of strategies. The measurement model used must provide measures that are both adequate (include all relevant factors) and that are not contaminated by inappropriate measures. Measures must also be used in a manner that is consistent with sound statistical principles.

Types of Quantitative Measures

Central Tendency Measures

Many statistical calculations aimed at finding "the number" out of a data set. The average rate is probably the most commonly sought value when using analytical data. For example, if the rate of turnover has varied over the last few years the organization might want to know if there are higher or lower rates of turnover in specific months of the year. Since the data must be aggregated in order to be compared the monthly average is usually calculated and used for the analysis. But when using an average, it is important to ask "average of what, calculated how?"

Typically, only turnover rates involving employees leaving the organization are of interest, so the average for each month will be based only on external turnover. But the count may be further altered if only voluntary turnover is to be considered. The averages may be broken down further, to focus on specific occupations that are critical. Another commonly performed analysis is the selection rate of various categories of applicants. If whites are selected at a much higher average rate than minorities this may represent statistically significant adverse impact on a protected class. When this the case the organization might break down the averages by relating each instance to a specific cause, assuming that can be determined.

The person selecting the basis upon which the average rates are calculated must ensure it is consistent with how the user wants if to be determined and that the user understands the method used. For example, if a compensation survey provides average pay rates for the survey sample they can be calculated on an incumbent-weighted or company-weighted basis (the same could be true for turnover rates or any other measure of interest). The incumbent weighted average is computed by adding up all the individual pay rates and then dividing that sum by the number of incumbents. The company weighted average gives the average paid by each company the same weight, no matter how many rates each of them reports. Large companies will have more weight on the incumbent weighted average while they will have the same weight as other reporting companies in the company weighted averages. The user will have to determine which of the two measures is most appropriate if they differ significantly. The same principle would apply to turnover rates and selection ratios.

Another measure indicating central tendency is the "median" – the middle rate in an array placed in ascending or descending order. For example, if there are 51 data points, the median rate is the 26th (from the top or from the bottom of the array placed in descending or ascending order by value). The median rate is identified by dividing the number of rates (n) plus one by two and then using the rate that holds that position in the array. Since it is middle rate, the median is often considered the best rate to use to represent the "typical rate." Also, the median is less affected by extremely high or low rates than is the average (mean).

However, the median is also a distributional measure and an uneven distribution can cause nonsensical results. For example, if the analysis covers seven annual turnover rates and those rates are 6%, 7%, 8%,18%, 19%, 20% and 20% the median is 18%, while the average is 14%. Users of reported results should be concerned about *why* a difference exists between the two measures and which is most relevant. And if the rates shown followed the sequence of years there is clearly an upward trend, with a sharp increase in year 4. This may render both the average and the median over the seven years inadequate for understanding what is happening. This illustrates the danger of aggregating data and obscuring patterns from those who must use the data. If the same data represented selection rates for seven different categories of applicant (male, female, white, minority, over 40, under 40 and all applicants) the average or median of all applicants would be meaningless measures, except for comparing each category to the total population. That is why a data scientist analyzing a data base must understand the significance of aggregating individual data points in different ways. If the average annual turnover rate for ten selected competitor organization is 10% it may be concluded that turnover is greater than that of competitors. However, one would have to know the lowest and highest rates (the range) and what the ten individual rates are in order to arrive at a conclusion about the organization's turnover rate.

This example illustrates that statistical measures may not produce a relevant answer, but only trigger examination of the measurements. Users must understand the nature of what is being measured and what does/does not make sense. Making sense of the data may require breaking the comparator sample down.

A third measure of central tendency exists … the mode. This is the most frequntly reported rate. It has little application in analyzing data relating to turnover rates or other data involving the aggregation of discrete values. Not all quantitative measures are useful for specific types of analysis.

Averages or medians can be used to compare two things as well. For example, most tourist books contain average monthly temperatures for destinations, to alert the traveler going to Chicago to pack either cotton shorts or down parkas, depending on the month. Averages and medians have wide application in pay administration as well. But if the level of analysis is too aggregated important information can be obscured. During the summer in Arizona the temperature can reach lofty heights at mid-day but can drop significantly once the sun goes down and many tourists have endured chilled arms and legs that stick out of their short pants and shirts when venturing out at night. Having taught many seminars I have found that an average temperature for the day in a conference center of 70 may not be ideal if the room was 55 in the morning and 85 in the afternoon. The level of detail must be appropriate if all useful information can be discovered.

Distribution Measures

Distribution measures are used to describe how individual values in a data array are distributed. The median (just described) is the most commonly used distributional measure. Quartiles and percentiles are other useful distributional measures. *Quartiles* break a distribution into quarters, while *percentiles* break it into hundredths (terciles into thirds, deciles into tenths, etc.). If a student graduates in the second quartile of the class, it means that student's grade point average ranks below 50% to 75% of his or her classmates and above 25% to 50% of them.

Surveys often report quartiles so the user knows generally how individual data points distribute between the lowest and the highest rate. The lowest and the highest rates are often outliers and useless to the user, but quartiles have a purpose. The quartiles enable the user to treat the "interquartile range" (range between the first and the third quartile) as the middle half of paid rates, and to use this as a test of "being in the ballpark."

Employee attitude surveys are commonly used to find out what employees believe or what their reaction is to a program or policy. For example, if a 9–80 work schedule (work 80 hours over 2 weeks in 9 days, rather than 10) is tried the organization is likely to be curious about how it is viewed by those involved. The organization may also wish to compare the results of its survey to normative data that provides the results in other firms. If the new program has a 75% approval rate and the average approval rate in competitive organizations is 81% this is useful information. It does not determine whether the 75% approval rate is viewed as a success or failure ... it may be taken as an affirmation of the decision to implement the program when the results are compared to expectations. The organization may know its employees generally dislike any kind of change so being this successful may be a triumph. It might be illuminating if the normative data were to be broken down in various ways. For example, if the vast majority of the sampled companies had approval ratings of over 90% but the average was dragged down by a few with 10–15% ratings, this could change the perception about whether the new program succeeded.

A distributional measurement tool that can be very valuable is the frequency distribution (a.k.a., histogram). This tool is typically in the form of a table or chart that describes how individual values cluster in predetermined categories. Table A1.1 shows the distribution of reported rates across a series of predetermined brackets. The vertical height represents the number (or percentage) of rates falling within each bracket and provides a picture of the nature of the distribution.

A histogram's graphic nature enables us to see patterns not evident in a numeric table and a quick glance at the example indicates that this is not a normal distribution. It looks like two normal distributions side by side. This pattern is called a "bimodal" distribution (two modes exist; one around 60% and another at the 75–80% bracket). An experienced survey analyzer would suspect that there is something going on that is not disclosed by the analysis and that further analysis is prescribed.

The first step in doing a more in-depth analysis is to find out if employee demographics explain this unsettling pattern. If it is older employees that have lower acceptance rates it might be due to the fact that they find the longer hours on the nine days worked over a two week period to be fatiguing; If it is younger employees with low acceptance it could be that parents with school drop off and pick up schedules could find the hours conflict with their schedules and this might explain the reason they had lower approval ratings. It is difficult to please everyone with anything you do but if there are employees with negative reactions it is important to find out who they are and what causes the lack of approval.

If an organization wishes to select among several options using employee feedback several approaches can be used. For example, employees might be asked to rank a set of potential actions based on the value they would place on each. It is assumed the organization views the alternatives to cost the organization the same, or that the organization is economically indifferent

Table A1.1 Frequency Distribution

Below 50%	50–55%	55–60%	60–65%	65–70%	70–75%	75–80%	80–85%	85–90%	90% &up
					X				
					X				
		X	X		X				
		X	X	X	X	X			
		X	X	X	X	X			
	X	X	X	X	X	X	X		
X	X	X	X	X	X	X	X	X	
X	X	X	X	X	X	X	X	X	X

to which is chosen. If the organization is willing to (1) give all employees a 2% pay increase, (2) add one day of vacation to the existing schedule or (3) offer a reduced employee contribution to health care costs, the responses will indicate which will be valued the most by employees. The decision could be made using one of several approaches. The approach ranked as # 1 by the most respondents could be selected. Or a weighed score could be computed, with # 1 ranks given 2 points, # 2 ranks 1 point and # 3 ranks no points. Or a Delphi approach could be used, which involves multiple iterations of feedback. After the first round the results could be tallied and fed back to employees and they would be asked to submit another ranking. This process could continue until a threshold level of convergence is reached (51% or more ranking one option # 1).

Relationship Measures

Relationship measures can be used to reflect the nature of relationships between two or more things. The most common measure is *correlation*. For example, the weight of adult males is correlated to height (correcting for age). This does not suggest one thing *causes* the other, but only they tend to covary. The coefficient of correlation measures the degree to which two factors covary: from 0 (no relationship) to 1.0 (perfect correlation). In the 9–80 example there may be a correlation with age and acceptance. But correlation can be a tricky thing to use in explaining *why* a relationship exists. We all have seen bizarre claims about A causing B based on a high correlation. If there is a high correlation between the price of coffee and the price of fruit both prices may be influenced by the weather patterns in South America, where both originate. And establishing causation has other requirements, one of which is that A must precede B, which then changes. An example would be using AI to analyze historical data to determine how room pricing impacts hotel occupancy rates. A correlation might be found between high prices and high occupancy rates, which would be surprising. But this is most likely due to the fact that hotels raise prices during the busiest periods. This does not justify raising prices and expecting occupancy rates to go up. This suggests that when using AI it is important to apply human scrutiny to the results.

Correlations can change over time. If the Staffing function uses a model for selecting new graduates that correlates each school with the performance of the graduates from that school it is often found that some schools have produced graduates that have tended to be successful at the organization more often. If there is an analysis every year the consistency with which a school's graduates continues to provide successful employees can be tested, to ensure changes have not altered the correlation. But if another analysis is done to determine whether grade point average/class standing correlates with subsequent success it might be discovered that considering that predictor is better than the school from which the graduates came. An astute evaluator might use both GPA and whether a person worked to earn the money for their education to improve the quality of selection decisions. Someone working a substantial number of hours and graduating with a 3.2 GPA might be preferred over someone with a 3.5 GPA who did not work. What the two prediction criteria are attempting to measure in this case would be both intelligence and conscientiousness, which research has shown are the two best predictors of performance. All of these are common correlations used by Staffing professionals, even though it is done informally.

The nature of the relationship between two or more variables can be explained by using *regression analysis*. Single-factor regression is a technique attempting to explain one variable using one other variable. For example, higher starting pay rates may impact the acceptance rate for job offers. The nature of the relationship can be expressed by calculating a regression formula that most accurately describes it. The relationship can also be displayed graphically. Start rates can be represented on the x-axis and the acceptance rates can be plotted on the y-axis of a graph. It is then possible to calculate a single factor linear regression formula that is the best fit to the pattern of the data points. The relationship would be perfect if all xs were on one straight diagonal line with higher vertical values when horizontal values increase. This pattern would indicate the relationship between acceptance rates and pay rates is positive (the higher the pay rates, the higher the acceptance rates). The simplest explanation of the relationship can be presented by drawing a straight line through the cluster of dots, inclining as it went from left to right.

The single-factor linear name for this regression is derived from the fact that one factor (starting pay rate) explains another factor (acceptance rate) and that it is a linear relationship. Software producing this chart also reports a coefficient of correlation enabling the user to determine what percentage of the variation in acceptance rates is explained by the pay rates. The number varies from 0.0 to 1.0 and for this type of application, the norm for acceptability probably ranges from .50 to .85.

If the relationship between the independent variable (pay rate) and the dependent variable (acceptance rate) is not linear, but rather some form of curve function, it requires the use of a nonlinear formula. This is a pattern frequently experienced when analyzing executive salaries, as the rate salaries increase is often faster than the rate at which organization size increases, creating an upward turning curve. Today's curve-fitting software selects the formula that produces the best fit between one variable and the other and provide a rank ordering of formulas based on how well they explain the relationship. It is prudent to test all data sets using such software, as operating under the assumption that a relationship is linear may force it to be so, as that formula will be applied. And if a straight-line assumption is used on a non-linear data set, the results are distorted.

One variable is often insufficient to explain another's behavior. In this case, one enters the world of multi-factor (multiple) regression analysis. If an organization is attempting to determine what best explains acceptance rates it may use multi-factor regression to test various possibilities. If acceptance rate is entered as the variable to be explained, several variables might be entered as possible determinants. The starting pay offered would be a leading contender. The job being offered may be another. And a flexible work schedule and location might be yet another. If those three variables are entered and the multiple regression model results show that they explain 95% of the variation in acceptance rates, it can be safely concluded that these factors influence acceptance. If all three factors were entered all at once it might be wise to test each one separately. This is possible using different types of multiple regression analysis. It may be found on further examination that the job offered had virtually no explanatory value and that the other two factors drive acceptance rates.

Another common application of multiple regression is to test the impact of HR programs on protected classes. Given today's legalistic environment, this is a good defensive technique, but it also is an opportunity to test for maladies such as racial bias or glass ceilings before trouble arises. In the previous example, the objective was to explain the impact of employee pay on selection rate. If the organization wanted to determine what factors had an impact on employee pay rates it might do a separate multiple regression analysis. For example, if age, gender and race were set as inputs to the equation, the results may provide usable information about whether or not these factors inappropriately influenced outcomes.

Determining The Impact Of Workforce Management Programs

Management attempts to formulate strategies that will have a positive impact on workforce effectiveness. As technology has advanced there are more tools available to use as evidence to support the contention that a new strategy or program had a positive impact on performance, turnover, employee satisfaction and other results. Evidence-based management is being used more often to replace "I think this will have a positive impact" claims with recommendations that are supported by relevant research and evidence generated by past trials.

Research methodology is even more obscure to most HR practitioners than quantitative analysis methods. This is largely explainable by the fact that even entry-level research courses tend to first appear in university curriculum only at the Master's, and perhaps PhD, level. But as the research being performed in areas directly related to the HR practitioner's world increased in value, it is unwise to remain uninformed about what makes sound research and how one can tell if it is prudent to act on reported results. When asked "is there any support for that or is that just an opinion" by senior management, the person recommending an action is well served by knowing the answer in advance. And support that is only the opinion of a consultant or the results of an action reported in the literature, or even a proliferation of articles on how successful the adoption of an "X" program was management may find this to be inadequate evidence. Recommendations based on high-quality research that is relevant to the issue is what practitioner should seek to support their proposals.

To determine if findings from a research study are believable and usable, there are two tests of that study: its internal validity and its external validity. Internal validity relates to how well the study was designed, and therefore whether the results can be believed to be valid in a specific context. External validity relates to where, and under what conditions, the findings will be likely to be the same.

The classic test of internal validity addresses how well various threats to the veracity of the results were controlled for. For example, we assume HR proposes a hypothesis that if people were given more responsible jobs, with appropriate amounts of latitude, that their job satisfaction would increase and that they would become more productive. One way to support that contention is to look to research results indicating the desired results occur when the proposed actions are taken. If one could find one or more studies to support the hypothesis, the strength of one's conviction would be contingent on the confidence in the studies on two fronts.

The first question to be answered when deciding on the validity of a study is "were the studies designed in a manner controlling against threats to internal validity?" The second would be "were the studies conducted in a context sufficiently similar to that of the subject organization so it is logical to assume the results would be similar?" This requires external validity, meaning that they would transfer to other contexts. What is important is to determine whether a similar result would be likely to occur in the context within which the practitioner means to take the same action. This defines the generalizability of results.

The internal validity threats include:

1. Events taking place during the study that might have caused the results (for example, benefits were improved during the time jobs were being enriched, positively impacting satisfaction).
2. Conducting the study when satisfaction is very low or very high relative to typical levels (for example, a layoff occurred before the study and morale is low enough that any change might be expected to improve satisfaction scores, particularly paying attention to employees and their needs).
3. Changes in the employee sample (For example, malcontents may have been encouraged to leave or chose to leave while the enrichment was going on and their satisfaction levels were among the lowest).
4. Expectations as to what jobs and the workplace will be like after the study, which might have inflated job satisfaction on a temporary basis.
5. Satisfaction might have improved but there has been insufficient time to tell if this will positively affect productivity.

The threats to external validity are well known to those versed in sound benchmarking. A study that resulted in improved satisfaction and productivity in one organization might not translate to the same results in the organization embarking on a similar job enrichment program (The author's paper titled "Human Resources Management Strategies: Can We Discover What Will Work Through Benchmarking," in the Second Quarter 2008 *WorldatWork Journal* explains this premise). The management style might differ from the organization(s) in the study (for example, supervisors might be more controlling and insecure about giving subordinates more latitude). The workforce might be from cultures that discourage employee initiative, which would be seen as disrespectful of the supervisor. The workforce may lack the knowledge, skills and abilities to effectively perform the jobs in their enriched form. And so on.

There is a tendency to prefer controlled studies conducted under laboratory conditions over field research, since internal validity can be achieved more easily in the lab. However, this bias can result in overlooking external validity/generalizability. A popular book recently claimed that research showed that extrinsic rewards can destroy intrinsic rewards.[1] But the evidence was a lab study that showed over a short timeframe people would throw tennis balls at targets longer if they were not paid. The rewards were insignificant, and the activity would be viewed by most as somewhat entertaining. It is the responsibility of those who would apply that research finding in an organization to decide if the context within which the lab study was conducted had any relevance to a situation where people spent years doing work that was not particularly enjoyable, for rewards that allowed them to sustain their standard of living. The book failed to point out that there is a substantial body of field research that refutes the lab result, showing the opposite result. Although one could argue that the lab study was more internally valid or "scientific" it could also be argued that the results would only be likely to be the same in a similar context. All that appears in the literature read by practitioners is not subjected to rigorous tests, such as peer review.

The safest haven for the organization trying to determine if research supports the hypothesis they are putting forward is the sample size of studies supporting it. If numerous studies resulted in similar outcomes, the confidence level can be assumed to be higher. A *meta-analysis* is a study of multiple studies and can provide more confidence in research results. The reporting of these findings is often in research journals, which may be opaque to those untrained in research methodology. But an advisor with academic training can often locate, synthesize research findings and guide the organization in developing a hypothesis supported by research. The advisor should also be capable of ensuring the desired change to an HR program or practice is designed in a controlled fashion maximizing the likelihood of successful implementation.

Increasingly, HR research is being reported in books that are accessible to those lacking the training in research methodology. The SHRM Foundation supported a research program examining the role of HR in mergers and acquisitions and what factors seemed to explain success and failure (a series of reports are available to all at no charge, accessible on the Foundations website).

Watson-Wyatt developed three human-capital indices for measuring the effect of HR strategies and programs on shareholder value. The Gallup organization has developed an enormous database to explore factors influencing employee satisfaction and effectiveness. The Conference Board does in-depth research reports on current issues. Models for measuring the HR function's effectiveness have been developed and tested and some have been reported in several popular books.

Perhaps none of these research programs would meet the test of an academic research journal but the studies just cited meet the test of admissible evidence and provide practical guidance to practitioners. It is this type of practical guidance that can help HR be more "scientific" in its application of research and quantitative analysis methods.

A dangerous tendency is the inclination to believe evidence that is consistent with currently held beliefs, while rejecting or avoiding evidence conflicting with their beliefs. Everyone is subject to this form of cognitive bias and professionals must make a conscious effort to remain open to research findings that bring into question the practices they have used with apparent success or that contradict what the user believes should be so. For example, research shows that intelligence is a better predictor of performance than conscientiousness. But we all have seen intelligent people who accomplish little, and hard workers who might be less gifted who get things done through persistence. Rooting for the latter does not make it so. A consolation to those disappointed in this finding is that neither of the two factors is strongly correlated, but when an individual has both there is a very high correlation with performance.

The behavioral research done during the past three or four decades has not demonstrated a strong causal link between employee satisfaction and motivation to perform at high levels. Even though this linkage seems to be consistent with common sense and with experience, the evidence is lacking. Evidence does indicate that employee satisfaction positively influences absenteeism and turnover, however, so employee satisfaction is still a worthwhile goal. It is important for professionals to be clear about the results satisfaction has been shown to impact, lest they mislead decision makers. Too many HR initiatives have produced positive results but have been viewed as failures as they did not produce the promised results. Research evidence can help guide HR to the correct path, but it is important not to try to force research to support desired results by stretching the conclusions it can support.

Although employee opinion surveys are a common approach to seeking understanding of how employees feel, they are also fraught with peril. As attitude surveys must frame questions in a technically sound manner for the results to be valid and actionable, this is not a technique to be undertaken by amateurs. A more fundamental concern is that sometimes results may not be actionable, as what employees report and what they act on may differ. Ed Lawler, a renowned researcher, reported recently on an employee attitudes survey performed by colleagues. It concluded that the most-desired feature of the work environment (work–life balance) had no significant correlation with the desired outcome (attachment to the organization). Most attitude surveys would have looked at the high rating of work–life balance and assumed that achieving it would have the desired results. The survey pointed out, according to Lawler, that having people rank the importance of things that are likely to be at least somewhat important to everyone has limited value, unless the researcher is willing to go the extra mile and determine if providing these things had any tangible value.

Even in this complex world, there is still hope for the practitioner who does not have the inclination or the time to go back for a master's degree in statistics. Sense can be made of the chaotic environment with effort and basic logic. Adequate published information enables one to gain adequate knowledge of research and quantitative analysis methods. Advanced software performs all statistical tests mentioned in this Appendix without demanding that the user understand the underlying equations. Finally, an increasing number of researchers are making their results accessible to people without advanced training.

There is, however, a problem for practitioners that lack basic skills in this area. The "let's try it and see how it works" approach is too slow and too costly today. An effective practitioner will take the time to find out how it has worked or is apt to work by accessing research results and evaluating all relevant evidence. The effective practitioner will demand that data be turned into information and will be capable of examining the quality of that information as it applies to the context within which it will be used. Workforce analytics have become a major focus for many organizations over the last few years, since executive management has increasingly demanded that recommendations be supported by relevant evidence. Artificial intelligence and machine learning have become valuable tools for discovering important relationships and in explaining them. More advanced technology has also increased the ability to predict outcomes, such as the likelihood of critical talent leaving the organization. But although data scientists are generating enormous bodies of analytical evidence human intuition, judgment and experience are needed to determine how this evidence is applied. It is critical that decision-makers understand the principles of sound quantitative analysis and that they are able to integrate evidence with business acumen and an understanding of human nature.

The Financial Impact of Human Resource Programs

Although the current focus is on using analytical tools to measure the results of programs and to predict what will be effective the financial impact of programs has always been an important consideration. Using cost-benefit analysis has been used as a management tool for as long as managers have made decisions. Even though a program might produce significant benefits those outcomes must be evaluated in light of the resources consumed. Whether the resource is financial, time or scarce talent it has a cost.

Minimizing turnover is a common objective for workforce management programs. Costco is willing to spend more on salaries and benefits than its competitors because management believes that it results in reduced turnover. Other organizations endure the turnover because they believe the costs of reducing it outweigh the benefits. Every manager and HR professional should be able to conduct rigorous analyses that lead to better decisions. But costing things like turnover, vacancies, absenteeism, worker dissatisfaction, customer churn and training/development programs can be difficult. Subjective (aka qualitative) judgments are sometimes necessary because cost cannot be expressed in financial terms.

The book *Investing in People*[2] provides a comprehensive guide to conducting rigorous analysis on HR programs. The models presented include both financial analysis and measures of impact on organizational effectiveness.

The Impact of Cognitive Bias on the Interpretation of Data Analysis

The Nobel Prize was awarded to Kahneman for his work with Tversky and others on the identification of cognitive bias and on the way in which humans think.[3] Since there must be a human intervention between data analysis and the use of the findings to deal with practical issues it is important to understand the nature of human cognitive processes.

The Kahneman research resulted in a model that predicts how cognitive input is processed. The model suggests that there are two types of thinking … System 1 (fast interpretation and acceptance of sensory input) and System 2 (calculative evaluation of input and determination of its meaning). System 1 will prevail unless the input causes the recipient to doubt it due to a conflict with expectations. It takes less effort, both mental and physical than System 2. System 2 is activated by doubt and attempts to evaluate the veracity of the interpretation made by System 1. Gladwell did additional research on System 1 thinking and its impact on cognitive processing.[4,5] When System 2 is activated blood pressure increases and pupils dilate, which are indicators of physical effort being required. Cognitive bias is unconstrained when System 1 is operative and compensating for that bias requires both knowledge that one is prone to it and effort to consciously override the distortions it creates.

Over 100 types of bias have been discovered and their implications identified. Some of those biases that are most relevant to talent analytics and talent management should be understood. These biases cause humans to:

Think others agree with them more than they actually do
Accept data/hypotheses that agree with what one believes/wants to be so more
    readily … and to resist contradictory evidence
Accept too readily conclusions based on inadequate samples
Rely on literature that reports only successes and not on failures

Believe that intuitive conclusions are valid

Overuse similarity as a simplifying heuristic

"candidate is great (thinks/looks like me)"

Assign weight to evidence based on its availability

"recency bias; familiarity bias"

Do not adequately consider regression to the mean

"why did the best performers last year seem to do worse this year?"

"giving a QB a huge raise because of one great year may prove to be foolish"

Assume quantitative data has higher validity than subjective data

See puppies and other shapes in clouds ... this is System 1 thinking (intuitive/automatic/emotional). Realizing that this is silly is System 2 thinking, which takes considerable effort to override the immediate perceptions triggered by System 1

Think the world makes much more sense than it does (the book *Fooled by Randomness*, by Taleb, exposes our vulnerability to believing there are rational explanations for events)

Sometimes answer a simpler question when we have no answer to a complex question – System 1 is puzzled, and System 2 goes to work

Can learn to apply System 2 control over impulsive conclusions reached by System 1 with training, but emotional intensity of the issue can make it harder

May use repetition of anything, even falsehoods, to make something seem more feasible

Are overly prone to assume causation when there is only correlation

Believe one is too intelligent to be prone to bias ... believe that rationality is used and overrides impulse"

Know less about how one thinks than one thinks (s)he does

Are primed to make associations by recent/repeated experience

Falsely believe that a "hot hand" in sports or in gambling exists

Believe a lot of experience makes one wiser about how to interpret evidence

The recognition that there is a tendency to be prone to bias does not necessarily lead to taking steps that help to correct for it. There are obstacles to accepting evidence that overturns fundamental beliefs that one might hold strongly for a long time. Admitting that one has been wrong is difficult, particularly if the person has publicly endorsed the now discredited assumptions underlying past decisions. There are "climb down" approaches to accepting errors. If a decision was made based on all evidence known at that time and subsequently research or experience demonstrates that the evidence is not still valid then it is difficult to criticize the person making the decision. But it is still difficult to admit one's fallibility.

Academic research often corrects itself. For decades researchers attempted to support the hypothesis that increasing employee satisfaction would have a positive impact on productivity. The studies frustrated these attempts, since they demonstrated a very weak correlation and failed to establish causation. What they did find is that increased satisfaction will have a positive impact on turnover and attendance, which is valuable information. But if someone makes management decisions relying on the assumption that increasing satisfaction will positively impact productivity the end result might be disappointing. Even though improved attendance and decreased turnover are hardly insignificant benefits if something else was promised and did not materialize the increased investment in programs to improve productivity could be viewed as a failure. Another reversal that has occurred has changed our beliefs about the relationship between satisfaction and performance. Field research that shows increased performance will tend to result in improved satisfaction, which is the reverse of what most of the earlier research attempted to establish ... it reverses the causal direction. This evidence suggests that early recognition and reinforcement of good performance will lead to increased satisfaction, which in turn will probably result in subsequent performance being positively impacted. So a virtual cycle is suggested, rather than the direct impact believed to exist, which can lead to investing in a way that facilitates both satisfaction and performance.

How decision makers process evidence can determine whether bias influences decisions. The concept that defines System 1 and System 2 thinking differentiates between "fast" and "slow" processing. If someone gives in to the tendency of making a snap judgment based on one input this may result in ignoring other evidence that is more important. We have a tendency to accept physical characteristics as being predictive of intelligence or competence and if the decision-making process is not structured to delay a conclusion until a search for all relevant evidence has been gathered and processed that tendency will drive the decision. Selecting one candidate for employment over another based on who is taller or who looks more like an athlete sounds ridiculous, but research evidence suggests this is more common than we would like to acknowledge. There is compelling research that establishes the least valid predictor of success is a one on one unstructured employment interview. Yet that is by far the most commonly used selection tool. Continuing to use a tool shown to be inadequate and expecting a better result is a form of madness.

By developing a decision-making model that prescribes a process demanding the consideration of all that should be considered the quality of decisions can be improved. Using all relevant evidence and assigning the appropriate weight to each input is the logical thing to do. But since cognitive bias is often subconscious it is hard to correct for something that is not known to exist. And shutting down instinct and quick judgment can be devilishly difficult. A defined process can help. Knowing that everyone is subject to bias can help. But even if one is dedicated to the principle of evidence-based decision making the execution of rational processes can be highjacked by our cognitive makeup. That suggests being less of a lone decider and involving others who might have different perspectives is a good idea. The individualistic culture in the United

States works against that but being right is usually more important than being able to take all of the credit for good decisions.

Notes

1 Pink, D. *Drive* (New York: Riverhead Books, 2009).
2 Cascio, W., Boudreau, J., & Fink, A. *Investing in People* (Alexandria, VA: Society of Human Resource Management, 2019).
3 Kahneman, D. *Thinking Fast and Slow* (New York: Farrar, Straus & Giroux, 2011).
4 Gladwell, M. *Blink* (New York: Little, Brown & Co., 2005).
5 Gladwell, M. *What the Dog Saw* (New York: Little, Brown & Co., 2009).

Index

Printed in the United States
by Baker & Taylor Publisher Services